ALL NECESSARY MEASURES?

IAN MARTIN

All Necessary Measures?

The United Nations and
International Intervention in Libya

HURST & COMPANY, LONDON

First published in the United Kingdom in 2022 by
C. Hurst & Co. (Publishers) Ltd.,
New Wing, Somerset House, Strand, London, WC2R 1LA
© Ian Martin, 2022
All rights reserved.

Distributed in the United States, Canada and Latin America by
Oxford University Press, 198 Madison Avenue, New York, NY 10016,
United States of America.

A Cataloguing-in-Publication data record for this book
is available from the British Library.

ISBN: 9781787385849

This book is printed using paper from registered sustainable
and managed sources.

www.hurstpublishers.com

Printed in Great Britain by Bell and Bain Ltd, Glasgow

CONTENTS

INTRODUCTION

More than a decade since the uprising that ousted Muammar Gaddafi, Libya remains deeply divided after another civil war, victim not only of the ambitions and corruption of its own elites but also of the involvement of rival external actors. Meanwhile, the chaotic collapse of the western intervention in Afghanistan, coming on top of the post-invasion tribulations of Iraq, demands further analysis of the forms and consequences of international intervention and non-intervention.

The 2011 intervention in Libya was initially regarded by some as a remarkable success: a first application of the doctrine of 'responsibility to protect' by the United Nations Security Council; the prevention of an impending massacre of civilians; a NATO operation that itself suffered no casualties and caused only very limited civilian deaths and damage to infrastructure; an opportunity for democratic forces to lead Libya out of forty years of dictatorship. This positive appraisal largely survived a difficult first year after the ousting of Gaddafi, with praise and relief when a first election in July 2012 was celebrated by Libyans and international supporters and appeared to result in a victory for 'moderates' over the Muslim Brotherhood, which had triumphed in Tunisia and Egypt.

Such optimism was soon dashed. Within weeks of the election, before a new government had been appointed, US Ambassador Christopher Stevens died in the jihadist attack on the American consulate in Benghazi; the new government that emerged from the elected congress was no more able than its predecessor to establish

1

its authority over the proliferation of armed groups; divisions among regions and cities, Islamists and others, split the country into rival governments and exploded into civil war; ISIS gained a foothold in the country; external intervention in support of contending parties escalated.

This tragic trajectory compels an assessment of the international engagement during and immediately after the uprising. Rival narratives compete. Russia asserts that the west should never have intervened to overthrow Gaddafi. Former President Obama maintains that the intervention was justified to protect civilians but failing to plan for the day after was the worst mistake of his presidency. For some, the lesson is less interventionism; for others, it is the need for any intervention to be followed by a more assertive international post-conflict role. One conclusion is despair: 'In Iraq, the US intervened and occupied, and the result was a costly disaster. In Libya, the US intervened and did not occupy, and the result was a costly disaster. In Syria, the US neither intervened nor occupied, and the result is a costly disaster.'[1]

Revisiting the international engagement in Libya from its February 2011 uprising to its first election in July 2012 provides no easy answers to the urgent question of how Libya can carry forward its emergence from its latest civil war, nor obvious lessons for future responses to crises elsewhere. But these are better served by a deeper and more nuanced analysis of that period than is found in the often superficial discourse today. In the pages that follow, I ask and offer personal answers to these questions: Was the international intervention in Libya a justified response to an impending massacre and wider threat to civilians, or were other motivations involved in seeking to oust Gaddafi and shape the future of an oil-rich country? What were the dynamics that brought about the resolutions of the UN Security Council, including the authorisation of military action? How did NATO act upon that authorisation, and did it exceed the mandate to protect civilians by seeking regime change? What role in the military victory of the rebels was played by the secretive special forces operations of bilateral actors, and with what consequences? Was there ever a possibility of a peaceful political transition being brought about by the mediation efforts of the UN, the African Union (AU) or others? How well informed, or how ignorant, were policy-makers about Libya and the regional implications of their decisions? What post-conflict planning was undertaken by the UN and other international actors, and by the Libyans themselves, and how did it play out during the first transitional government? Should and could there have been a major peacekeeping or stabilisation mission to provide security during the transition, instead of a 'light footprint' of the international community? Was the first national election held too soon? Who should and could have done more to help bring the proliferation of armed groups under government authority and achieve their integration into state security forces or demobilisation?

In trying to answer these questions, I do not claim to be either an entirely objective observer, or an expert in Libya or the region. When the Arab uprisings began, I shared enthusiastically the hope that they would bring respect for human rights to countries where they had long been being violated by repressive regimes. Heading missions to Egypt and Tunisia as secretary-general of Amnesty International at the beginning of the 1990s, I had been personally involved in putting our evidence of arbitrary detention and torture to those governments, including in meetings with Presidents Hosni Mubarak and Zine El-Abidine Ben Ali themselves. With my colleagues, I had engaged with human rights activists across the region, working closely with the Arab Lawyers Union and the Arab Organisation for Human Rights, as well as local civil society organisations. I had not myself been to Libya, but it was while I headed Amnesty that in 1988 the Libyan General People's Congress adopted Gaddafi's 'Great Green Document of Human Rights in the Era of the Masses'. Many prisoners were released; Gaddafi commuted death sentences, proposed an end to capital punishment, and appeared on television tearing down prison walls.[2] Seeking to make the most of any opening, after years of reporting 'physical liquidation' of opponents abroad and televised executions, torture and secret detention in Libya, we sent a delegation to meet Gaddafi. He suggested that he might join Amnesty and that we should move our headquarters to Libya. But imprisonment without trial continued, and before long executions resumed and torture was again being reported.

I had no inkling that I was to become involved with Libya when the February uprising began there, or when the UN Security Council adopted its first sanctions against the Gaddafi regime, or when it authorised military action. I followed these events only through the media, with no privileged information. My views on past military interventions were mixed. I had seen the consequences of the failure to intervene when I led a UN human rights field operation in post-genocide Rwanda. I had headed the UN mission that conducted the 1999 self-determination referendum in East Timor (now Timor-Leste) and that hung on amid the subsequent violence until the mandating of the Australian-led military deployment, which I encouraged and warmly welcomed.[3] I had strongly opposed the illegal US–UK invasion of Iraq, resigning my long-standing membership of Tony Blair's Labour Party. I was acutely aware through the experience of colleagues of the disastrous post-conflict failings of international actors in Iraq and Afghanistan. But watching developments in Libya from afar, I shared the view that military action was justified to protect civilians when Gaddafi had failed to respond to international condemnation and sanctions. And I was motivated to do whatever I could to support the 'Arab Spring'.

My involvement in Libya came about because of my prior responsibilities in UN peace operations. It was at the end of March 2011, just days after Secretary-General Ban Ki-moon had agreed at the London Conference on Libya that the UN would 'lead the coordination of humanitarian assistance and planning for longer-term stabilisation', that I was asked by the UN's Department of Political Affairs—the department with which I had worked when heading missions in East Timor and Nepal—to come to headquarters to support forward planning on Libya. I became special adviser to the secretary-general for post-conflict planning in Libya from April 2011 until Tripoli fell to the rebels. I then went almost immediately to Tripoli, becoming in September 2011 special representative of the secretary-general on the ground in Libya, establishing the UN Support Mission in Libya (UNSMIL) and heading it for its first year. I agreed to establish the mission and then to see it through to the election but believed that a longer-term role required someone with regional understanding and language skills that I lacked.

As the tenth anniversary of the uprising was approaching, I wanted to reflect on the period of my involvement. It seemed to me that many references to 2011–12 missed or distorted aspects of the events in Libya and the dynamics among the international actors. I scrutinised literature that has since emerged, including the memoirs of participants. I sought the recollections and retrospective views of a substantial number of Libyan actors, former UN colleagues, persons with relevant responsibilities in some of the involved governments and organisations, and independent experts. I did not carry out formal interviews, but these conversations greatly assisted me in judging what can be relied upon in the literature and in confirming or modifying my own recollections and views.

There are many aspects of the period that I do not address in what follows. I do not attempt to analyse the dynamics among Libyans themselves,[4] both because I am not competent to do so and because my focus is on the international engagement. I do not attempt a full narrative of events—only enough of the story of what happened to provide the basis for my assessment of the international role. I am heavily reliant on the accounts of others; I have referred to those sources that I believe are the most reliable. I conclude with a personal reflection on the views that I held at the time, and my reassessment today.

Ian Martin
London, January 2022

1

THE CASE FOR INTERVENTION
AND THE SECURITY COUNCIL MANDATE

It has become common for Libya and Iraq to be coupled together as leading examples of the failure of western intervention. Whatever the ultimate judgement on each intervention, no purported parallel could be less apt.

The 2003 invasion of Iraq to oust Saddam Hussain was a gratuitous decision by George W. Bush, supported by Tony Blair. The 2011 Libyan uprising, like the neighbouring uprisings of the Arab Spring, took western leaders by surprise. The west had largely made its peace with Muammar Gaddafi after he agreed to decommission Libya's chemical and nuclear weapons programmes and settled legal proceedings regarding the 1988 Lockerbie bombing, and had come to value Libya as an ally in its counter-terrorism efforts. It was major sections of the Libyan people who decided that they would no longer put up with his regime, and it was their uprising and Gaddafi's reaction to it that compelled external actors to consider their own responses.

Even as the uprisings in Tunisia and Egypt headed towards the ousters of Presidents Zine El-Abidine Ben Ali and Hosni Mubarak, there were few expectations among either Libyans or Libya experts of a similar uprising in Libya.[1] Gaddafi's combination of an effective state machinery of repression and distribution of Libya's oil riches to maintain the standard of living of its population was assumed to be able to contain dissent. Gaddafi condemned events in Tunisia; but amid expressions of discontent on social media, demonstrations that included occupations of empty and unfinished flats in protest at housing shortages, and some arrests, he engaged in meetings to try to calm tensions. The regime began talking of increasing salaries, and he sent his son al-Saadi to try to head off demonstrations in Benghazi.[2] No evidence has emerged of encouragement of an uprising by any of the western governments that had been happily back in business with Libya and welcoming the counter-terrorist cooperation of its security services (despite their record of violating human rights)[3] before the events of mid-February took them by surprise. Frederic Wehrey cites US diplomats as saying that the CIA representative at the US embassy in Tripoli, 'concerned with preserving his agency's counterterrorism relationship with the regime, was the most forceful in arguing against the likelihood of serious unrest'.[4] As Alison Pargeter writes: 'Even the most seasoned of Libya-watchers were stunned that the Libyans were finally able to shake off the fear and to rise up en masse.'[5]

Gaddafi's response to the uprising

The outbreak of the Libyan uprising in Benghazi, with the arrest of the lawyer Fathi Terbil on 15 February 2011 and a 'Day of Rage' on 17 February, has been well described in several detailed accounts.[6] The uprising began with peaceful demonstrations that were quickly met with lethal force. The International Commission of Inquiry on Libya mandated by the UN Human Rights Council found that Gaddafi's forces engaged in excessive use of force against demonstrators in the early days of the protests, leading to significant numbers of dead and injured: the nature of the injuries indicated a clear intention to kill, and the level of violence suggested a central policy of violent repression.[7] Its report described shootings of protesters in Benghazi, Misrata, Tripoli, Al Zawiyah and Zintan. Human Rights Watch relayed contemporary accounts of killings of demonstrators in Benghazi, Al Bayda, Ajdabiya and Derna in eastern Libya, and in Misrata, with an estimated death toll of at least 233 in four days to 20 February, followed by at least sixty-two dead after random firing at protesters in Tripoli on 20–21 February.[8] The commission was later informed by doctors that between 20 and 21 February over 200 bodies were brought into morgues in Tripoli. Further shootings took place in Tripoli after Friday prayers on 25 February, when deaths were probably far greater than on 20 February, with wounded persons being shot in the head and later in hospital.[9] Amnesty International found that in eastern Libya, where most of the casualties were in Benghazi and Al Bayda, some 170 people were killed and more than 1,500 injured between 16 and 21 February alone; scores of them were unarmed protesters, while others were killed in the context of armed clashes.[10] The Office of the Prosecutor of the International Criminal Court (ICC) said there was credible evidence that 500–700 civilians died as a result of shootings in February.[11] The ICC Pre-Trial Chamber found that there were reasonable grounds to believe that there was a state policy designed at the highest level aimed at deterring and quelling the February demonstrations by any means, including the use of lethal force. It characterised this as a widespread and systematic attack against the civilian population, constituting crimes against humanity, in which hundreds of civilians were killed by the security forces and hundreds injured, primarily as a result of shootings, and hundreds arrested and imprisoned.[12]

Elements of Gaddafi's army in the east quickly threw their lot in with the uprising, while civilian rebels and individual military defectors took up arms to take and defend control of their cities, attacking police stations and other symbols of the regime. It became impossible to distinguish those who had remained unarmed among the growing numbers of dead and injured, but the commission rejected the regime's claim that it was only after demonstrators had acquired arms that security forces began using live ammunition. In Al Zawiyah, the situation turned violent after the 32nd Brigade under Gaddafi's son Khamis arrived to regain control of the city and fired on still peaceful protesters.[13] Elsewhere, civilians became victims of bombardments, including with Grad rockets and cluster munitions, and other indiscriminate use of force. Amnesty

International reported that Gaddafi's forces often targeted residents in opposition-held areas who were not involved in the fighting:

> They fired indiscriminate rockets, mortars and artillery shells as well as cluster bombs into residential neighbourhoods, killing and injuring scores of residents. On several occasions they fired live ammunition or heavy weapons, including tank shells and rocket-propelled grenades (RPGs), at residents who were fleeing—in what appeared at times to be a policy of 'shoot anything that moves.' Such attacks were particularly widespread in Misratah, but in some cases also took place elsewhere, such as in and around Ajdabiya, when al-Gaddafi forces regained control of the area.[14]

Cities retaken by Gaddafi's forces, including Al Zawiyah and Zuwara, faced a campaign of reprisals, including enforced disappearances. In Tripoli and Zintan, Gaddafi's forces raided hospitals and removed people injured in the protests. In the Nafusa Mountains area, scores of people disappeared when they ventured out of opposition strongholds, particularly around checkpoints established by Gaddafi's forces, from late February onwards. A detained BBC team gave first-hand testimony of torture of those allegedly involved in the uprising in Al Zawiyah,[15] and televised 'confessions' and later testimony confirmed torture and ill-treatment. Amnesty International noted that the practice of abducting individuals deemed as opponents or critics of the political system, followed by a denial of their arrest and the concealment of their fate and whereabouts, was a recurring feature of Gaddafi's rule.[16] This early pattern of behaviour of Gaddafi's forces is relevant to the assessment of what could have been expected if they had gone on to retake Benghazi.

The regime's rhetoric was uncompromising from the outset. In a televised speech on 20 February, Saif al-Islam Gaddafi—until then the hope of reformers—declared that the army would support his father to the last minute: '[W]e will fight until the last man, the last woman, the last bullet.' A close adviser, Mohamed al-Houni, later revealed that he had drafted for Saif the elements of a conciliatory speech; it seems that this had been put aside after discussions within the Gaddafi family.[17] The eventual unscripted speech did criticise the actions of the army in Benghazi, saying that it had been under stress and was not used to crowd control, and made reference to the possibility of new media laws, civil rights and a constitution. But it also accused the protesters of being drug addicts, and its ultimate tone was belligerent. Al-Houni would write in an open letter:

> I was at your side for over a decade … [Then] one unfortunate night, at one frightening moment, came that speech in which you threatened the Libyan people with civil war, the destruction of the oil industry, and the use of force to decide the battle. You chose your side in the conflict very clearly: you chose the side of lies.[18]

In a later interview in an Arab newspaper, Saif said: 'When the situation was good and perfect, I acted as an oppositionist, reformer, and everything. But when people step over red lines, I beat them with the boot. I beat them and beat their fathers too.'[19] The significance of Saif's speech in dashing hopes of a peaceful transition is attested by Mustafa Abdul Jalil, Gaddafi's former justice minister who became chairman of the rebels' National Transitional Council (NTC):

> I was counting on Saif Al-Islam's speech to be balanced. It was a speech prepared for him by a man called Mohamed Abdel-Muttalib Al-Houni. If he had made this speech to the people, he would have been able to replace his father and things could have been resolved amicably and a constitution could have been drafted according to the people's needs … But Saif Al-Islam came out with threats and said the country would be divided. It was a speech that was not expected.[20]

Two days later, Muammar Gaddafi made his first public speech since the beginning of the uprising. He referred to rebels as 'rats'[21] and alleged that young protesters had been given hallucinogenic drugs. He cited past actions by other governments, including Yeltsin's attack on the Duma, the crushing of demonstrators in Tiananmen Square with tanks, deaths in the FBI siege at Waco, and the American destruction of Fallujah: '[T]he unity of China was more important than those people in the square; the unity of the Russian Federation was more important than those in the building.' He threatened the death penalty for anyone who used force against the authority of the state. He concluded by saying that he would march with his supporters 'to purify Libya inch by inch, house by house, home by home, street by street, person by person, until the country is cleansed of the dirt and scum'.

His speech had an immediate impact on those who would play leading roles in the later intervention. It was televised while the UN Security Council was holding its first meeting on Libya. UK Prime Minister David Cameron was on a scheduled trade promotion trip to the Gulf, accompanied by executives from eight British arms manufacturers; he had diverted for a hastily arranged six-hour stopover in Cairo to visit Egypt's Tahrir Square[22] and the following day watched Gaddafi's speech in a hotel room in Doha: he judged Gaddafi 'defiant, deranged—and determined'.[23] A private insight into the mind of Gaddafi around this time is to be found in former UK Prime Minister Tony Blair's transcripts of two phone conversations on 25 February, in which Gaddafi claimed that the rebels in Benghazi wanted to name it 'Al Qaeda Emirates' and were paving the way for Bin Laden in North Africa. He maintained that there was no bloodshed and no fighting except when rebels attacked police stations, but he would have to arm the people and get ready for a fight against 'a campaign of colonisation'.[24]

International condemnation

The actions of the regime were unresponsive to a chorus of condemnation and sanctions short of military intervention. On 22 February, the Arab League condemned the use of force against civilians and suspended Libya's participation in the league. This was echoed on the same day by the General Secretariat of the Organisation of the Islamic Conference (OIC). On 23 February, the AU Peace and Security Council condemned the indiscriminate and excessive use of force and lethal weapons against protesters, and called on the Libyan authorities to ensure the protection and security of citizens. On 25 February, the UN Human Rights Council held an emergency session, condemning the violence, establishing its commission, and recommending that the General Assembly should suspend Libya from the council, which the assembly did on 1 March.

In New York, the UN diplomatic community was greatly impacted by the defections of Libya's representatives. Deputy Permanent Representative Ibrahim Dabbashi, supported by most members of the mission, had called a press conference on 21 February at which he called for referral of Libya to the ICC and imposition of a no-fly zone. Still acting formally on behalf of the Libyan government from which he had defected, and without the authority of the permanent representative, Dabbashi managed to call for a meeting of the UN Security Council. When it met on Libya for the first time on 22 February, both Dabbashi and Permanent Representative Abdurrahman Shalgam, a former foreign minister and close associate of Gaddafi, claimed to represent the Libyan government. In the end, Shalgam addressed the meeting, saying that he had been trying to persuade senior members of the government to stop the bloodshed but telling reporters that he continued to support Gaddafi, his childhood friend.[25] The council issued a press statement (an action that requires unanimous agreement of a negotiated text), condemning the use of force against civilians and repression against peaceful demonstrators and calling on the government of Libya 'to meet its responsibility to protect its own population'. By the time the council met again on 25 February, the defections had culminated in that of Shalgam himself. In open session, after Secretary-General Ban Ki-moon had briefed the council, he made an impassioned speech calling for the UN to save Libya with 'a swift, decisive and courageous resolution', to be embraced by a weeping Dabbashi.[26] In his memoir, Ban describes this as 'the most incredible moment of diplomatic history I had ever witnessed'.[27]

On 26 February, the council adopted its first resolution on the situation, Resolution 1970. The UK, which introduced the draft, included in it every sanction short of a trade embargo or the use of force: an arms embargo; a travel ban and assets freeze on senior members of the Gaddafi regime; referral of the situation in Libya to the ICC. Forcing the pace of negotiations over thirty-six hours with deliberate speed, the UK nonetheless expected more resistance from other members than it received. When it tabled the resolution for vote without prior agreement of the US to the ICC referral, the US complained forcefully about what it regarded as an unfriendly act. Reportedly, a majority of members initially favoured only a threat of referral, arguing that a referral might complicate a negotiated political solution, but were swayed by a letter from Shalgam.[28] To the surprise of the UK and France, the ICC referral became the first to be agreed by the Security Council unanimously, despite five members—permanent members China, Russia and the US, along with India and Lebanon—not being party to the Treaty of Rome. A US proposal to authorise 'all necessary measures'—i.e. the possible use of force—to provide humanitarian assistance did prove a step too far. At Russia's insistence, the resolution stated that the council was acting under Article 41 of the charter, referring to 'measures not involving the use of armed force'. Samantha Power, then President Barack Obama's UN and human rights adviser and later US permanent representative at the UN, described the passing of the resolution as 'probably the best example in history of governments hastily using a vast array of "tools in the toolbox" to try to deter atrocities'.[29] But before long, the implications of an arms embargo for supplies to the rebels, and of the ICC referral for efforts to persuade Gaddafi to step down, would lead some western policy-makers to wonder whether they might not have rushed to deploy all tools before fully considering their implications.

The immediate goal was to check the ongoing repression, but all these condemnations, and very many others from individual governments, had little effect in persuading the regime to exercise restraint. It persisted in its military efforts to recapture cities where it had lost control, with some of the heaviest March attacks taking place in Al Zawiyah, Misrata and Ajdabiya. Its forces faced armed resistance from rebels who at this stage had limited weaponry with which to confront assaults involving the use of heavy weapons, although they quickly gained access to some of the regime's arsenals. On 5 March, the Interim Transitional National Council (later the NTC) formed by the rebels held its first meeting in Benghazi, appointing Mustafa Abdul Jalil as its chairman and designating Mahmoud Jibril to head a Crisis Management Committee that was to manage foreign affairs; this later became an Executive Committee with quasi-governmental responsibilities, with the

NTC operating like a legislature responsible for setting policy.[30] The NTC immediately requested that the international community 'fulfil its obligations to protect the Libyan people from any further genocide and crimes against humanity without any direct military intervention on Libyan soil'. The following day, Secretary-General Ban announced the appointment of former Jordanian Foreign Minister Abdel-Elah Al-Khatib as his special envoy, tasked with consulting with the Libyan parties, neighbouring states, regional organisations and other stakeholders, and exploring how best to resolve the crisis in Libya.

Towards military intervention

As fighting continued, the international response intensified. Increasingly, it focused on the possibility of a no-fly zone, albeit with little realistic analysis of the implications or limitations. Most accounts of the path towards UN Security Council authorisation of military intervention highlight the roles of France, the UK and the US, but some of the earliest calls came from the Arab world. On 26 February, an open letter to world leaders from Arab non-governmental organisations from eighteen countries, and a public statement from some thirty-four Arab intellectuals—the latter headed by the Egyptian former judge of the International Court of Justice and later foreign minister of Egypt and secretary-general of the Arab League, Nabil Elarabi, and including the Libyan writer, Hisham Matar—called for contingency plans for international intervention, under Arab regional leadership, to provide protection for civilians, including, if necessary, a no-fly zone.[31] The overwhelming majority of Arab media was 'almost aggressively' in favour of intervention.[32] The first intergovernmental organisation to call for a no-fly zone was the six-member Gulf Cooperation Council (GCC) on 7 March, reiterating its call when its foreign ministers met on 10 March. On 8 March, the OIC condemned Libya's repression, which it said contravened Islamic values, and called for an emergency meeting of its foreign ministers to consider recommendations including a no-fly zone. On 12 March, the Arab League met at ministerial level and called upon the UN

Security Council to impose immediately a no-fly zone and to establish safe areas in places exposed to shelling.

The leading role among Arab states was played by Qatar, which happened to hold the rotating presidency of the Arab League. In preceding years, Qatar had been enhancing its role as a potential new leader in the region and as an international actor through its mediation initiatives in multiple contexts, as well as through the high profile of Al Jazeera. Although it had been as unprepared for the sudden developments of the Arab Spring as others, as Al Jazeera's saturation coverage moved on from Tunisia and Egypt's Tahrir Square to the Libyan uprising, Qatar's leadership quickly saw the opportunity to be at the forefront of Arab opinion and become the key interlocutor with the west.[33] It was aided in its rapid response by the ruling family's monopoly of decision-making and the near absence of political demands at home, while its openness to Arab political exiles gave it links to opposition leaders, including some key Libyan actors. Thus, 'Qatar's diplomacy was at the forefront of attempts to bring together the regional and international dimensions of policy responses to the Arab Spring.'[34] Its role was not lost on Gaddafi, who concluded his 22 February speech with a denunciation and warning to Qatar: 'You may regret this when it is too late. People who live in glass houses shouldn't throw stones. Who are you?!'

At this juncture, there were no divergences regarding Libya among Qatar, the UAE and Saudi Arabia, although the latter was more preoccupied with developments in Bahrain and Yemen. The ability of the Gulf states to take the lead among the Arabs was aided by the self-absorption of Egypt, the regional heavyweight with the greatest interests in Libya, including a huge contingent of migrant workers. Arab leaders who had been insulted by Gaddafi had little inclination to defend his regime,[35] and resistance by Syria and Algeria was not sufficient to prevent the no-fly zone call. Eleven of the twenty-two members of the league were represented at the 12 March meeting at ministerial level, six of them being countries of the GCC.[36] Some reports add Sudan and Yemen to states opposed to the resolution,[37] but the Omani foreign minister, who chaired the meeting, told journalists that '[n]o-one objected, but there was a partial reservation of one or two countries fearing full scale military intervention'.[38] Diplomats were quoted as saying that Arab League Secretary-General Amr Moussa manoeuvred his way around Article VI of the Arab League's statutes, which requires such decisions to be taken unanimously, by couching the resolution as an appeal to the UN Security Council.[39] The closeness of Qatar and the UAE to France, the UK and the US reflected the security ties they had been developing and that would play a role in the military cooperation among them that lay ahead. Western diplomats encouraged the calls from the Arab League,[40] but suggestions that western would-be interveners arranged the cover of regional support—Cameron later wrote of the Arab League's 12 March resolution that 'William Hague [his foreign secretary] reached a breakthrough in the Arab world'[41]— understate the early initiatives of the Gulf states. To the contrary, the Arab League, Qatar, the UAE and other Arab foreign ministers were active in their telephone diplomacy with Washington in particular, calling for Gaddafi to go.

However, the public calls from the Arab and Islamic world displayed initial ambiguity regarding military intervention.[42] At the same time as the Arab League's resolution called on the Security Council to impose a no-fly zone, its preamble rejected 'all forms of foreign intervention in Libya'; Moussa maintained that a no-fly zone would be a humanitarian measure to protect Libya's civilians and foreigners in the country, and not a military intervention.[43] The OIC statement stressed 'the principled and firm position of the OIC against any form of military intervention to Libya'. Meanwhile, Arab intervention of a different kind was going ahead: from 14 March, GCC Peninsula Shield Forces, initially from the Saudi Arabian National Guard, followed by units from the UAE and Qatar, were dispatched to Bahrain, where the ruling Al-Khalifa family was putting down a popular uprising and sectarian clashes with grave human rights violations by its security forces, including deaths from excessive use of force, torture and arbitrary detention. Qatar also offered to play a mediating role in the context of a US initiative, but this was rejected by the government of Bahrain.[44] Some have suggested that the Gulf rulers saw their support for the

Libyan uprising as a way of diverting criticism of their own lack of democracy; in any event, a largely Shia uprising threatening a Sunni monarch was seen very differently from the revolt against Gaddafi, who had alienated most other Arab rulers.

The AU was unambiguous when it met at the level of heads of state and government on 10 March. It rejected 'any foreign military intervention, whatever its form'. While underscoring the legitimacy of the Libyan people's aspirations for democracy and political reform, it noted the stated commitment of the Libyan authorities to embark upon reforms; and its strong condemnation of the indiscriminate use of force and lethal weapons extended to 'the transformation of pacific demonstrations into an armed rebellion'. It set out a four-point road map calling for urgent African action for

> (i) the immediate cessation of all hostilities, (ii) the cooperation of the competent Libyan authorities to facilitate the timely delivery of humanitarian assistance to the needy populations, (iii) the protection of foreign nationals, including the African migrants living in Libya, and (iv) the adoption and implementation of the political reforms necessary for the elimination of the causes of the current crisis.[45]

Its 23 February decision to send an assessment mission to Libya, which had not yet been implemented, was upgraded to become the establishment of an ad-hoc High-Level Committee comprising five heads of state and government, as well as the chairperson of the AU commission.

The international debate about a no-fly zone intensified among the governments that might be expected to enforce it, before heading towards the UN Security Council. On 28 February, Cameron told the House of Commons that the UK was working with allies on plans for a no-fly zone. France began to make stronger statements in favour of military action. On 10 March, Cameron and French President Nicolas Sarkozy sent a joint open letter to the Council of the European Union calling for continued planning, which could include a no-fly zone or other options against air attacks, 'as the situation evolves on the basis of demonstrable need, a clear legal basis and firm regional support'. The same day, Sarkozy received representatives of the NTC, which had itself called for a no-fly zone; he announced France's recognition of the NTC as the legitimate representative of the Libyan people, taking other governments by surprise.[46]

Reluctance or outright opposition to military intervention remained strong on the part of many governments. Among countries that would play significant roles in later events, Turkey's Prime Minister Recep Tayyip Erdoğan described a potential military intervention as 'unthinkable ... an absurdity',[47] while Foreign Minister Franco Frattini told Italy's Parliament: 'We cannot have war, the international community should not, does not want and cannot do it.'[48] France and the UK were unable to get support for a no-fly zone when NATO defence ministers met on 10 March, from European Union heads of government on 11 March, or from G8 foreign ministers on 14 March: in each case, one of the most significant voices of opposition was that of Germany, while the US remained non-committal. Cameron says he found Europe 'in a peacenik mood'.[49]

In New York, France and the UK had nonetheless begun working towards a second Security Council resolution that would authorise a no-fly zone. Obtaining authorisation for any military intervention was assumed to be a major challenge, yet the effectiveness of a no-fly zone alone was being questioned. The UK Chief of the Defence Staff General David Richards

> was clear from the beginning that curtailing Gaddafi's air power alone through the imposition of a no-fly zone would be insufficient to make a decisive difference ... but for some reason I had a hell of a job trying to convince David Cameron of this ... I made equally ineffective progress with the Foreign Office on this point.[50]

Cameron claims that he recognised that a no-fly zone was not a solution in itself but would be 'a foot in the door' for the sort of action from the air that could stop Gaddafi, and the later shift in proposed council authorisation to 'all necessary measures' was 'what I'd wanted from the beginning'.[51] Sarkozy and his advisers did not believe in the effectiveness of a no-fly zone, which was opposed by France's military planners, and saw it as a cover for their real design: 'Diplomatically, the No Fly Zone will serve as a screen for the French to achieve their true purpose: targeted strikes that Nicolas Sarkozy and his entourage consider alone capable of making Gaddafi submit.'[52] In his meeting with NTC representatives, Sarkozy had told them that a no-fly zone would be insufficient and a further military operation would be necessary. Asking for their discretion, he said that if France could not get a Security Council resolution, together with the UK it would find other ways of legitimising it, perhaps through the Arab League and with an ad-hoc coalition.[53]

After the Arab League's 12 March resolution, Lebanon called for informal consultations of the Security Council on 14 March, and joining with France and the UK, circulated a draft text on 15 March that included authorisation of a no-fly zone. US Permanent Representative Susan Rice had so far roundly rejected this during the council's consultations,[54] but France forced the pace towards a vote; with the debate in Washington not yet resolved, Rice told French Permanent Representative Gérard Araud that the US would not follow France into 'your shitty war'.[55] But together with the advance of Gaddafi's forces towards Benghazi, this urgently required a decision by Obama as to whether the US would support and participate in military action.

President Obama decides

Obama had repeatedly called for Gaddafi to step down, and Secretary of State Hillary Clinton had said on 28 February that no option was off the table, including a no-fly zone, although she was herself undecided. But while Obama 'shared the impulse to save innocent people from tyrants, I was profoundly wary of ordering any kind of military action against Libya', finding 'the idea of waging a new war in a distant country with no strategic importance to the United States to be less than prudent'.[56] Having been warned by Gulf leaders that his call for Mubarak to step down in Egypt threatened stability elsewhere, such as Bahrain, he was 'scornful of the Arab League's hypocrisy'.[57] Within his administration, there was both opposition to any military intervention and understanding of the limitations of a no-fly zone. The internal debate has been described in detail by key participants in their memoirs—now including the president himself—as well as by journalists who interviewed them; the accounts are consistent in all essential respects.[58] Three things stand out: the strongly argued opposition of Secretary of Defense Robert Gates; the evolution of the views of Clinton as she engaged with other international actors and representatives of the NTC; and the careful weighing of information and arguments by Obama as he came to his own judgement.

Gates believed that what was happening in Libya was not a vital national interest of the US; that the US should not attack a third Muslim country in a decade to bring about regime change; that the US military was tired and overstretched; and that conflict in Libya might be protracted rather than a short, easy fight. 'A no-fly zone would be of limited value and never prevented Saddam from slaughtering his people.'[59] In addition to her discussions with NATO allies, Clinton engaged with Arab leaders to assess whether they would be participants in military intervention rather than mere cheerleaders and met NTC Executive Chairman Jibril in Paris on 14 March, concluding that 'there was a reasonable chance the rebels would turn out to be credible partners'.[60] By the time a divided National Security Council (NSC) met on 15 March, Clinton was ready to support intervention.

In the NSC meeting, Obama questioned the information and options he was presented with. He asked what percentage of attacks Gaddafi's forces were carrying out by air, to be told this was negligible. He probed the human rights implications, asking what was known about what was happening to civilians in the towns Gaddafi was recapturing.[61] When Chairman of the Joint Chiefs of Staff Mike Mullen described why a no-fly zone would have little effect on the movement of ground forces or in protecting innocent civilians, he asked why they were even discussing what France and the UK were proposing at the UN: 'In other words, we are being asked to participate in a no-fly zone that will make everyone look like they're doing something but that won't actually save Benghazi.'[62] Clinton, Rice, Power, Deputy National Security Adviser Ben Rhodes and Vice President Joe Biden's National Security Adviser Tony Blinken were among those favouring intervention; Biden himself, White House Chief of Staff

William Daley, National Security Adviser Tom Donilon, Mullen and other senior officials shared Gates' opposition. Obama ended the meeting by saying that he was not yet ready to make a decision, but 'here's the one thing we are not going to do—we're not going to participate in some half-assed no-fly zone that won't achieve our objective'. He demanded 'real options for what an effective intervention would look like' by the time a smaller NSC meeting would convene in a few hours.[63]

Against the advice of his senior advisers other than Clinton and Rice, Obama then decided upon military action that would include targeting Gaddafi's heavy weapons and forces threatening civilian areas. This was to be conditional upon three things: first, Security Council authorisation for a robust mandate to protect civilians—as Rice had suggested, the French and the British would be asked to back off their proposal for a no-fly zone so that the US could put an amended proposal for a broader mandate; second, the participation of Arab League countries; and third, limiting the US role to an initial one, with the Europeans thereafter carrying the bulk of the load.[64] He told Gates that the decision had been a 51–49 call for him.[65] Gates would later write that he had considered resigning over Libya; he had decided not to as he was so close to the end of his tenure and it would just look petulant, but he was frustrated that he had tried to raise all the issues for which the administration was later criticised—an open-ended conflict, an ill-defined mission, Gaddafi's fate, and what came after him, but the president 'had not been interested in getting into any of that'.[66]

The Security Council authorises all necessary measures

Discussions within the UN Security Council were transformed. The next day, the US announced its position and the council began to discuss a text that would authorise 'all necessary measures' to protect civilians. Rice quotes her address to the private council session:

> We will not support a simple no-fly zone, which will do nothing to stop the forces massing on the ground heading for Benghazi. With the robust mandate we seek, we will take out Libyan air

defenses, their heavy weapons—like tanks, artillery, and air-craft—and halt advancing columns of soldiers. This would need to be an unfettered mandate to protect civilians, and I don't want any ambiguity about what we intend to do with it. This will be an air war to save innocent lives. The US is prepared to join militarily with like-minded countries in a coalition to enforce the resolution to save innocents.[67]

The sudden change in the US position initially led the French and British representatives to suspect that Washington might be raising the stakes in order to provoke a Russian or Chinese veto and avoid being itself blamed for failure.[68] Once they were assured that this was not the case, the three countries worked together from capitals as well as in New York to ensure passage of the new text. Russia offered an alternative draft resolution calling for a ceasefire, but this gained little traction and was soon dropped.

The major hurdles for the adoption of the resolution were the avoidance of a veto from Russia or China, and the assembling of at least nine positive votes in the fifteen-member council. In the light of the strong criticism that would soon come from Russia, there has been considerable speculation over its decision to abstain rather than veto. The key foreign policy decision-maker in Moscow was President Dmitry Medvedev. Medvedev had expressed some sympathy for the uprisings in Tunisia and Egypt when questioned at Davos in January. On 9 March, Biden met Medvedev in Moscow: the then US ambassador recalls that Medvedev hinted that he would not block western military intervention in Libya with a veto, and that he shared US analysis about the probabilities of a humanitarian disaster.[69] After Obama had made his decision, he called Medvedev on 16 March to obtain confirmation that there would be no Russian veto;[70] Sarkozy too lobbied Medvedev to abstain.[71] Obama found that Medvedev had serious reservations about any western-led military action that could lead to regime change, but he also 'wasn't inclined to run interference for Gaddafi'.[72] Suggested explanations for Medvedev's decision include his personal rapprochement with the US and the west; a genuine humanitarian concern, or avoidance of blame for blocking intervention if there were a massacre in Benghazi; a desire for good commercial relations with a new government that might emerge; and/or anticipation that the west might be heading into a quagmire.[73] Medvedev's divergence from the views of Prime Minister Vladimir Putin and other senior officials seems to have been real.[74] Russia's ambassador to Libya cabled his dissent, and when fired by Medvedev, declared publicly that the president was acting against Russia's interests.[75] Only a few days after the resolution was passed and the bombing began, on 21 March, Putin denounced the UN resolution, likening it to 'a medieval call to crusade'; this provoked Medvedev to call talk of crusades 'unacceptable' and to defend his 'qualified decision' not to veto, saying that

> Russia did not use its power of veto for the simple reason that I do not consider the resolution in question wrong. Moreover, I think that overall this resolution reflects our understanding of events in Libya too, but not completely ... everything that is happening in Libya is a result of the Libyan leadership's absolutely intolerable behaviour and the crimes that they have committed against their own people.[76]

A 23 March declaration by the State Duma said that the deputies considered that the decision to abstain was appropriate in that situation: 'This option maintained the cohesion of the international community in rejecting military repression of the civilian population of Libya, while leaving intact the message sent to the Libyan leadership to protect its citizens.'[77] Obama thought that it was inconceivable that Putin hadn't signed off on Medvedev's decision to have Russia abstain, or that he had failed to understand its scope at the time, and concluded that his decision to make his handpicked successor look bad was 'a sign ... that Putin intended to formally retake the reins in Russia'.[78]

China's decision-making is characteristically more opaque, but a dominant consideration in this as in other contexts was its respect for the position of regional groups. The difference between the positions of the Arab League and the AU, as well as known disagreements within each, posed a problem but confirmed that abstention was the safest course. Despite its consistent defence of sovereignty, China had no particular sympathy for Gaddafi; it was stung by the reference in his 22 February speech to the crushing of demonstrators in Tiananmen Square, and the People's Liberation Army had had to carry out a major evacuation of some 36,000 of its citizens working on projects in Libya. In any event, China would have been unlikely to cast a veto alone when Russia had decided not to do so.[79]

Of the council's remaining members, the most crucial were the three African countries—Gabon, Nigeria and South Africa: if they abstained in line with the opposition of the AU to military intervention, they would deny the resolution the necessary nine votes. South African President Jacob Zuma had been designated a member of the AU's High-Level Committee to implement its road map; Obama called him personally to secure his support, which he gave despite warnings by his foreign ministry that a mandate for 'all necessary measures' might be a pretext for regime change.[80] Nigeria had made clear that it would align itself with South Africa.[81] All three African members voted for the resolution, which was adopted on 17 March with ten positive votes and five abstentions: Brazil, China, Germany, India and Russia.

Among the countries that abstained, Russia, India and China complained in their public explanations of the vote that questions that had been asked during negotiation of the resolution had gone unanswered: how and by whom the no-fly zone would be enforced; and what would be the rules of engagement and the limits on the use of force. India noted that the council had not yet had any report from UN Special Envoy Al-Khatib, who had visited Tripoli for the first time from 13 to 16 March, or briefing about his assessment. Germany saw great risks regarding the possibility of large-scale loss of life and a protracted conflict. Brazil feared that the use of force could exacerbate tensions on the ground and change the narrative away from the spontaneous, homegrown nature of the popular movement in North Africa and the Middle East. Not only those who abstained but also Nigeria and South Africa emphasised the political path to conflict resolution through the AU High-Level Committee and the UN special envoy. Lebanon expressed the hope that the resolution 'will have a deterring effect, ensure that the Libyan authorities move away from using all forms of violence against their own people, and avert the use of force'.[82]

Four aspects of Resolution 1973 are of particular relevance to later controversy. The first, of course, is the wide scope of its mandate regarding the use of 'all necessary measures'. This extended to 'civilians *and civilian populated areas* [emphasis added]' under threat of attack, and did not set any limitations on the use of force by member states 'acting under the authorisation nationally or through regional organisations or arrangements'. It merely required them to inform the secretary-general immediately of the measures they took pursuant to the authorisation, which were to be immediately reported to the Security Council.

Second, in deference to Arab and other sensitivities regarding external intervention, and to underline a distinction from the unauthorised invasion and subsequent US/UK occupation of Iraq, the resolution explicitly excluded foreign occupation. Initially drafted as 'while excluding an occupation force', the resolution's language was strengthened at Lebanon's request to more emphatically 'excluding a foreign occupation force of any form on any part of Libyan territory'.[83]

Third, all necessary measures were authorised 'notwithstanding paragraph 9 of resolution 1970 [i.e. the arms embargo]'. This would later be argued to permit arms supplies to the rebels, although it is not clear whether this was a conscious intention when the resolution was drafted. The purpose of arms supplies would in any event still be limited to the protection of civilians and civilian-populated areas and be subject to the obligation of member states to report all measures taken to the secretary-general.[84]

Fourth, although the resolution's main provisions related to military action and strengthening sanctions, late additions demanded a ceasefire and stressed the need to intensify efforts to find a solution to the crisis. Early drafts had referred only to the Arab League and not at all to the AU: the final resolution referred to intended visits to Libya of the UN special envoy and of the AU High-Level Committee 'with the aim of facilitating dialogue to lead to the political reforms necessary to find a peaceful and sustainable solution'. Pressed for by South Africa, this language may have helped to secure its vote, and stood first in the operative paragraphs of the resolution, but the intended visits were only 'noted' rather than being welcomed or supported.

As the council negotiated and then prepared to vote on Resolution 1973, the tone of Gaddafi's rhetoric had remained defiant.[85] His forces had retaken Al Zawiyah, were shelling Misrata, and had entered Ajdabiya, from where they would advance towards Benghazi. Speaking on the radio on 17 March, the day the resolution would be adopted in New York, he repeated the image of cleansing:

> They are finished, they are wiped out. From tomorrow you will only find our people. You all go out and cleanse the city of Benghazi. A small problem that has become an international issue. And they are voting on it tonight … because they are determined. As I have said, we are determined. We will track them down, and search for them, alley by alley, road by road, the Libyan people all of them together will be crawling out.

He promised amnesty for those 'who throw their weapons away' but 'no mercy or compassion' for those who fight. He told Benghazi residents that soldiers would search every house in the city—'we will find you in your closets'—but people who had no arms had no reason to fear, telling his troops not to pursue any rebels who dropped their guns and fled when government forces reached the city.[86]

In response to the adoption of Resolution 1973, the Libyan government issued a statement agreeing to an immediate ceasefire and sent a letter to the president of the Security Council saying that, 'being keen to comply with the ceasefire, [it] is fully prepared for the deployment of international monitors to oversee it'. Prime Minister Al-Baghdadi Ali Al-Mahmoudi urgently called Ban asking him to intervene; there was no doubt, Ban said, that the Libyans were trying hard to ward off military action.[87] But no signs were reported of the cessation of military action on the ground: the bombardment of Misrata never stopped, and at 3 a.m. on the morning of 19 March Gaddafi's forces moved on Benghazi, rocketing the town from the Ajdabiya road to the south-west.[88] That day, France convened the first 'Friends of Libya' meeting in Paris, and in the evening launched the first air strikes, followed swiftly by the US and the UK.

Reflections

The case that intervention was necessary to prevent a 'massacre' or 'bloodbath' in Benghazi has been questioned.[89] Those who maintain that a massacre was unlikely advance a number of arguments. The long history of repression during Gaddafi's four decades in power did not include massacres, with the single exception of the killing of 1,200 or more inmates in Abu Salim prison in 1996. In the immediate context of the uprising, there had not been large-scale killing of civilians as Gaddafi's forces had retaken cities such as Al Zawiyah and Ajdabiya. Gaddafi had used his sons to try to calm the events in Benghazi and had threatened only those using weapons while promising to protect unarmed residents. There had not been attacks on civilians from the air, as had been alleged in making the case for a no-fly zone.

There is no doubt that there was substantial exaggeration both in media reporting and in the rhetoric of the uprising's supporters. On 21 February, Al Jazeera reported that Libyan military aircraft were bombing anti-government protesters in Tripoli; the report, which was taken up widely in other media, seemed to be given credibility when two Libyan air force pilots defected to Malta with their jets and were reported to have said they had been ordered to bomb protesters in Benghazi.[90] But Gates and Mullen later said they had no confirmation of attacks on civilians from the air, and French Foreign Minister Alain Juppé said it appeared to be untrue. The regime did use air power in zones where civilians were present, but its intentional use against civilians was never established.[91]

It was also on 21 February that Dabbashi described the regime's actions as 'genocide', a quite inappropriate use of the term that would be repeated by others. Rice told the Security Council that a failure to vote for the second resolution would be 'another historic failure of this Council to prevent a potential genocide'; she believed that atrocities were certain and maintained that Obama 'should not allow what could be perceived as his Rwanda to occur'.[92] White House Middle East strategist Dennis Ross was widely reported as saying: 'We were looking at "Srebrenica on steroids".'[93] Sarkozy's adviser Jean-David Levitte testified that 'from the outset, the head of state has decided not to allow a new Rwanda or a new Srebrenica at the gates of France'.[94] Richards recalled that in London 'the decision was taken ... that it would be a stain on our conscience forever if we allowed another Srebrenica; I remember a lot of talk about Srebrenica.'[95] Such repeated comparisons with Srebrenica and Rwanda seem in retrospect wildly overblown. But there is ample evidence, from both contemporary references and subsequent memoirs, that the experience of Rwanda and Srebrenica, some of it first-hand, weighed heavily on policy-makers in Washington, London, Paris and beyond: the then foreign minister of Norway later reminded critics, 'as politicians, we belong to a generation that has the disastrous experiences of Rwanda and Srebrenica with us'.[96] Rwanda's President Paul Kagame said the intervention was the right thing to do: 'No country knows better than my own the costs of the international community failing to intervene to prevent a state killing its own people.'[97] Bosnia and Herzegovina was now one of the ten members of the Security Council voting for Resolution 1973. There is no evidence that the fears were a fabricated excuse for intervention for other reasons: they were real, not a pretext.

Gaddafi had a long record of executions, disappearances and reprisals against opponents, and the behaviour of his forces in retaking cities that had rebelled was in fact far from reassuring. What might happen in Benghazi—the epicentre of the uprising, with a long history of mutual hatred towards Gaddafi, and a population of perhaps 600,000—could hardly be argued from the experience of Ajdabiya, a relatively small city much of whose population had fled before it was retaken. There were claims from within Gaddafi's forces that their instructions were, to say the least, inconsistent with an undertaking to target only those who had taken up arms, and they hardly constituted a disciplined force that would be likely to respect such an undertaking. But perhaps above all, it was the violent language of so much of Gaddafi's speeches, from 22 February to the eve of the advance on Benghazi, that seemed to support the apprehension about what might take place if it went ahead. Whatever the objective assessment might be, especially with the benefit of hindsight, there can be no doubting the subjective fears at the time, both in Benghazi and among external actors. The International Committee of the Red Cross withdrew staff from Benghazi on 16 March, saying that it was 'extremely concerned about what will happen to civilians, the sick and wounded, detainees and others who are entitled to protection in times of conflict'.[98] Libyans who were in Benghazi as Gaddafi's forces reached its outskirts testify to the grim expectations of residents, many of whom were trying to flee the city.

The Libya intervention must also be understood in the wider context of the Arab Spring. The ousters of Ben Ali and Mubarak in two neighbouring states had led to expectations of rapid transitions elsewhere. There was a strong concern that if Gaddafi succeeded in crushing the uprising in Libya, this would be a major setback to a trend towards democratic reform in the Arab world. As Obama put it: 'The democratic impulses that are dawning across the region would be eclipsed by the darkest form of dictatorship, as repressive leaders concluded that violence is the best strategy to cling to power.'[99] At this early stage, the many declarations that Gaddafi must go were indications that his departure was assumed to be inevitable, rather than that regime change had already been decided upon as a strategic military objective. The focus of hasty decision-making amid multiple crises in the region was to stop the killing, while the encouragement of defections was expected to herald the collapse of the regime, without any plan for a protracted military campaign.

Testimony to the climate of opinion in the Arab world has emerged from a surprising source: Osama Bin Laden. Documents seized from his home in Pakistan in the raid by US Special Forces include an account of family discussions in which his nineteen-year-old daughter tells her father that 'people await your position about the West's intervention in Libya'. Jihadi leaders had consistently pointed to the west's support of Muslim dictators, yet in Libya the west intervened in support of the people against the dictator. 'This is a very difficult position', Bin Laden admitted, conceding that the 'people rejoiced' at the intervention. Jihadis, he told his daughter, 'have no option but to remain silent'.[100] After initial enthusiasm for the revolutions, he lamented that al-Qaeda and other jihadi groups were mostly on the sidelines.[101]

The western governments that spearheaded the intervention made their decisions under great time pressure, with their Middle East diplomats and specialists trying to keep up with several other complex and fast-moving situations for which they had been unprepared—including in Tunisia, Egypt, Bahrain, Yemen and Syria. There was no anticipation of a protracted involvement, and thus no real attempt at strategic analysis and planning prior to intervention; if there had been, it would have found that understanding of Libya was particularly limited.[102] The isolation of the Gaddafi decades had limited both diplomatic engagement and academic research; the focus of recent western interest was largely restricted to counter-terrorism cooperation and trade opportunities. Many of the issues that eventually emerged as most critical appear to have been considered little, if at all: the extent of Gaddafi's support, the inclusiveness of the NTC, the relevance of Libya's tribes. Within the AU and among Libya's neighbours, there was concern about the potential implications for the region, especially the Sahel: Chad's President Idriss Déby Itno warned against 'opening the Libyan Pandora's box',[103] and Algeria was equally concerned that it would pay a price for destabilisation in the region and used its influence with the AU and individual African countries to try to avert regime change. Yet there is little evidence of such concerns among western policy-makers, even in France, which might have been expected to consider consequences it would eventually confront in the Sahel. There was some questioning of the extent to which Islamists were involved in the uprising, but the early assessment was that they were not the dominant force.

Was there an alternative course of action that could have halted the advance on Benghazi and the risk of further imminent bloodshed? As the bombing began, the AU High-Level Committee was preparing to fly to meet Gaddafi. A Norwegian mediation team had already been in Tripoli under the auspices of Saif, and as Resolution 1973 was adopted he asked them how military action could be averted. Many voices were calling for a ceasefire and dialogue. But Gaddafi's record and his rhetoric surely meant that only his own decision to order a clear halt to the actions of his forces in the east and in the assault on Misrata, and to show a serious openness to dialogue, would have averted the bombing. The question of whether there was ever a real possibility of a negotiated transition is one that would persist throughout the months ahead as the military campaign became prolonged.

2

ALL NECESSARY MEASURES

NATO'S OPERATION UNIFIED PROTECTOR
AND THE GROUND WAR

Implementation of the UN Security Council authorisation of 'all necessary measures to protect civilians and civilian populated areas' has been highly controversial, amid little transparency and some obfuscation and secrecy. The main charge has been that NATO and the intervening states went beyond civilian protection to pursue regime change and in doing so violated or exceeded the council mandate. NATO has also been accused of reluctance to investigate and acknowledge the number of civilian deaths caused by an intervention mandated to protect civilians. Those acting under the mandate were required to report to the secretary-general and thus to the Security Council, but post-action reporting enabled no effective oversight of the authorisation to use force, and together with the weak monitoring of the arms embargo, this raises major questions of accountability. The lack of transparency regarding extensive bilateral military operations, including deployment to Libya of covert special forces, has impeded analysis of their role and its implications.

The attacks begin

From 19 to 20 March, US, French and British missile strikes obliterated Gaddafi's air force; attacked his armour and troops on the ground, reversing the advance on Benghazi; and destroyed command and control installations, including in Tripoli.[1] While transition to a NATO operation was being debated and planned for, the leading interveners were joined in the assault by some ten other NATO member states, plus Qatar and the UAE—the latter after it was talked out of threats to withdraw its willingness to participate because of US criticism of the GCC operation in Bahrain.[2] Rice had put the Security Council clearly on notice that 'we will take out Libyan air defenses, their heavy weapons—like tanks, artillery, and aircraft—and halt advancing columns of soldiers'.[3] But the extent of the attacks on command and control installations took many by surprise and contributed to an immediate storm of criticism. They included a strike on Gaddafi's Bab al-Azizia compound in Tripoli. Although General Carter Ham, the head of US Africa Command (AFRICOM), said it was aimed at a command centre within the extensive compound and not at Gaddafi himself, this led to public disagreement over whether Gaddafi was a legitimate target.[4] In the UK, Defence Secretary Liam Fox said that Gaddafi could potentially be targeted, while Chief of Defence Staff Richards said 'absolutely not', whereupon Prime Minister Cameron reproached Richards along the lines of '[y]ou do the fighting, I'll do the talking'.[5] The UK position was that while removing the Libyan leader was not an aim of the UN resolution, were it to be necessary to do so in order to fulfil the resolution's aim of protecting civilians, it would be legal.[6] US Defense Secretary Gates later said 'I can't recall any specific decision that said, "Well let's just take him out," [but] I don't think there was a day that passed that people didn't hope he would be in one of those command and control centers.'[7] By the time NATO assumed full command on 31 March, Gaddafi's air force had been destroyed and Benghazi saved from attack, but the siege of Misrata continued, while regime forces had retaken Ajdabiya and were adapting their tactics to make attack from the air more difficult, discarding military vehicles and switching to technical vehicles similar to those used by the rebels.[8]

Immediate criticism of the attacks was encouraged by regime allegations of civilian casualties, mostly without confirmation by independent sources or objective investigation on the ground. Arab League Secretary-General Amr Moussa was quoted as saying that '[w]hat is happening in Libya differs from the aim of imposing a no-fly zone, and what we want is the protection of civilians and not the bombardment of more civilians', but he was brought back into line by reminders of his support for Resolution 1973 and plans for its implementation.[9] Russia and China were quick to condemn the strikes: Medvedev remonstrated against Putin's fierce criticism referring to 'a medieval call to crusade',[10] but Russian spokespersons repeatedly stated that the mandate was being exceeded. Similar statements by Brazil, India and South Africa meant that by 23 March all five of the BRICS[11] had joined in the criticism and, as all were currently members of the UN Security Council, heated debate was soon opened up there.[12] Zuma's decision to support adoption of Resolution 1973 did not prevent him saying that South Africa 'rejected any foreign intervention, whatever its form', while former President Thabo Mbeki bitterly denounced the way that

[t]he countries of the West, acting through the UN Security Council, have used their preponderant power to communicate the message to Africa that they are as determined as ever to decide the future of Africa, regardless of the views of the Africans, much like what they did during the years of the colonial domination of our continent.[13]

Transition to NATO

Meanwhile, debate about whether the continuing military action should become a NATO operation was complex and sometimes stormy. France would have preferred the continuation of a coalition operation outside NATO—it feared that negative views of NATO in the Arab world would undermine support there and that countries within NATO that had opposed or been hesitant about the operation, such as Germany and Turkey, would inhibit it. But the US and the UK, the two countries that had launched the military campaign with France, were both insistent that it could only be effectively conducted in the NATO framework, and this was conclusive. Clinton explained that 'NATO assuming the responsibility for the entire mission means that the United States will move to a supporting role ... We are supporting a mission through NATO that was very much initiated by European requests joined by Arab requests.'[14] Obama was blunt in spelling out the limitations of US participation; Cameron describes a video call:

> On the one side of the split screen I saw Obama, clearly frustrated that he had been sucked in—blindsided by a bargain that asked for American support only in the initial phases, but that would now clearly require it in the long term. He said he would find it more difficult to trust us again. On the other side of the screen was an emotional Sarkozy. 'I can't believe you're doing this,' he said to Obama, as he set out the limits of America's involvement.[15]

France initially agreed that the maritime arms embargo should be a NATO operation before then conceding that NATO should also enforce the no-fly zone while still preferring that the more aggressive interveners would separately carry out attacks on ground forces and installations. But it was persuaded by the US and UK of the difficulties of two parallel missions. NATO command and control were also strongly favoured by Italy, Norway and the other member states that had agreed to take part: the Arab participants agreed that it was not an obstacle for them, and Germany agreed to abstain rather than obstruct an operation it had opposed. There had been open tension between France and Turkey, which resented not being invited to the meeting Sarkozy had convened in Paris on 19 March; it had been critical of military intervention and publicly cast aspersions on France's motives.[16] But having initially opposed NATO taking responsibility, Turkey moved towards wanting to have a share in influencing events through its membership of the alliance. Clinton played a key role in brokering agreement among France, Turkey, the UK and the US. Its basis was that NATO would conduct the military campaign, while the political lead would be in the hands of a separate contact group, limiting the role of the full North Atlantic Council (NAC).[17]

NATO had been planning for four potential operations: humanitarian relief, enforcement of the arms embargo, a no-fly zone and/ or a 'no-fly zone plus' or 'no-drive zone'. In the event, planning for a humanitarian operation was taken up by the European Union (although the EU's plans were never to be activated by a UN request). NATO proceeded to adopt two operational plans within its overall 'Operation Unified Protector': one for the arms embargo, activated on 23 March, and the other for the no-fly zone plus: 'Protection of Civilians and Civilian Populated Areas Under Threat of Attack in Libya', activated on 31 March.[18] With the US wanting to keep a low profile, and potential objections to either France or the UK providing the commander of the operation, the appointment went to Canadian Air Force General Charles Bouchard.[19]

Within NATO, the NAC and the countries that would participate in the campaign discussed its limits. The NAC agreed that the stipulation in Resolution 1973 against any foreign occupation force should mean no boots on the ground at all: NATO's spokeswoman declared that '[t]here is going to be no presence on the ground … There is going to be no foreign military intervention on the ground.'[20] There was also a total ban on direct communications with any national forces operating in Libya or with the opposition's forces.[21] This had already been anticipated in the interpretation of the protection of civilians mandate by Carter Ham: 'Our mission is not to support any opposition forces. So while we have reports from people who are reported to be in the opposition, there is no official communication or formal communication with those in this so-called opposition that are opposing the regime's ground forces.'[22]

The military objective: protection of civilians, supporting the rebels, regime change?

The debate about targeting Gaddafi had already intensified the issue of whether regime change was an objective of NATO's operation, and there were early denials. Belgium declared that '[s]iding with the rebels to liberate towns is not in our mandate';[23] its foreign minister stated that 'it is not the intention to use military force until Gaddafi has relinquished power. If Gaddafi were still there when the violence against the civilian population stops, then Resolution 1973 will have been effective.'[24] As he assumed command, Bouchard stated that the 'aim is to protect not help rebels'.[25] In a major speech explaining his actions on 28 March, Obama said that

> [j]ust as there are those who have argued against intervention in Libya, there are others who have suggested that we broaden our military mission beyond the task of protecting the Libyan people, and do whatever it takes to bring down Qaddafi and usher in a new government. Of course, there is no question that Libya—and the world—would be better off with Qaddafi out of power. I, along with many other world leaders, have embraced that goal, and will actively pursue it through non-military means. But broadening our military mission to include regime change would be a mistake.[26]

The 'Friends of Libya' meeting that Sarkozy had convened in Paris on 19 March as military action began was followed up by a London Conference on 29 March, which established itself as a Contact Group that would meet thereafter to bring together supporters of the intervention in the presence of representatives of the NTC, with the chair rotating among leading states.[27] A key aspect of potential support to the rebels, the supply of arms, was discussed in London. NATO's Secretary-General Anders Fogh Rasmussen was clear: 'The purpose of the arms embargo is to stop the flow of weapons into Libya … We are there to protect the Libyan people, not to arm them.' The same view was taken by Norway, Belgium and Italy, the last saying it would be an 'extreme measure which would divide the international community'.[28] But the international community was already divided on the issue. Clinton said that the US interpretation was that Resolution 1973 amended or overrode the absolute prohibition of arms to anyone in Libya, so that there could be legitimate transfer of arms if a country were to choose to do that; it was reported that Obama had already signed a presidential 'finding' authorising covert support to the rebels, and in a television interview he said that the US had not ruled out providing weapons.[29] Foreign Secretary William Hague told the UK Parliament that although there were differing views internationally, the government's legal advice was that Resolution 1973 'would not necessarily rule out the provision of assistance to those protecting civilians in certain circumstances'.[30] When Qatar hosted the Contact Group on 13 April, the intention to provide arms to the rebels became more explicit: the emir told CNN that if the opposition asked for weapons, 'we are going to provide them'.[31]

Immediately after the Doha Contact Group meeting, on 14 April, foreign ministers of NATO and non-NATO contributors to Operation Unified Protector met and strongly endorsed the call for Gaddafi to step down. Resolution 1973 had not defined any end state for implementation of its mandate, but the governments agreed that NATO's operation would continue until three conditions were met:

> (1) All attacks and threats of attack against civilians and civilian-populated areas have ended; (2) The regime has verifiably withdrawn to bases all military forces, including snipers, mercenaries and para-military forces, including from all populated areas they have forcibly occupied, entered or besieged throughout all of Libya ...; (3) The regime must permit full, safe and unhindered humanitarian access to all the people in Libya in need of assistance.[32]

The same day, an op-ed article co-signed by Cameron, Obama and Sarkozy declared that

> [o]ur duty and our mandate under U.N. Security Council Resolution 1973 is to protect civilians, and we are doing that. It is not to remove Qaddafi by force. But it is impossible to imagine a future for Libya with Qaddafi in power ... so long as Qaddafi is in power, NATO must maintain its operations so that civilians remain protected and the pressure on the regime builds ... Qaddafi must go and go for good.[33]

Officially entitled 'Libya's Pathway to Peace' but carried elsewhere under the headline 'The Bombing Continues until Gaddafi Goes',[34] the op-ed signalled that the line between protection of civilians and regime change, between the authorised military objective and the political objective, was getting blurred.

NATO was clear that its targeting must go to the greatest possible lengths to avoid civilian casualties. This had been anticipated before the handover: Defence Secretary Fox had set the Collateral Damage Estimation for UK strikes at zero, reportedly without consultation with Cameron and to his fury.[35] The NAC applied a zero-casualty stipulation to the NATO concept of operations: no target could be engaged unless every effort had been made to reduce the prospect of civilian casualties to zero.[36] This applied both to planned deliberate strikes, identified and cleared in advance, and to dynamic strikes, based on information discovered during the sortie. For planned strikes on fixed targets, thirty minutes of observation was required to ensure that the site was free of civilians, and smaller precision munitions were used in place of larger bombs to minimise collateral damage.[37] Strict adherence to the rules of engagement meant that NATO was unable to strike some 70 per cent of the targets in its database.[38]

Protecting civilians by avoiding civilian casualties was one thing: applying in practice the requirement that each and every target must be justified in terms of protecting civilians was another, and it was here that mission creep began. After the 14 April NAC decision, the NATO striker group is said to have 'decided that Qaddafi's forces were fair game anywhere in Libya as long as attacks against civilians were occurring somewhere because those attacks posed an intrinsic threat to the Libyan populace'.[39] Publicly, NATO's spokesperson made clear that the alliance was not only targeting the forces that were directly threatening the civilian population: '[W]e also at the same time attack his … what we call, in military terms, second echelon forces, so forces that are further away from the population, that are gathering, that are massing, that are starting to move towards a civilian area.'[40] The French were relieved that the criterion for strikes was to protect civilians threatened 'or likely to be threatened', so that command centres and the 'second echelon', which were the heart of their targets, could be struck.[41] When the regime reported that Gaddafi's youngest son, Saif al-Arab, had been killed along with three of Gaddafi's grandchildren in a NATO strike, NATO confirmed that it had hit a command and control building in Tripoli, and not a residential building as the regime claimed.[42]

The Naples headquarters of the operation still

> had to resist the pressure from individual nations or influence from senior civilian or military leaders which sought to bring about a change in the fundamental targeting philosophy. The slow progress of the operation—which was perceived as a 'stalemate'—gave

these politicians the necessary excuse to push for more aggressive targeting.[43]

Already in April, British and French Foreign Ministers Hague and Juppé called on NATO to be more aggressive as its efforts were not sufficient.[44] In mid-May, UK Chief of Defence Staff Richards called for more intense military action and a change in NATO's rules of engagement: 'At present Nato is not attacking infrastructure targets in Libya ... But if we want to increase the pressure on Gaddafi's regime then we need to give serious consideration to increasing the range of targets we can hit.'[45] Bouchard resisted pressure for attacks on infrastructure—only one road was hit in seven months, in a UK dynamic strike mission that gave him cause for concern.[46] Throughout the summer, delegations from NATO countries recommending targets such as oil refineries and pipelines, highways, government buildings, civilian infrastructure, the water network and even individual leaders connected to the regime were all 'met with Bouchard's intransigence and staff dismissal given that not a single target was consistent with the prescribed target sets or with the authorized rules of engagement'.[47] But there was particular criticism of NATO targeting when on 30 July three satellite dishes of Libyan state television in Tripoli were struck, with UNESCO Director-General Irina Bokova deploring an attack she called 'unacceptable'.[48] NATO, however, said that the airstrikes aimed to degrade Gaddafi's

> use of satellite television as a means to intimidate the Libyan people and incite acts of violence against them ... Striking specifically these critical satellite dishes will reduce the regime's ability to oppress civilians while at the same time preserve television broadcast infrastructure that will be needed after the conflict.[49]

Pressure on NATO for more intensive bombing also came from the rebels—publicly and directly, as well as through France and the UK. There was particular frustration with the inability to stop the regime's artillery bombardment and constant ground attacks on Misrata. The NTC's military commander, General Abd al-Fattah Younis, declared on 5 April that 'if NATO wanted to free Misrata, they could have done that a few days ago' and again on

14 April complained publicly that 'NATO is disappointing us';[50] he went to Paris and Brussels to press his case. In retrospective interviews,[51] rebel commanders expressed exasperation at NATO's aversion to striking targets in densely crowded urban areas and acknowledged trying to provoke Gaddafi's artillery into firing in the direction of civilians so that NATO would strike. But there was also what Frederic Wehrey characterises as 'grudging acknowledgement' of the pressure on NATO not to make a mistake. When NATO bombing killed groups of rebels, mistaking them for regime troops, the NTC was forgiving.[52]

As the interpretation that the protection of civilians required removing the regime that posed the threat to them gathered steam, participating countries varied considerably in the nature and extent of actions they were undertaking. Only eight NATO countries were involved in all aspects of the operation: Belgium, Canada, Denmark, France, Italy, Norway, the UK and the US.[53] Red-card holders for each of the participating nations had the right to veto the use of its assets proposed for a particular mission if it was not in accordance with national policy.[54] Reportedly, national red cards were often played, and considerable differences across the alliance also arose about the rules of engagement: after the end of the operation, Bouchard acknowledged that 'we would find ourselves with certain nations being uncomfortable with certain targets ... What was important was that all the targets were addressed as necessary.'[55] The Netherlands and Spain participated only in the enforcement of the no-fly zone and not the bombing campaign. Sweden, which had joined the operation from outside NATO, was restricted by its parliament to the task of creating and upholding the no-fly zone and had to work out what were legally and politically acceptable activities within this mandate until it was rewritten when it was renewed in late June.[56] Norway had no such limitations: it was a contributor to air–ground operations and carried out 15–18 per cent of the bombing in the first part of the campaign, and about 10 per cent during the operation as a whole. The evaluation by its retrospective Libya Commission attributed Norway's withdrawal from the operation on 1 August to 'practical reasons related to the operational ability of the Air Force to support other

Norwegian contributions to international operations', but the decision was taken in a context of some domestic criticism, and the commission noted that Norway had had little opportunity to influence the political direction of the campaign.[57] Turkey participated only in the arms embargo.

From France and the UK, Sarkozy and Cameron pushed for military victory. Cameron's retrospective account described NATO as focusing on 'wider targets that would help the Libyan rebels'. He himself was 'commissioning work on military options—precision targeting, the mentoring of NTC commanders ... constantly trying to keep the pressure up ... exasperated that too many parts of government seemed more concerned about a future Libya war inquiry than about the war itself'.[58] His military commander, General Richards, refers to Cameron's 'highly effective leadership' as single-minded:

> We had far too many meetings on Libya in the space of six months—and we were constantly getting into what I called the 'tactical weeds' as Cameron sought to micro-manage the campaign ... I told him that being in the Combined Cadet Force at Eton was not a qualification for trying to run the tactical detail of a complex coalition war effort in Libya.[59]

The then UK ambassador to Libya, exiled to London, observed that political involvement in the operational detail 'led to an over-emphasis on short-term results and a focus on day-to-day political headlines rather than the longer-term strategic objectives given higher priority by departmental experts'.[60] Sarkozy too was said to have a voracious appetite for detail. In Washington, Defense Secretary Gates also complained about micromanagement by White House national security staff, recalling that the same day the military campaign began, he started to get questions at a principals' meeting from National Security Adviser Donilon and White House Chief of Staff Daley about the targeting of Libyan ground forces: 'I angrily shot back, "You are the biggest micromanagers I have ever worked with. You can't use a screwdriver reaching from D.C. to Libya on our military operations."'[61]

In May, France and the UK began to deploy attack helicopters, which along with the Predator drones the US had added in late

April, were able to fly at much lower altitude and make precision strikes in conflict zones, adding significantly to the risk to regime forces.[62] The French pressed for speeding up strikes once targets had been identified and had an ally in Rasmussen, who felt that Bouchard had yet to make full use of the rules of engagement.[63] It seems, moreover, that the actions undertaken by the most aggressive nations did not stop at those authorised as part of the NATO operation. France in particular had insisted on retaining some direct operational control of its forces.[64] The account co-authored by the director of operations for Operation Unified Protector refers to tensions 'between planned, approved NATO operations and unscheduled unauthorised national activities', and 'indications that individual nations were directing autonomous tactical action outside the scope of current operational priorities. Some of these were skating on the edge of the interpretation and subsequent implementation of the NAC-endorsed plans, target sets, rules of engagement and collateral damage.'[65] Sarkozy was impatient with the UK's agonising over legality regarding helicopter strikes: 'There are endless discussions among the English as to whether they are or are not purely within the resolution. As a result, down below, the targets don't wait for the lawyer's report to take cover.'[66] Norway's Libya Commission noted that the Norwegian authorities realised that despite the transfer of responsibility to NATO, countries that participated in the operation could not be prevented from also carrying out their own missions under national command, and this became a 'demanding' issue, in particular because of different attitudes to practical cooperation with the rebel forces.[67] In the final stages of the operation, NATO HQ had to apply 'unremitting pressure on the contributing nations to go the last mile and not withdraw forces or reverse their transfer of authority to go under national command for autonomous operations'.[68]

Special forces and the ground war

Although NATO had decided that Resolution 1973's exclusion of a foreign occupation force should mean no boots whatsoever on the ground, it could be interpreted to mean that 'ground forces can be used as long as they do not exercise effective control over the territory'.[69] NATO's public assurances that there was going to be no military presence on the ground in Libya and no communication with the rebels were quickly seen not to apply to individual countries. The involvement of UK special forces started before the military campaign was authorised, when in early March a team of eight persons in civilian clothes with arms in their luggage was taken prisoner by bemused rebels some 40 kilometres south of Benghazi. Reportedly, they comprised two MI6 agents and six members of the special forces.[70] They had been dropped by helicopter while others were finding no great difficulties in making their way to Benghazi by land or sea—an NTC contact asked a British journalist: '[W]hy did they come in through the window when they could have come in by the door?'[71] The embarrassment was compounded when Libyan state television broadcast a recording of the UK ambassador explaining to an NTC representative that they were sent ahead of a UK diplomatic liaison team 'just to find if there was a hotel, if everything was working, if there was somewhere they could stay ...'[72] As well as western personnel establishing contact and seeking intelligence on the rebels, Egypt was reported to have begun providing weaponry and training to the eastern opposition forces even before the passage of Resolution 1973.[73]

Significant deployments of military advisers began after Operation United Protector was under way. France, the UK and Italy sent letters on the same day, 26 April, in almost identical terms, to the UN secretary-general, informing him that each had sent a small team of military advisers to mentor and advise the NTC 'on how it might organise its internal structures, prioritise its resources and improve communications'.[74] UK Foreign Secretary Hague told Parliament that 'our officers will not be involved in training or arming the opposition's fighting forces, nor will they be involved in the planning or execution of the NTC's military operations or in the provision of any other form of operational military advice'.[75] Asked if this was a first step towards directly arming the opposition, Defence Secretary Fox told the House of Commons Defence Committee:

We have been careful that this is mentoring, not training. As I said, that comes inside the legal advice we get to make sure that we are always safely inside Resolution 1973. Our mentoring role is to ensure that the opposition forces are able to organise themselves better, that their logistics are better and the communications are better. We believe that that is vital to their stated role and their ability to help protect the civilian population better. So it is not a first step, or intended to be ... In terms of training and supplying weapons, there is clearly an arms embargo that applies to two sides.[76]

Italy's explanation to its Parliament was that it would be sending ten 'military instructors, which, together with an equal number of instructors supplied by France and Great Britain, will be inserted in the military command structure to be created by the National Transitional Council in Benghazi'. The UK assurances seem to be contradicted by Italy's description of the duties of the Italian military mission, which were listed as 'supporting the Libyan staff of the Benghazi operations center (OC) in acquiring autonomous capabilities in planning, organising and carrying out military operations'.[77]

No such notification of provision of military personnel, nor of transfer of weapons, was given to the UN by Qatar, although its special forces were among the first in Benghazi and would be the most numerous across the country. For NATO, Bouchard maintained that

[o]ur actions were not coordinated with the NTC. It was not in my mandate, and our mandate remained the protection of civilians ... But in many ways, parallel to whatever NATO will be doing, nations have got their own right to do certain actions that may not necessarily be shared with the Alliance itself.[78]

As Wehrey points out, NATO's self-denying abstention from direct liaison with the rebels had the effect of increasing dramatically the influence played by the individual NATO member states.[79] Early in NATO's operations, a Qatari liaison officer 'constituted the only conduit for transmitting and receiving coherent communication to and from the rebel forces via his national sources'.[80] This was important in avoiding the repetition of early incidents where rebels were the victims of NATO strikes. But as the operation continued, and the presence of various special forces became increasingly significant alongside the rebels in different parts of the theatre, the channels to NATO developed and coordination deepened through the militaries that were both on the ground and participating in Operation Unified Protector. The French had a single special forces officer discreetly placed close to Bouchard who passed intelligence through their red-card holder, while the UK opened a special forces cell alongside NATO's air operations centre.[81] In breaking the siege of Misrata, British and French advisers called in coordinates to NATO command centres via radio or satellite phone.[82] On occasion, there was direct communication between French special forces on the ground and French aircraft taking part in NATO operations.[83] In July, Naples received 'a visit by a small cadre of advisers who under national auspices had been operating in Benghazi', providing valuable input.[84] In NATO headquarters, the special forces were an open secret: 'Everybody knew but we never spoke about it.'[85] Bouchard met NTC Chairman Mustafa Abdul Jalil 'in his Canadian, not NATO, capacity'.[86]

Supplying weapons and the arms embargo

There was an early challenge to NATO's interpretation of the arms embargo as its naval operation encountered movements of weapons to Misrata, sometimes with the involvement of western special forces. Enforcement of the embargo seemed to depend on the nationality of the NATO vessel involved in inspecting cargo. French vessels were reported to be escorting rebel supplies from Benghazi to Misrata, but in early April, Turkish and Canadian NATO ships turned back Libyan vessels, which they searched and found to be carrying arms and ammunition as well as humanitarian supplies. NTC members 'went berserk', and the UK representative in Benghazi set out to 'knock NATO heads together'.[87] Eventually, the NAC issued legal advice that vessels moving from one Libyan port to another, even if through international waters, were not breaching the embargo by a transfer of weapons that originated in and returned to Libya.

Qatar had been open at the Doha Contact Group meeting about its intention to provide weapons; in fact, it had already smuggled in its first supplies after receiving appeals from NTC representatives in Doha on 22 March. After the Contact Group meeting, it began flying supplies into Benghazi and Tobruk.[88] By the end of the fighting, Qatar is reported to have provided more than 20,000 tons of weapons, flying in at least eighteen weapons shipments, as well as funding a dozen other shipments, mostly of ammunition, via Sudan.[89] The military materiel delivered included French anti-tank weapon launchers. From Benghazi, supplies were shipped across to Misrata,[90] and arms from Qatar were also smuggled into the Nafusa Mountains from Tunisia.[91] The UAE remained discreet about its role but in June began flying supplies to the Nafusa Mountains airstrip it had constructed with US support.[92]

The UK, the US and France for the most part preferred that arms should be provided by Qatar and the UAE, rather than open themselves to controversy regarding the interpretation of the arms embargo. The UK refrained from directly providing lethal supplies, but its special forces were involved in ensuring their movement to where they were needed, and it provided telecommunications equipment and protective body armour.[93] The US also provided non-lethal supplies, but its legal advice was that its Arms Export Control Act did not allow it to provide lethal assistance,[94] although one report alleges that the US did eventually 'cross the line' into lethal assistance.[95] The Qataris reached an early understanding with France on issues of end-user certification, but the UAE was initially constrained by the US, which preferred that they ship weapons of non-US origin, although this objection was lifted by June.[96]

Sarkozy responded personally to NTC appeals for military assistance. When he received Younis in Paris on 13 April, he promised a response through 'allies' to the list of arms required, as well as more French instructors; the NTC was already pressing for supplies to the rebels in the Nafusa Mountains.[97] France itself air-dropped arms to the rebels in the Nafusa Mountains in early June; according to the report by *Le Figaro* that made this public some weeks later, the delivery consisted of rocket launchers, assault rifles, machine guns and anti-tank missiles.[98] The operation had been planned in secret, and there was consternation in Paris and international criticism when it became public.[99] France had not consulted its NATO partners, but NATO had been notified of its flight plans. A military spokesperson said that, as the situation for the civilians on the ground worsened, they had dropped 'arms and means of self-defence, mainly ammunition'; the arms were 'light infantry weapons of the rifle type', dropped over a period of several days 'so that civilians would not be massacred'.[100] It was only after the public controversy that France reported to the UN secretary-general on 30 June that it 'had airdropped self-defence weapons for the civilian populations that had been victims of attacks by Libyan armed forces, in the absence of any other operational means of protecting these populations under threat'.[101] It asked the Sanctions Panel of Experts to keep confidential the details it subsequently provided. France again intervened to ensure the supply of arms, this time through Qatar, after Sarkozy received a delegation from Misrata on 20 July.[102]

Even if Resolution 1973 did override the absolute prohibition on providing arms, as some had argued, it still required measures taken under its authority to be notified to the UN secretary-general by the member state concerned, as the belated French notification recognised. Neither Qatar nor the UAE notified the UN of transfers of weapons or provision of military personnel.[103] In an eventual response to the Sanctions Panel of Experts in February 2012, Qatar 'categorically' denied that it supplied the rebels with arms and ammunition, maintaining only that it had sent a limited number of military personnel to provide military consultation to the revolutionaries, defend Libyan civilians and protect aid convoys, and that it had supplied those Qatari military personnel with limited arms and ammunition for the purposes of self-defence.[104] The UAE did not respond to letters from the panel. A leaked email from the UAE Ministry of Foreign Affairs to its mission at the UN, as the panel continued to pursue its enquiries in 2015, advised 'I think we should be slightly careful in replying to the Libya Panel. The fact of the matter is that the UAE violated the Security Council resolution on Libya and continues to do so.'[105] The panel concluded that 'these States never intended to utilize the provisions of the sanctions regime to deliver arms and ammunition and therefore provided this materiel to the Libyan opposition in breach of the arms embargo'.[106] The panel established that NATO provided three flights from Tirana to Benghazi carrying military materiel from the UAE with deconfliction numbers, so presumably NATO had deconflicted other flights with arms supplies for the rebels: the panel had been informed that around twenty flights had delivered military materiel from Qatar.[107] NATO told the panel that there was no basis to refuse deconfliction unless there was a specific reason to believe that a given flight contained goods in violation of the embargo.

Of Libya's neighbours, Tunisia and Sudan facilitated the flow of weapons to the rebels. Tunisia also allowed its territory to be used for recruitment and training and as 'a safe place where the rebels and their Arab and Western backers could plan'.[108] President Omar al-Bashir boasted in October of the extent to which Sudan had supplied weapons.[109] According to an account based on information from Sudanese military and intelligence sources, Sudan not only sent vehicles with heavy and light weapons to the southern town of Kufra but despatched an infantry battalion and a tank company to help the rebels take control there, while its Darfuri opponents, the Justice and Equality Movement (JEM), fought on the side of Gaddafi. Sudan continued to provide the rebels with weapons and ammunition, communications equipment, intelligence officers and trainers.[110]

Advancing to Tripoli

The operations of special forces soon extended from an initial focus on developing the NTC operations centre in Benghazi and the defence of the eastern front, to the siege of Misrata and the fighting in the Nafusa Mountains.[111] By mid-May, a small French team established a constant presence in Misrata, and by early June, a British team of four arrived; according to Misratan commanders, they played a crucial role in breaking the siege.[112] By June, Qatari and Emirati advisers arrived in the Nafusa Mountains, soon followed by the French and British. Wehrey summarises their role and significance:

By nearly every account, the arrival of foreign ground advisers had a transformational effect on air–ground coordination. They built trust, provided training, and corroborated targeting information provided by Libyan networks of spotters and informants that reported to the operations rooms. They helped smooth the political and regional divisions within the rebels' ranks. They proved instrumental in major breakthroughs on the Nafusa front, Misrata, and the liberation of Tripoli.[113]

This arrival of special forces in Misrata and the Nafusa Mountains was the outcome of a strategic decision by the countries most committed to delivering a rebel victory. Even in April, the NTC representatives who had met Sarkozy had pointed to the potential of an eventual attack on Tripoli from the mountainous regions to its south.[114] But it was several weeks later when, according to Richards, as the long haul from the east showed no likelihood of early victory, 'a key moment came when we made the switch from focusing the main opposition military effort from the eastern half of the country to the west'.[115] Four countries—France, the UK, Qatar and the UAE—now decided to coordinate the support of their special forces to the rebels:

> A top secret plan was drawn up, to be coordinated by a special ops cell in Paris at the offices of the French operational headquarters (CPCO). Allied special forces and intelligence officers would be sent into areas such as Misrata and Zintan—twelve teams of four to six, plus support infrastructure—to assist with rebel activity, tactical advice and targeting intelligence.[116]

As Cameron describes it:

> With our allies France, Qatar and the UAE we ended up steering the ramshackle Libyan army from a secret cell in Paris, providing weapons, support and intelligence to the rebels planning an assault on Tripoli. This quartet of countries—known internally as the Four Amigos—focused on training, equipping and mentoring effective militias in the west. Though this was known to NATO and the US, once again we were operating outside the traditional structures.[117]

Despite the coordination among 'the Four Amigos', the manner in which support was provided to the rebels saw divergences that were to have long-lasting consequences. The first Qatari arms supplies were delivered to Younis as the NTC's military commander, but soon Qatar was steering its supplies to Islamist networks, both in the east and later in the Nafusa Mountains, although Qatar's own concern over unclear authority among the rebels apparently contributed to the NTC's creation of a Ministry of Defence to seek to control weapons transfers.[118] The UAE and Qatar backed rival operations rooms in the east, with a third in Dubai backed by the US AFRICOM as well as by the UK and the UAE.[119] In the Nafusa Mountains, Qatar favoured Nalut, to whose rebels it had provided assistance and training as early as April, while the UAE delivered its aid to Zintan. The operations room set up by the Emiratis in Zintan became the region's key liaison with NATO, while the Qataris subsequently set up separate operations rooms there and elsewhere in the Nafusa Mountains, helping to coordinate the mountain communities and support the rotating deployment of Qatari special forces 'to fight alongside and coordinate rebel advances with the NATO air campaign'.[120]

The western special forces were perhaps more constrained than the Qataris from fighting alongside the rebels. But the UK special forces team was said to have 'strayed beyond its training facility, with single men or pairs accompanying the NTC commanders that they had been training back to their units. They dressed as Libyans and blended in with the units they mentored.'[121] The head of the Zintan forces, Usama al-Juwayli (who would become defence minister in the interim government), 'was assisted by British soldiers who accompanied him throughout the advance on Tripoli, advising him on tactical options and marking the targets for the NATO aircraft when they attacked Gaddafi's stubborn defenders.'[122] French special forces accompanied rebel fighters as they advanced, 'not without running great risks'.[123] One rebel said that 'the French were moving with us everywhere, by foot and car. They returned fire on several occasions.'[124] There was some embarrassment when a team of six armed western soldiers was seen operating alongside rebels on the Misrata frontline in an Al Jazeera video on 29 May.[125]

The complicated story of the fall of Tripoli has been extremely well detailed elsewhere.[126] It was the culmination of the triangular cooperation of the rebels, the special forces on the ground and NATO. For months, various groups that the NTC struggled unsuccessfully to reconcile were developing different plans for taking and securing Tripoli and discussing these with their main foreign advisers and supporters.[127]

NATO operations had increasingly extended from preventing attacks by Gaddafi's forces to supporting rebel advances. NATO strikes, guided by ground advisers, covered the rebels' advance out of Misrata and enabled them to envelop Gaddafi's forces.[128] Misratan forces would attack Tripoli from the north, while the rebel groups that had been training and fighting in the Nafusa Mountains would sweep in from the south. NATO helicopters supported rebels in close engagements and interdicted regime reinforcements: British Apache helicopters were pivotal in supporting the final assault on Tripoli.[129] A detailed description of the UK's air operations shows how they 'were designed to accompany the rebels' advance on Tripoli'.[130] As Richards recalled it: 'From the air, we concentrated on Tripoli and on using our bombing raids to open a corridor for the rebels as they moved toward the capital.'[131] The US stepped up its airstrikes, and its Predator drones provided round-the-clock surveillance to NATO and to the British and French special forces on the ground, after a decision that opened up the sharing of more sensitive information.[132] During the final attack on Tripoli, there was direct contact between NATO and the rebel operations rooms, as NATO actively supported rebel movements on the ground with strikes and overhead intelligence.[133] On 20 August, the NTC gave the signal for the long-planned uprising in Tripoli, and on 23 August the rebel fighters converged on Gaddafi's Bab al-Azizia compound. A significant deployment of Qatari special forces—perhaps around seventy—had fought with them, and some appeared in filming of the rebels' celebrations.[134]

After the fall of Tripoli

Once Tripoli had fallen at the end of August, some members of the Security Council argued that the NATO mandate should be terminated, but the NTC—no longer rebels, as the NTC had now been seated at the UN General Assembly after a contested 16 September vote[135]—made clear that they wanted NATO's support to continue. The operation was extended on 21 September for up to another ninety days. Addressing the Security Council, NTC Executive Chairman Mahmoud Jibril said that Gaddafi's battalions continued to kill innocent civilians in three regions, 'and therefore the very foundations of resolution 1973(2011) remain valid'.[136] Bouchard said that threats from the regime continued: 'Their forces are still dangerous, orders continue to be given and violence against the population continues.'[137] NATO provided air support to the NTC forces that attacked the last pro-Gaddafi strongholds of Sirte and Bani Walid and isolated the remaining pockets of the regime, destroying targets as they attempted to move: '[T]he continued presence of advisers on the ground working alongside the rebels ensured that deliberate dynamic targeting was continually refined and sustained.'[138]

As the NTC forces closed in on Sirte, NATO said that it had no evidence of civilians being targeted or improper behaviour by NTC forces; the NTC had repeatedly shown their intent to allow the civilian population to escape and attempted to resolve the situation through political means, while the remaining Gaddafi forces had shown no willingness to let the civilian population escape or protect the city.[139] But it is likely that a significant proportion of the civilian population of Sirte, as of Bani Walid, having been pro-Gaddafi, would have feared the NTC forces. NATO had declared as Operation Unified Protector began that the mandate to prevent attacks on civilians 'applies to both sides, whoever targets risks becoming a target. We will apply the mandate across the board.'[140] A senior NATO planner is quoted as confirming that 'we were prepared to strike anti-Qadhafi forces if they had targeted civilians. Toward the end of the war, in Sirt, we came very, very close.'[141] There were several reasons why NATO failed to act against rebel crimes: they occurred in densely populated areas where NATO already had difficulty distinguishing between the different factions; air strikes would endanger more civilian lives; and rebel crimes were disorganised and scattered: 'That notwithstanding, the alliance was accused of applying a double standard in Libya.'[142]

The taking of Sirte was, in fact, not without atrocities: Human Rights Watch found fifty-three bodies, apparently of Gaddafi supporters, at an abandoned hotel in an area of the city that had been under the control of anti-Gaddafi fighters from Misrata; some had their hands bound behind their backs when they were shot.[143] Already in August, a grim period of human rights violations against the people of Tawergha, who had fought with Gaddafi's forces as they committed grave abuses in Misrata, had begun after the rebel forces broke out of Misrata and destroyed their town; its inhabitants fled, and many were taken into long-lasting detention and subjected to ill-treatment.[144] There were also reprisals in the western mountains, where the Mashashiya tribe, accused of siding with Gaddafi and providing a base for his forces, suffered a similar fate at the hands of Zintan, being driven out of what became 'lifeless neighbourhoods in a ghost town'.[145]

Meanwhile, the focus of some of the special forces had switched to the search for Gaddafi.[146] UK Defence Secretary Fox stated on 25 July that 'I can confirm that NATO is providing intelligence and reconnaissance assets to the NTC to help them track down Colonel Gaddafi and other remnants of the regime'; NATO's spokesperson, however, maintained that 'NATO does not target specific individuals ... there is no military coordination with the rebels.'[147] Within NATO, Bouchard declared that his mandate made no mention of arresting Gaddafi, still less of eliminating him.[148] When, however, on 19 October NATO received the first clear indication that Gaddafi was in Sirte, it increased its air surveillance. In the early hours of 20 October, his convoy was identified fighting its way out of the city and was initially struck from a US drone, then by two French fighter jets.[149]

Bouchard told a press briefing that NATO 'had no idea' that Gaddafi was onboard the convoy; they were concerned that forces from Sirte would join up with the remnants of forces from Bani Walid and move into another built-up area where part of the civilian population would be held hostage. There were rocket and machine guns on some of the pickup trucks, and the NATO assessment was that there was a clear potential threat to the population.[150] But as the NATO command team watched Gaddafi's convoy driving into rebel lines, instead of the usual thirty or so in its bunker, there were over 100 watching: 'And then, when Qadhafi was captured … that was such a moment of release.'[151] Gaddafi and his son Mutassim briefly survived the missile strikes, to be murdered by fighters from Misrata.[152] Operation Unified Protector ended on 31 October.

Reflections

Assessment of the military action that followed the passage of Resolution 1973 requires judgements of the extent to which it caused civilian casualties; of whether NATO went beyond the mandate to protect civilians to bring about regime change; of the legitimacy of involvement of external special forces in the ground war; and of whether the UN arms embargo was violated. The nature of the action would have major implications for future possibilities of Security Council authorisation of the use of force and far-reaching consequences for what followed in Libya.

Civilian casualties and rebel abuses

At the conclusion of the NATO operation, Rasmussen stated that there had been no confirmed civilian casualties.[153] This statement was already contradicted by credible media reports, and Russia attacked it, as well as its apparent endorsement by Secretary-General Ban,[154] proposing in the Security Council that there should be an investigation under UN auspices into civilian casualties caused by NATO bombing. This had some support from China, Brazil and South Africa, while NATO members of the council countered that these were being investigated by the Human Rights Council-mandated International Commission of Inquiry, as well as being within the jurisdiction of the ICC. Angry exchanges continued as Russia persisted in pressing the issue in the council, including in open session in the presence of the Libyan prime minister in March 2012.[155]

The commission's March 2012 report concluded that NATO 'conducted a highly precise campaign with a demonstrable determination to avoid civilian casualties'. It noted that the Libyan government had deliberately misstated the extent of civilian casualties, on one occasion moving the bodies of children from a hospital morgue to the site of a NATO airstrike. Nevertheless, the commission documented five airstrikes where a total of sixty civilians were killed and fifty-five injured; at four of these five sites, NATO's characterisation of them as 'command and control nodes' or 'troop staging areas' was not found to be reflected in evidence at the scene and witness testimony. NATO did not provide detailed evidence for why these sites were considered legitimate targets, because such evidence was member state, not allied, in origin.[156] The commission called on NATO to conduct investigations in Libya and to apply its guidelines for compensation of victims.[157] Reports by Amnesty International and Human Rights Watch also acknowledged NATO's efforts to minimise the risk of causing civilian casualties, but were more critical. Amnesty documented a total of fifty-five named civilians killed, including sixteen children and fourteen women, with reports of twenty more, as well as additional incidents of civilian casualties reported to have occurred in circumstances where it was difficult to distinguish between combatants and civilians.[158] Human Rights Watch investigated eight NATO air strikes hitting residential homes in which it found that twenty-eight men, twenty-four children and twenty women lost their lives, and dozens of other civilians were wounded.[159] More recent research by Airwars concluded that NATO strikes killed between 223 and 403 civilians in 212 events of concern that it reviewed.[160]

In its response to the commission, NATO said that 'the targeting and strike methods employed in OUP were as well-designed and as successfully implemented to avoid civilian casualties as was humanly and technically possible'.[161] Given that NATO employed a total of 7,642 air-to-surface weapons during the seven-month campaign, there can be no doubt that the precautions taken resulted in remarkably few civilian casualties and very limited damage to civilian infrastructure, comparing favourably in these respects to military campaigns elsewhere, including Kosovo. NATO did not, however, serve itself well by its initial denial of any civilian casualties whatsoever, or by its failure to investigate on the ground once this became possible.[162] M. Cherif Bassiouni, the first chair of the commission, wrote elsewhere (with co-authors) of 'vague responses' and notes that NATO made investigations difficult. It failed to specify which countries were involved in particular strikes and claimed that individual nations were responsible for their own assessment of the alleged incidents. However, seven of eight countries involved in the strikes responded that the issue should be referred to NATO because 'the operation was conducted under NATO command'.[163]

The intervening nations were also vulnerable to the charge that they did not display as much concern regarding abuses during the conflict by some of the rebels they were supporting as they did regarding those of the regime. Amnesty International drew attention to abductions and killings as groups of armed rebels hunted for Gaddafi loyalists suspected—rightly or wrongly—of being involved in attacks or past repression.[164] African migrant workers in Libya were victims of serious human rights violations, which were rightly a consistent concern of the AU. Many were the victims of attacks seemingly motivated by suspicions that they served as mercenaries with the pro-Gaddafi forces; several nationals of sub-Saharan countries were brutally attacked and killed.[165] During the fighting, the NTC and leaders of some rebel groups responded to representations with commitments to respect human rights, and gave human rights organisations access to some of those detained, but their control was limited. Although the prosecutor of the ICC said that he would investigate war crimes by both sides, the eagerness with which he seized on allegations of a policy by Gaddafi to encourage rape, with hundreds of victims, and the provision of 'Viagra-type medicaments' to his forces, did nothing to enhance a perception of objectivity when they went unsubstantiated.[166] It was Misratan fighters who committed abuses in Sirte and Tawergha,[167] and one study concludes that 'a perception that the rebels were immune from the purview of the Prosecutor was strongly reinforced by the Prosecutor's visit to Misrata in April 2012, when he was photographed standing on a tank at a NATO bombing site'.[168]

Exceeding the mandate?

NATO insisted that it did not exceed the mandate of Resolution 1973, to protect civilians and civilian-populated areas. It was supported in this by Ban, when he declared in December 2011 that NATO's military operation had been strictly within the resolution's mandate.[169] Bouchard was adamant that the operation did not engage in regime change: 'We stayed well inside our mandate.'[170] Increasingly, defenders of the military campaign argued that there had come to be no distinction between protection of civilians and regime change: Gaddafi's refusal to end his military action meant that only the end of his regime would ensure the protection of civilians. Among later considered judgements, Norway's Libya Commission endorses this argument (although Norway had ended its participation before the taking of Tripoli, Sirte and Bani Walid): '[T]he Commission believes that Norway's military efforts against targets that weakened the Libyan regime's military capability did not go beyond the formal framework for the mandate the Security Council had given … it was necessary to weaken the Libyan regime's military capability in order to protect civilians.'[171] Some participants were frank that a humanitarian intervention 'morphed' into regime change. Richards told the House of Commons Inquiry that the UK decision-makers were focused on regime change by April: '[A]t some point, regime change, in shorthand, became the accepted means of ensuring that the civilian population of Libya would not be threatened into the long term, so it became … an ineluctable change of mission, for me.'[172] After the military victory, leading interveners indulged in ill-advised triumphalism, with no pretence that they had sought anything else. On the fall of Tripoli, Cameron told friends that he had 'just won a war'.[173] When told of Gaddafi's death, Clinton joked 'We came, we saw, he died.'[174] Gates' successor as defense secretary, Leon Panetta, records slipping up when 'I said what everyone in Washington knew but we couldn't officially acknowledge: that our goal in Libya was regime change.'[175] Juppé declared that 'the objective that we had, that is to say, to accompany the forces of the NTC in the liberation of their territory, has now been achieved'.[176]

One persuasive analysis of the legality of the NATO operation distinguishes among three phases. In phase one, NATO launched air strikes to halt attacks by Gaddafi's forces on Benghazi, Ajdabiya,

Misrata and elsewhere: these were in accordance with the protection mandate. Phase two covers NATO military operations during the stalemate between the combatting forces; although Resolution 1973 did not establish a basis for destroying Gaddafi's military forces, 'there may be a fine line between what could be considered a lawful destruction of capacity to threaten civilians ... and general impairment of the regime's army'. Phase three covers NATO airstrikes while the rebels advanced on territories controlled by Gaddafi's forces: these went beyond the mandate, as the areas held by Gaddafi's forces were obviously not under threat of attack by him—it was the rebels themselves who posed a threat of attack on civilians and civilian-populated areas.[177] NATO's arguments that its support for the rebels' attacks on Tripoli, and after its fall, on Sirte and Bani Walid, were necessary to protect civilians are unconvincing.

Secrecy in the ground war

These arguments, moreover, do not address the external involvement in the ground war. All military assessments agree that the ground war was crucial. Richards writes of the importance of what he calls a 'proxy land force', crediting the rebel forces themselves, along with Qatar and the UAE, while disclosing little about the role of the UK's 'small teams'.[178] French General Benoît Puga, Sarkozy's chief of military staff, who had been at the centre of the operation of the 'Four Amigos' coordinated from Paris, declared that the special forces 'went to snatch victory with their guts'.[179] NTC Chairman Abdul Jalil was generous in his tribute to Qatar on his post-victory visit to Doha: Qatar, he said, had planned the battles that paved the way for NTC fighters to gradually take over Gaddafi-held towns and cities and had been 'a major partner in all the battles we fought'.[180]

The secrecy of the special forces operations makes it impossible to give definitive numbers of those who were deployed by each of the countries involved. Qatari Chief of Staff Major General Hamad bin Ali Al-Attiyah said later that the numbers of Qataris deployed were 'hundreds in every region', although this could have been an exaggeration.[181] Other accounts suggest a range of fifty to 150

Qataris on the ground at any one time, with a team of sixty assisting the rebels in setting up command centres in Benghazi, Zintan and Tripoli.[182] Regarding other Arab special forces, one estimate suggests twenty from the UAE, while an unknown number of Jordanians provided training.[183] UK special forces (including supporting elements) may have built up from twenty to twenty-two in late March to thirty to forty by June.[184] Estimates of the deployment of French special forces are similar. The early Italian military mission to Benghazi was reported to be additional to the role carried out by Italian intelligence and special forces,[185] and one account reports that by October there were at least forty operatives from a crack unit of Italy's Parachute Brigade.[186] Obama's directive that there must be no US boots on the ground excluded the insertion of any military personnel, even in civilian dress and for diplomatic protection,[187] but the US is reported to have inserted elements of the Special Activities Division of the CIA,[188] and to have had personnel present in Misrata and Zintan, in addition to the AFRICOM presence in Dubai.[189]

Measures taken under Resolution 1973 by member states were required to be notified to the UN secretary-general and by him to the Security Council. Following initial notifications of action by individual states that preceded Operation Unified Protector, NATO submitted regular reports. But there were no notifications of later bilateral military action, deployment of special forces or supplies of arms, beyond the notifications of the initial teams of military advisers sent by France, Italy and the UK, of non-lethal supplies, and of the French arms drop in June. The Sanctions Panel of Experts was in no doubt that non-notified supplies of weapons violated the arms embargo. But since the special forces operations and other military assistance were not officially declared, their legality has been little debated.

Accountability

What is clear is the lack of effective accountability, in several respects. It is impossible to believe that there would have been the necessary votes in the Security Council, let alone the withholding of vetoes by Russia and China, if the full extent of the military campaign had been foreseen. The argument made by Rice in response to Russia, that she had made clear that there would be air–ground action, applies only to taking out Libyan air defences and heavy weapons and halting 'advancing columns of soldiers'—phase one, in the foregoing analysis, but not phases two and three. Once the mandate had been given, the reporting by NATO—which was dutiful in its regularity, but entered into none of the difficult questions of the justification of its targeting—did not allow for serious scrutiny by the council, where there was only squabbling. Although NATO held regular press conferences in Brussels where it was questioned closely by journalists regarding details of its actions,[190] it never appeared before the council for a briefing or consultations. Not only were the bilateral roles of intervening countries not reported; they were deliberately concealed. Indeed, there was outright dissembling—as late as July, Sarkozy was declaring that there were no French special forces on the ground in Libya: the ambassador in Benghazi 'has aides, we have observers, because we need intelligence, but there are no special forces'.[191] The UK gave notification in April of its initial military assistance team, and in October of the new team it was sending to assist the interim Libyan authorities, but remained silent about the presence of its special forces during the fighting. Qatar was formally denying its massive breaches of the arms embargo in February 2012, long after they had been widely reported, while the UAE remained silent.

For the UN, the lack of effective scrutiny and accountability regarding the implementation of a Security Council mandate for the use of force by member states, individually or collectively, should be an important issue of concern. The immediate consequence of this being made so obvious—although not for the first time—by the case of Libya, is that it is highly unlikely that the council will again grant a mandate for 'all necessary measures' when arguments are made for humanitarian intervention. Already at the beginning of June 2011, Russian Foreign Minister Sergei Lavrov said:

> If somebody would like to get authorization to use force to achieve a shared goal by all of us, they would have to specify in

the resolution who this somebody is, who is going to use this authorization, what the rules of engagement are and the limits on the use of force.[192]

This has now been widely discussed in analyses of the implications for 'the responsibility to protect' in general, and the case of Syria in particular.

For democratic countries, the secret role of special forces raises major questions of domestic as well as international accountability. As one military analyst writes:

> The Libya campaign has constituted a litmus test for the use of SOF working alongside secret intelligence case officers in covert teams specifically created for the purpose … but is this an acceptable route for democracies to follow in the long run, and what does it imply for transparency and accountability in connection with military action?[193]

* * *

A number of features of the intervention had lasting consequences for Libya's subsequent travails and beyond. The arming and training of different armed groups outside any chain of command aggravated the later challenge of asserting state authority over them. The rivalry of Qatar and the UAE, and the factions favoured by each, would continue to deepen Libyan divisions. France and the UK would take little continuing responsibility for a situation they had done so much to shape, while the US would continue to stand back. Disregard for a Security Council arms embargo and its reporting requirements would become increasingly blatant. NATO airstrikes had blown open Gaddafi's stockpiles, contributing to the outflow of weapons from Libya to the Sahel and elsewhere. Victory had been delivered by external actors to a disparate set of armed groups that had not had time or been required to evolve their own common leadership or strategy, and to the NTC, prematurely recognised as representing the Libyan people ahead of any national dialogue, undermining both the military and political imperatives to forge greater unity as a basis for post-conflict state-building.

3

A NEGOTIATED TRANSITION?

Attempts to bring about a political transition through negotiation began in the short period before military intervention was authorised and launched, in an effort to avert it, and became protracted once that had failed. All the multiple approaches were ultimately unsuccessful: was there ever a possibility that they could have succeeded?

Efforts to promote dialogue between the Gaddafi regime and the emerging rebel leadership began as the international condemnation of his response to the uprising mounted. The early speeches of Gaddafi and Saif were not encouraging,[1] to say the least; nor were formal government communications. A letter signed by Foreign Minister—and former intelligence chief—Moussa Koussa was sent to the president of the UN Security Council on 2 March, stating that 'the Libyan authorities are committed to conducting a comprehensive national dialogue, and the relevant bodies are engaged in making preparations for such dialogue, that is to be begun as soon as possible'. But the first version was promptly withdrawn, and the substituted letter of 3 March drew back from any exceptional national negotiating process:[2]

The political system and social structure of Libya allow opportunities for dialogue at any time. The Popular Social Leadership committees and the Secretariat of the General People's Congress are

making efforts in that regard, enabling prominent Libyans, including lawyers, intellectuals, journalists and bloggers, to raise any
item that they wish to discuss in complete freedom.

Meanwhile, at its first meeting on 5 March in Benghazi, the
NTC declared itself 'the sole national representative of Libya with
all its social and political strata and all its geographical regions'.
This was inevitably an unrealistic claim. It initially brought together
in eastern Libya a group that Peter Bartu, who engaged with the
NTC in Benghazi for the UN from April 2011, describes as 'an
eclectic mix of notable families, lawyers, academics, young activists, serving diplomats, former ministers and security chiefs, government reformers, and diaspora leaders, some of whom had long
opposed Mu'ammar al-Qadhafi'.[3] It chose as its leader Mustafa
Abdul Jalil, a former judge and reforming minister of justice, and
it quickly established an Executive Committee[4] headed by Mahmoud
Jibril, a US-trained economist who had been close to Saif while
serving in the Gaddafi regime as head of the National Planning
Council and the National Economic Development Board. Jibril was
based in Doha and from the outset travelled extensively to fulfil his
responsibilities for the foreign relations of the NTC. Maintaining
some cohesion between the NTC leadership in Benghazi and Jibril
and other spokespersons in the diaspora would be one challenge;
another would be ensuring effective representation of cities that
remained under regime control, especially Tripoli; and a third
would be the ideological tensions that emerged between more and
less Islamist members. The uncertain cohesion would pose com-
plications for external interlocutors and negotiators who engaged
with 'the NTC'. But as Bartu observes, the NTC did meet a critical
threshold of legitimacy for the Libyan revolutionary movement:
'Significantly, no one ever challenged the NTC for leadership of
the revolution despite often severe criticisms as to how it organised
itself, the opaque manner in which it took decisions, and the way
it engaged with external patrons and managed domestic affairs.'[5]

As the pressure on the regime intensified, a spate of defections
accelerated.[6] There were multiple reports of those in the circle
around Gaddafi contacting potential interlocutors to open some
negotiation, but the extent to which they carried the authority of

Gaddafi himself was uncertain. Some of those involved would before long defect themselves: Koussa defended the regime's response before the AU on 10 March and voiced its acceptance of a ceasefire on 18 March but fled into exile—via an intelligence debriefing in the UK—on 28 March.

Early efforts

Norway was contacted on behalf of Gaddafi's family on 9 March and initiated a mediation effort that was the first to get to Tripoli and continued for months after the military intervention, which Norway would join as a member of NATO.[7] The Norwegian mediation team had week-long meetings in Tripoli from 11 March; the team was there when Resolution 1973 was adopted and left just before bombing began, after encouraging an anxious Saif to seek a ceasefire. A key interlocutor on behalf of the regime in this and other negotiations was Mohammed Ismail, an aide to Saif, who also met the UK government in London at the end of March, once military action was under way.[8] The leading NTC representative in contact with Norway was Ali Zeidan, then based in Europe and a later prime minister.

The appointment of Abdel-Elah Al-Khatib as UN special envoy had been announced on 6 March. It was not well received by South Africa and other Africans who saw the choice of a Jordanian as a tilt towards the Arab League rather than the AU, and others were sceptical as to the seriousness of the expectations of his mediation. On 13 March, he flew to Tripoli, accompanied by senior UN political, humanitarian and human rights officers, where he met Koussa and other officials; however, a proposed meeting with Gaddafi himself did not take place after Al-Khatib insisted on being accompanied in the meeting. He pressed for a ceasefire and an end to violence, as called for in Resolution 1970, but was discouraged from proceeding to Benghazi at a time when he was told that the government was concluding operations against the rebels there.[9]

The AU ad-hoc High-Level Committee, mandated by the 10 March AU Peace and Security Council (PSC), was composed of the presidents of Mauritania (chair of the PSC, and of the committee), Republic of Congo, Mali, South Africa and Uganda, and AU Commission Chairperson Jean Ping. It met for the first time in Nouakchott on 19 March, after which it was planned that its members would fly on 20 March to Tripoli, and on to Benghazi. By then, Resolution 1973 had been adopted by the UN Security Council, with the votes of the three African members including South Africa; although the resolution merely 'noted' the AU's decision to send the High-Level Committee, several members had urged efforts to seek a peaceful solution.[10] When Sarkozy convened his 'summit for the support of the Libyan people' on 19 March, the AU interpreted this as a snub, since France knew that the AU leaders were to meet that day, and Ping declined to go to Paris 'for a photo opportunity'.[11] From the Paris meeting, Ban was given the unhappy task of phoning Ping to tell him that bombing was beginning and the no-fly zone was being imposed, a message also communicated less diplomatically by the US: the High-Level Committee could therefore not proceed to Libya.[12] The committee formally expressed regret that it was denied the permission it had requested to fulfil its mandate.[13] The AU sought to recapture the lead among international actors through a threefold initiative: proposing to convene a meeting between the Libyan authorities and the NTC to discuss the AU roadmap; a coordinating meeting of international organisations—the Arab League, OIC, EU and UN; and a regional consultation involving Libya's neighbouring countries.

It can be argued that the imminence of Gaddafi's attack on Benghazi left no time for diplomacy and the negotiation of a mutual, monitored ceasefire: only an immediate and very visible halt to the regime's military operations might have postponed military action. But immediately thereafter, as one commentator later noted, 'a more subtle dictator could have put the three principal allies under far greater political pressure when the Arab League blanched as it confronted the realities of what it had advocated, and voices in Europe and the US warned of a dangerous military stalemate'; instead, Gaddafi 'played into their hands by continuing with his delusional bluster and threats'.[14]

This nonetheless leads to the question of whether a pause in the bombing, once Benghazi had been successfully protected and the serious intent of the intervening countries had been demonstrated, might have afforded a second opportunity for mediation. One person who thought so was UK Chief of Defence Staff General Richards. He later told a UK parliamentary inquiry that he tried to build into the military campaign 'checkpoints during the campaign when politics could have reasserted itself':

> I felt that my political masters and those in America and Europe should at least have had an opportunity to pause, perhaps have a ceasefire and have another go at the political process ... Would we then be able to persuade Gaddafi to negotiate? ... In the military campaign plan we had built in a pause after Benghazi if we were successful on Benghazi.[15]

His proposal for a pause did not, he said, get much traction in London, and was not accepted by 'our allies'. US Defense Secretary Gates would also later argue 'I think if we could have prevented a massacre in Benghazi and basically held there, we would have been better off.'[16] But this does not seem to have been considered within the Obama administration, although the president might have been more favourable to the possibility than Cameron and Sarkozy.

The AU remained determined to pursue its roadmap, beginning with a ceasefire. However, its attempt to bring together regime and NTC representatives foundered. Only Gaddafi's representatives came to Addis Ababa to meet the committee on 25 March; there they reiterated acceptance of the roadmap, including a ceasefire and deployment of a monitoring and verification mechanism. On the same day, the AU's consultative meeting took place, with broad representation of international organisations, members of the UN Security Council, Libya's neighbours, African and other states, but not at a level that indicated a willingness of the non-Africans to accept an AU lead. The communiqué from the meeting papered over the cracks of the diverging approaches,[17] and the AU went on to convene a 31 March technical consultation, in which the UN, Arab League, OIC and EU participated, regarding modalities for an early ceasefire and the establishment of an operational monitoring mechanism.

The countries favouring military intervention had, however, set off on a very different course from that proposed by the AU. Following on from Sarkozy's Paris meeting, the UK convened the London Conference on Libya on 29 March, with high-level participation of the UN, the Arab League, the OIC, the EU and NATO: the AU was invited but did not attend, nor did any of its member states, so that of Libya's near-neighbours, only Morocco was present. The conference decided to establish a Libya Contact Group. As well as coordinating the international response on Libya, it declared that this would provide a focal point for contact with the Libyan parties. Its first meeting would be convened by Qatar, and its chairmanship would thereafter rotate between the countries of the region and beyond it. The AU was expected to participate, but clearly the leading role would be elsewhere.[18]

Ahead of the London Conference, Italy attempted to prepare a peace plan to present along with Germany; this envisaged a cease-fire monitored by the UN and a humanitarian corridor. France was prepared to encourage this if it involved Gaddafi going into exile, but no one close to Gaddafi could envisage this.[19] At the beginning of April, Deputy Foreign Minister Abdul Ati al-Obeidi, who was about to succeed Koussa, travelled to Greece, Turkey and Malta as special envoy for the regime. At his first stop, the Greek foreign minister said that 'it appears that the regime is seeking a solution'.[20] Gaddafi's spokesman declared that '[w]e are ready for political solutions: constitution, election, anything', but 'the leader has to lead this forward'.[21] Prime Minister Erdoğan had signalled that Turkey had ambitions to mediate an early ceasefire, warning of the situation becoming another Iraq or Afghanistan,[22] but Turkey's early criticism of military action and apparent unwilling-ness to join it resulted in protests outside its consulate in Benghazi with slogans including 'Erdoğan, don't talk to Gaddafi.'[23] After al-Obeidi's visit to Ankara, Erdoğan sent an envoy to Benghazi and in a 7 April speech set out a roadmap with three elements: a cease-fire and withdrawal of regime forces from cities under siege; secure humanitarian zones; and a comprehensive democratic change and transformation process establishing a constitutional democracy with free elections.[24] Abdul Jalil unenthusiastically endorsed the plan, but the NTC was unhappy that Turkey envisaged Gaddafi remaining in a symbolic post with Saif leading the transition. The initiative came to nothing.[25] Meanwhile, the main attention of the intervening countries was devoted not towards mediation and possible ceasefire, but on the assumption of the military campaign by NATO from 31 March and support to the NTC.

The AU and the UN

The AU High-Level Committee finally visited Tripoli on 10 April—the delegation comprised Presidents Mohamed Ould Abdel Aziz of Mauritania, Denis Sassou Nguesso of the Republic of Congo, Amadou Toumani Touré of Mali and Jacob Zuma of South Africa; the foreign minister of Uganda representing Yoweri Museveni; together with the AU Commission Chairperson Ping and Commissioner for Peace and Security Ramtane Lamamra. They had the first face-to-face meeting of any international representatives with Gaddafi. Alex de Waal gives an account of the lengthy meeting based on his interviews with senior AU officials:

> Gaddafi insisted that his country was a victim of aggression and that Africa should stand on his side. He spoke at length about his unhappiness with the 10 March PSC communiqué and rejected accusations that his army and security services had killed civilians. Instead, he accused the demonstrators of being drug addicts, criminals and Al-Qaeda-linked terrorists. Gaddafi adamantly opposed any visit to Benghazi by the AU leaders. In response, the four presidents insisted that the communiqué was fair and that attacks against civilians had to stop. Touré reminded Gaddafi that he had advised other African leaders to enter into dialogue with opposition groups, and said that the Libyan government similarly had no choice but to negotiate with the NTC. The African leaders emphasised that any solution had to be based on democracy and human rights. They also argued that Libya lacked the means to stand up to the international coalition and that its leader should therefore be realistic about his options. Finally, they told Gaddafi that they would continue to Benghazi whether he liked it or not.[26]

Gaddafi eventually told the committee that he accepted the roadmap, including a cessation of hostilities, monitoring and dialogue.

With the significant exception of Zuma, the other members of the delegation proceeded to Benghazi. The mood in Benghazi was heightened by ongoing bombardment of Misrata after the delegation had left Tripoli, and they were received with demonstrations rejecting negotiations with Gaddafi.[27] Although working-level discussions towards a joint communiqué seemed positive, there were divisions within the NTC, and the committee had to conclude that 'due to a political condition put forward by the TNC as a prerequisite for the urgent launching of discussions on the modalities for a ceasefire, it was not possible, at this stage, to reach an agreement on the crucial issue of the cessation of hostilities'.[28] NTC Chairman Abdul Jalil told a news conference that the AU initiative 'does not include the departure of Gaddafi and his sons from the Libyan political scene; therefore it is outdated'. An NTC participant said that they were told to reject the AU plan by representatives in Benghazi of some intervening countries who 'threatened ... to withdraw their support for the opposition if they accepted intervention by the African Union. They were not willing at all to reach a peaceful solution to the conflict.'[29] The NTC did send representatives to a ministerial-level meeting of the committee in Addis Ababa on 25–26 April, where the Libyan government was represented by its foreign minister; but while the latter was still said to reiterate unconditional acceptance of the roadmap, the NTC could only be said by the AU to have thanked it for its efforts and committed itself to study the roadmap more thoroughly.[30]

By the time of the 10 April AU visit, UN Envoy Al-Khatib had had his first discussion with NTC representatives in Tobruk on 21 March and had visited Tripoli and Benghazi from 31 March to 1 April; he made further visits on 17–18 April and 29 April. He summarised his talks with the parties when he briefed the Security Council on 3 May. Both sides had stated that they were ready to cease all hostilities if there was a genuine desire on the part of the other party to do the same. However, the Libyan authorities required NATO attacks to stop, with an agreed date and time for simultaneous ceasefire under the supervision of impartial monitors. Thereafter they would hold discussions about elections, democracy and constitutional reform. For the NTC, on the other hand, a ceasefire would not be sufficient to end the conflict if it was not directly linked to the departure of Gaddafi and his family, with whom it would not negotiate. The difficulty, said Al-Khatib, lay in 'how to link a credible and verifiable ceasefire with a lasting political process that would remain inclusive of all relevant parties'.[31]

Coordination between Al-Khatib and the AU was constrained by the latter's mistrust of a mediator from Jordan, which had joined the NATO operation, and by the UN being fully implicated in the approach of the Contact Group, while the AU and some of its member states—most notably, South Africa in the divided Security Council—became increasingly critical of the military campaign. The discussion of Libya at the 21 May consultative meeting between the UN Security Council and the AU Peace and Security Council in Addis Ababa was stormy. An extraordinary session of the Assembly of the AU on 25 May gave expression to some of the divisions among African leaders in their attitudes to Gaddafi and the intervention.[32] However, it reiterated the approach of the AU roadmap, not only calling for a monitored ceasefire but demanding an immediate pause in the fighting and the NATO-led air campaign; this, it said, was defeating the very purpose for which it was authorised in the first place—the protection of the civilian population—and further complicating any transition to a democratic dispensation in Libya, while adding to the threats facing countries of the region. It expressed deep concern at 'one-sided interpretation' of the Security Council resolutions and military and other actions on the ground, which it said—to the anger of NATO's secretary-general—were outside the scope of the resolutions. It expressed 'Africa's surprise and disappointment at the attempts to marginalise the continent in the management of the Libyan conflict.'[33] Ban was present, as well as Al-Khatib, and followed up his several phone conversations with Gaddafi's Prime Minister Al-Mahmoudi with a meeting with the Libyan foreign minister. The Libyans again proposed a ceasefire and elections, the outcome of which they said Gaddafi would respect.

On 31 May, Zuma went for a second time to Tripoli, this time unaccompanied by and without coordination with other members of the High-Level Committee, for another lengthy meeting with

Gaddafi. Gaddafi was prepared only to accept 'not being part of the negotiating process'. Jibril, who had been to see Zuma before the visit, would later express disappointment with what he said was a change in his position after the meeting.[34] But the patience of some members of the committee was running out: on 7 June, its chairperson, President Abdel Aziz of Mauritania, said that Gaddafi could no longer lead Libya—he must be made to leave without causing more damage.

Meanwhile, Al-Khatib had continued his efforts with visits to both parties, dialogue with NTC representatives at meetings of the Contact Group, and attempts to orchestrate coordinated pressure from other external actors. From the end of May, he began to advance proposals of his own for a political transition: a power-sharing transitional mechanism where each side would provide two people and collectively agree on a neutral chairman or interim president to oversee an interim government and a comprehensive ceasefire. He was offered a face-to-face meeting with Gaddafi on 7 June, but once he was in Tripoli, the Libyans said that Gaddafi could not leave his place of hiding due to NATO bombings. Al-Khatib was taken to a meeting at a hotel with Saif; NATO later said that the meeting with Saif was at a location that it had not cleared, which had meant a 'close call' for the envoy.[35] The parties agreed to study his proposals, but the impasse over Gaddafi's departure was unchanged. Efforts to persuade Gaddafi to leave Libya were made yet more difficult when on 27 June the ICC issued a warrant for his arrest, as well as warrants for Saif and intelligence chief Abdullah al-Senussi.

The AU's position and pursuit of its roadmap were repeatedly spelled out during UN Security Council consultations by South Africa, and in a public presentation to the council by Mauritania's foreign minister in mid-June, when members were unable to reach consensus on a statement proposed by the African members. During that month, the AU drafted detailed proposals for a framework agreement on a political solution. These were discussed in a coordinating meeting with the UN, Arab League, OIC and EU, but the other international organisations were not persuaded to adopt them as a common position. They were endorsed by the AU

Summit on 30 June–1 July, although debate was heated; Ethiopia, Rwanda, Nigeria and Senegal were reluctant to endorse a ceasefire call, which was also lobbied against by UK diplomats.[36] The proposals were presented to the Libyan parties, with the intention of convening negotiations in Addis Ababa under the joint auspices of the AU High-Level Committee and the UN special envoy, and were shared with the UN Security Council.[37] The summit resolved that AU member states should not cooperate in the execution of the ICC arrest warrant against Gaddafi and requested the Security Council to use its power to defer the ICC process. Regime representatives came again to Addis Ababa in mid-July, but there was no response from the NTC to the AU proposals or invitation.

Russia engages

While voicing its strong criticism of the NATO military campaign in the Security Council and publicly, Russia joined in efforts to persuade Gaddafi to make way. It coordinated with Zuma as a fellow member of the BRICS; and at the G8 meeting, where Medvedev had a lengthy bilateral meeting with Obama on 26 May, Russia accepted the collective statement that Gaddafi's regime had lost its legitimacy and he had to go. At a news conference, Medvedev said:

> If he makes this responsible decision himself—and this would be useful for the country and for the Libyan people—then we can talk about how it can be done, what country will take him under what conditions, and what he can keep, and what he should lose. But in any case, international society does not see him as the leader of Libya now.[38]

Russia's special envoy to the Middle East and North Africa, Mikhail Margelov, then made June visits to Benghazi and Tripoli. He tried to persuade the NTC to join the negotiations proposed by the AU, while they in turn urged Russia to join the Contact Group. In Tripoli, he met Al-Mahmoudi, but although he expressed cautious optimism after his visits, positions remained unchanged.[39] Immediately before Margelov's visit to Tripoli, Gaddafi had been televised playing chess with the Russian president of the International Chess Federation, Kirsan Ilyumzhinov: Margelov said he had asked him to pass the message to Gaddafi that he was near-ing an endgame.[40] Medvedev met with Zuma in Sochi on 4 July, where he also had discussions with NATO Secretary-General Rasmussen during the NATO–Russia Council meeting, while Ilyumzhinov made a second visit to Tripoli, but was again told that Gaddafi would not leave Libya.[41]

Final attempts

As the date approached for the fourth Contact Group meeting, to be held in Istanbul on 15 July, there was mounting concern among its members that there was a military stalemate on the ground, and thus a growing interest in a political solution. France and the UK had been dismissive of the AU's efforts, and their formal state-ments in the Security Council welcoming the work of Al-Khatib had not been reflected in any pressure on the NTC to be more responsive to his proposals. They preferred to pursue bilateral contacts, utilising relationships between intelligence services, to seek Gaddafi's departure and thus a negotiated victory. As their parliament considered extending its military operation, French ministers spoke publicly about the need for a political solution and communications with regime emissaries but said that these did not constitute direct negotiations.[42] A claim by Saif that Sarkozy had met a special envoy from the regime was denied, but Gaddafi's chief of staff, Bashir Saleh, had indeed had a ten-minute meeting at the Elysée on 6 July, where Sarkozy had reminded him of the fate of former President Laurent Gbagbo of Côte d'Ivoire after he refused to give up power when offered an alternative to prosecu-tion at the ICC.[43] In a meeting with the AU, Foreign Minister Juppé now encouraged its efforts. The UK's engagement with the regime remained secret, but Cameron maintains that he 'pushed and pushed for a deal to be offered to Gaddafi—an "exit with hon-our"—using political links built up historically between our coun-tries'. Amid various suggestions for where Gaddafi might be hosted in exile, the UK development minister sounded out Equatorial Guinea, which was not a party to the ICC.[44]

On the eve of the Istanbul Contact Group meeting, Turkey's foreign minister publicly proposed what he called a 'third way' between the approach of the AU—which he described as leaving Gaddafi in power to implement the reforms demanded by the opposition—and that of France—which he said favoured arming the regime's opponents and overthrowing it by force. Turkey's plan, he said, included finding Gaddafi a safe haven and establishing a joint governing council between regime representatives not implicated in war crimes and members of the opposition.[45] He said the plan was developed in cooperation with UN officials, and indeed it resembled Al-Khatib's proposals, while being consistent with the approach Erdoğan had set out for Turkey's diplomatic contacts with the Gaddafi regime early in the conflict. The Contact Group meeting declared that Gaddafi and certain members of his family must go; until then it would deal with the NTC as the legitimate governing authority in Libya, pending a transition process that would include 'the potential participation of select members of the previous bureaucracy as stipulated in the NTC Road Map'. In doing so, it again endorsed a roadmap presented by the NTC's Executive Committee Chairperson Jibril to the second Contact Group meeting in May, which provided for the inclusion of technocrats and high-ranking officers from the regime in an interim government, but it was far from certain that this represented the agreed policy of the NTC. The Contact Group reaffirmed the UN's leading role in facilitating dialogue and called on all actors to coordinate with its special envoy.[46]

Norway and the United States

One actor that had not coordinated with, or indeed informed, the UN or the AU of its mediation efforts was Norway. After the departure of the Norwegian mediators from Tripoli as bombing began, the regime's team came several times to Oslo, including meeting face-to-face with NTC representatives. By late April, there was provisional agreement on a document providing for a peaceful transition of power: its first line stated 'Colonel Gaddafi has decided to leave power and step aside and to end the first phase of the revolution.'[47] Norway's Foreign Minister Jonas Støre spoke to Saif on the phone to confirm backing for the plan, and the

Norwegian team believed that Saif and other key figures favoured a negotiated outcome but that Gaddafi himself was isolated and surrounded by people who filtered the information that reached him. Once the rebels were on the offensive, they became less willing to negotiate.[48]

Norway had kept the US informed of its continuing mediation attempt and had conveyed the importance the Gaddafi regime attached to the position of the US, but the latter pulled back from a possible meeting in May with regime representatives. Washington had been wary of talking directly to the regime for fear of undermining other negotiators and allowing Gaddafi to exploit any differences but was being told that he misinterpreted this unwillingness to engage him as a sign of ambivalence about his future.[49] In this context, US and Norwegian representatives proceeded immediately from Istanbul to Tunis, where they met—separately—with regime representatives on 16 July. The Libyan interlocutors included both Saleh and Ismail, together with the deputy foreign minister and Gaddafi's 'interpreter and adviser'. The US side, headed by Assistant Secretary of State Jeff Feltman, said that they were there to emphasise that it was time for Gaddafi to step down on his own and to discuss modalities for his departure. The Libyans insisted that Gaddafi was more of a symbol than a political leader, and that the best way forward was the AU roadmap: ceasefire first, then negotiations without preconditions or foreign intervention. The Americans affirmed the Contact Group decision that there should be no separate roadmaps or channels of communication other than Al-Khatib, but noted to themselves that working with the AU would be very important in the days ahead: '[I]f the Africans stiffen their spines, then the Libyans would be really cornered.'[50]

The impasse

Gaddafi's departure had long been the central issue in any negotiated transition. The NTC had been willing to envisage a transition involving some of those who had remained with the regime: after all, leading NTC figures, including Abdul Jalil, had broken with it only when the uprising began, while Jibril had been a close, but disillusioned, collaborator of Saif. The extent to which Saif had identified himself with his father's response, beginning with his speech of 20 February, had dashed hopes that he could now be a reformer. But the first NTC roadmap envisaged including in a transitional arrangement some who had remained with the regime but did not have 'blood on their hands'. In a retrospective interview, Abdul Jalil named respected figures with whom the NTC could have achieved reconciliation.[51] He also revealed in early July that a month previously he had offered through Al-Khatib that if Gaddafi resigned and withdrew his forces, he could stay in Libya, at a place determined by the NTC and under international supervision of all his movements.[52] Such an arrangement—which was unsurprisingly controversial within the NTC—was again referred to as a possibility by Abdul Jalil in late July, but he quickly said the offer had expired.[53]

After the flurry of contacts in July, what prospects there might have been of a mediated outcome receded, as rebel advances in the west broke the apparent stalemate and the focus of the NTC and its supporters became the fall of the regime in Tripoli itself. In Benghazi, the NTC was preoccupied with internal debate about the roadmap to be followed once Gaddafi stepped down and was in turmoil after the assassination of its military commander, General Abd al-Fattah Younis.[54] In what turned out to be his last visits to Benghazi and Tripoli on 25–26 July, Al-Khatib found both sides still emphasising maximum demands. NTC members would not engage in talks for the establishment of a new transitional entity while the existing regime was still in place, and Al-Mahmoudi reiterated that the government was not ready to engage in a political process that implied the stepping down of Gaddafi, demanding that NATO first stop its military actions. The NTC was at last persuaded, in part by the US, to respond to the AU by sending a delegation headed by Jibril to meet the High-Level Committee in Addis Ababa on 9 August. But mediation attempts were effectively over, and military victory was imminent.

Reflections

Was this inevitable? To have achieved the greatest possibility of a negotiated transition, the efforts of all those with influence on either side of the conflict would have needed to be more effectively coordinated. The AU, especially in the person of Zuma, had the advantage of access to Gaddafi himself and could most directly tell him he had to step down. The western backers of the NTC—principally France and the UK—could have conditioned their support on its willingness to negotiate with the regime, but they were as determined as the NTC itself that Gaddafi must go and were committed to a path to military victory that left the NTC little incentive to compromise. If they had been more seriously invested in the mediation of Al-Khatib and less dismissive of the AU, their own messages to the parties could have been supportive of a coordinated process. But a mediation adviser who met senior UK officials in late April found no appetite for any initiative that sought to mediate a negotiated settlement with Gaddafi:

> According to UK government experts then, defection was the key to success and any attempt to present potential defectors with an alternative diplomatic scenario was counter-productive to the ultimate objective of removing Gaddafi from power ... I soon realised that the government's support of the UN's mandate to the exclusion of all others was based more on the UN's inability as opposed to ability to effect reconciliation.[55]

Obama would probably have been more open to a mediated outcome than Sarkozy and Cameron but was letting the Europeans lead. In the absence of a mutually agreed ceasefire, either Gaddafi or NATO could have paused their military action to test the willingness of the other side to talk realistically: neither was willing to do so.

Reflecting on Norway's efforts, then Foreign Minister Støre accepts not knowing whether Gaddafi would have stepped down or if the rebels would have accepted a deal, but he also says that major western nations were not interested in a negotiated settlement:

> I felt that the mindset in London and Paris didn't have openings for really reflecting on the diplomatic option ... Had there been in the international community a willingness to pursue this track with some authority and dedication, I believe there could have been an opening to achieve a less dramatic outcome and avoid the collapse of the Libyan state.[56]

This view is shared from within the AU Commission:

> A consensus could have been achieved had the west approached the AU in a more subtle and respectful way … a closer coordination and honest and respectful conversation between the AU and the west would have made it possible to build sufficient international leverage to compel Gaddafi to accept to exit the scene with the required security guarantees for himself and his close associates.[57]

An angry Zuma told the Security Council in September that 'the AU initiative to ensure a political rather than military solution to the Libyan crisis was deliberately undermined' despite the decision in Resolution 1973 to support the AU roadmap, and 'such blatant acts of disregard for regional initiatives have the potential to undermine the confidence that regional organizations have in the United Nations as an impartial and widely respected mediator in conflicts'.[58]

That said, there is reason to doubt that Gaddafi would ever have been willing to give up the real power he wielded—at the same time as he repeatedly said he held no offices to resign from, which added to the mediators' difficulties in seeking a symbolic stepping aside; let alone that he would have agreed to leave Libya. The tone of his speeches remained defiant and belligerent throughout: there was no moment when he offered an olive branch to his opponents, whom he consistently denounced as 'traitors'.[59] Those who had been close to him testified to his state of mind: Koussa said from his exile that 'he knew Qaddafi as well as anyone, and believed in the spring of 2011 that the mercurial Libyan leader was living in his own world, determined to fight to the end'.[60] Libyan officials were said to have admitted after the war that at no time did Gaddafi's family or inner circle think they would be defeated: they suffered from 'supreme arrogance and miscalculation'.[61] Sarkozy's adviser Jean-David Levitte testified, on the basis of French intelligence contacts, that '[t]o our knowledge, the colonel never showed the slightest intention to negotiate. We never received a message that he understood what we were saying, that he was thinking about his resignation or that he considered opening negotiations.'[62]

In such a context, it is hard to assess what effect, if any, the referral to the ICC and its indictments of Gaddafi, Saif and Senussi may have had on mediation efforts.[63] The ICC referral can hardly be said to have had the desired effect of deterring further war crimes, although together with the Security Council sanctions it may have contributed to the defections from the regime. Saif's aide Mohammed Ismail later said that 'we were open to power sharing, but the minute that happened it was hard to go forward'.[64] The indictment added to the difficulties of attempts to find a country of exile for Gaddafi, but it seems he was never open to this, although there is some evidence from interviews with his chief of security that it contributed to Gaddafi's eventual frustration that he had no options for escape.[65] One might expect that Saif's UK and other western connections would have made him more sensitive to potential consequences, but after he had thrown his lot in with his father, he had little leeway for moderation. Saif mocked the court in light of the willingness of states to negotiate a way around the indictments:

> It's a fake court. Under the table they are trying to negotiate with us a deal. They say if you accept this deal we will take care of the court. What does that mean? It means this court is controlled by those countries that are attacking us every day! It is just to put psychological and political pressure on us. That's it. Of course, it won't work. The court is a joke here in Libya.[66]

The indictments did have an effect on the other party to potential negotiations, the NTC, further delegitimising the regime and emboldening the rebels.[67] As Jibril later put it: 'Many saw the warrant for Gaddafi as effectively labelling him an international war criminal, thus providing clear moral support for the opposition.'[68]

Attitudes within the NTC hardened over the months of fighting. Those whom Al-Khatib met in Tobruk on 21 March seemed open to a negotiated process of reform. There were some intra-Libyan efforts at dialogue with some of those close to Gaddafi.[69] But as more blood was shed, such as in the bitter battle for Misrata, so the pressures not to 'betray the revolution' grew, and pent-up hatred of Gaddafi and his decades of repression found its expression. Those who had been reformers inside the system were joined by long-term opponents returning from exile, and Islamist fighters became a major element among the armed groups. Jibril and others who represented the NTC in its external relations had little room to compromise, even if they had wanted to.[70]

The NTC also had legitimate fears about the possible implications of a ceasefire and a transition with Gaddafi still in Libya. A ceasefire might become the basis for de facto division of the country. Gaddafi's skill in manipulating divisions among Libyans to maintain his dominance over a period of forty years might outwit a rebellion composed of diverse individuals who hardly knew each other, which had had no time to develop strong and united leadership.

The marginalisation that the AU had protested left it feeling bitter as its persistent efforts petered out. It had consistently emphasised that it was Africa that would be the most affected region, exposed to the risks that continued fighting in Libya posed to regional stability and security, as migrant workers, former mercenaries and weapons crossed its borders: Chad's President Déby could soon say that 'my fears, alas, were not unfounded'.[71] It also found its motives caricatured by those who alleged that it sought to protect Gaddafi and his regime, perhaps because of his past largesse to some African states and leaders.[72] In fact, Gaddafi's behaviour in Africa had left him few friends.[73] Moreover, as Ping maintained, the AU had reacted creatively to the uprisings in Tunisia and Egypt, basing its response not on a dogmatic interpretation of its rejection of unconstitutional changes of government but 'on the need to contribute to the attainment of the overall AU objective of consolidating democracy in the continent'. From the very start, it made clear that any solution to the Libyan crisis had to be based on the fulfilment of the legitimate aspirations of the Libyan people for democracy, respect for human rights and good governance. In striving to secure a Libyan consensus on inclusive transitional institutions until elections were held, it 'clearly implied Colonel Qaddafi's relinquishing power to those institutions'.[74] But it resented those outside the region declaring publicly that an African head of state must step down.

However, those who claimed a lead for Africa in the Libyan crisis perhaps did not sufficiently recognise that Libya did not identify itself only as an African country: its Arab identity was at least as strong. Many Libyans resented the way Gaddafi had squandered their country's resources on his African ambitions; together with Gaddafi's use of mercenaries from sub-Saharan Africa, this contributed to Libyan racism towards black Africans, of which there were many victims in 2011. In his reflections, Ping deplored the reluctance of some members of the international community to fully acknowledge the AU's role and said that lasting peace on the continent could only be achieved if efforts to that end were based on the full involvement of Africa and a recognition of its leadership role.[75] But the circumstances of Libya in 2011 suggest that what was needed was a complementarity of UN and AU efforts, with consistent support from all actors. While this too might have failed, foundering on Gaddafi's extreme obduracy and the virulence of the hatred he had engendered among many Libyans, it was far from what was tried.

4

THE DAY AFTER

POST-CONFLICT PLANNING

The decision to intervene militarily in the Libyan conflict had been made to prevent what was envisaged to be a humanitarian catastrophe and with an expectation that Gaddafi's downfall would quickly follow those of Ben Ali and Mubarak. There was an almost complete absence of strategic thinking, accompanied by an extremely limited understanding of Libya among decision-makers.[1] As the conflict became protracted, and was assumed likely to culminate in regime change, to what extent did the main actors engage in post-conflict planning? Obama declared that failing to plan for the day after was the worst mistake of his presidency.[2] One academic commentator told the UK House of Commons Inquiry that there was 'not a bit' of post-conflict reconstruction planning.[3] What efforts were in fact made, by whom, and what constraints did they face?

The leading western countries that intervened were conditioned by their experiences in Afghanistan and Iraq to be determined to avoid becoming responsible for a prolonged post-conflict role. Although he had reluctantly joined France and the UK in the intervention, Obama was also adamant that the Europeans would carry the main responsibility: '[B]ecause North Africa was in Europe's backyard and not ours, we would also ask the Europeans to pay for much of the post-conflict aid that would be required to rebuild Libya and help the country transition to democracy once Gaddafi was no longer in power.'[4] The London Conference of 29 March, which established the Libya Contact Group, promptly passed the buck to the UN, agreeing that 'participants welcomed the UN Secretary-General's offer to lead the coordination of humanitarian assistance and planning for longer-term stabilisation'.[5]

The role of the United Nations

Within the UN, while the Office for the Coordination of Humanitarian Affairs (OCHA) assumed the humanitarian respon-sibility, Secretary-General Ban decided to designate a special adviser for post-conflict planning, and I was appointed to this role.[6] My initial understanding of the challenge, based on my first read-ing, did not, I think, underestimate it, and was set out to colleagues as follows:

> Even on the most optimistic set of assumptions regarding the transi-tion to a new government in Libya, the challenges which it will face will be among the greatest of any post-conflict contexts. Libya has been variously described as 'an accidental state' and as having 'a tradition of rejection of states'. Following a particularly brutal period of colonial rule, and then wartime destruction and occupa-tion, it was created out of distinct entities at the behest of great power interests and agreed to by the provinces only because they feared other alternatives. Its political independence was not the result of a struggle which forged a sense of national identity. Neither its experiment with federalism under the 1951 Constitution nor the turn towards a centralised state from 1963 to 1969 saw sound insti-tutional development. Under Qadhafi, the rejection of the normal institutions of a state, of representative democracy or of any inde-pendent civil society became a matter of policy; in theory, people have managed themselves without state institutions, while the real power has been a narrow circle of family, tribe and intimates around the Leader, supported and kept in place by a number of security sector institutions and the Revolutionary Committees. The last elections of any kind were in 1972.[7]
>
> The stateless state was in charge of all economic and social activity. An immensely resource-rich economy was badly managed, with

efficiency and real concerns for development yielding to the political imperatives of the regime—handouts to keep the population quiescent and more substantial outlays for its coalition of supporters inside the country and allies outside. The economy has been highly dependent on expatriates, while domestic unemployment has been estimated at 30 per cent; the east of the country clearly feels that it has not properly shared in its wealth. The emergence of a professional military was prevented in favour of a popular army and militias with members of Qadhafi's tribe and family in sensitive positions; there has been no Ministry of Defence since 1969. Freedom of expression and association have existed neither in law or in practice, and arbitrary detention, torture and disappearances have persisted. Steps towards economic liberalisation and legal reform in recent years have been personalised in the role of Saif al-Qadhafi and were yet to be institutionalised. While Libya has many skilled professionals, the challenge of developing the institutions of a modern democratic state is immense.[8]

The UN had a standing agreement with the World Bank and the European Union regarding a Post-Conflict Needs Assessment Framework for post-conflict countries, within which the three entities would collaborate in carrying out in-country assessments, in conjunction with national authorities. But since the in-country assessments envisaged by this agreement could not commence in Libya while the conflict raged, the UN set in motion what I decided to call a 'pre-assessment process'—not yet calling it post-conflict planning, since planning would require as interlocutors those Libyans who would have authority to govern after the fighting. Its objective was to bring together all parts of the UN system to seek to understand relevant features of pre-conflict Libya, the likely effects of the conflict itself, and thus expectations for post-conflict challenges. Cross-UN sub-groups examined the political process, the security apparatus, rule of law and human rights, economic recovery, public administration, service delivery and physical infrastructure and distribution networks. The economic recovery sub-group was chaired by the World Bank, and discussions were held with the EU and the International Monetary Fund (IMF).

The UN's understanding of Libya, like that of other international actors, was limited: its in-country presence had been a small one, both because of the closed nature of Gaddafi's Libya and because its wealth made it, in UN terms, a 'net contributing country', limiting the UN funds that could be provided and thus confining the work of UN agencies largely to a few government-funded projects. The pre-assessment process did, however, draw on the knowledge of the small UN country team, which had been evacuated from Libya, as well as the humanitarian agencies that now had some access to the country. Recognising the limitations of the UN's own knowledge, the UN engaged a leading scholar of contemporary Libya as consultant to the process.[9]

It was obviously important to learn the views of Libyans themselves on the desired post-conflict role of the UN and of the wider international community, but which Libyans? While the conflict continued, its outcome uncertain, the UN's engagement with Libyan actors was a sensitive issue. France had been the first government to recognise the NTC as 'the legitimate representative of the Libyan people', and as time went on, other governments accorded different degrees of recognition; but critics of the intervention, including of course some in the Security Council, regarded such recognition as premature. The formal position of the Security Council, as well as the AU, was to seek a ceasefire and a political solution that would meet 'the legitimate aspirations of the Libyan people', and Special Envoy Al-Khatib was attempting to mediate a peaceful transition involving the NTC and what remained of Gaddafi's government, which might feature some interim power-sharing. The UN team and I engaged with members of the NTC in Benghazi,[10] at Contact Group meetings and elsewhere to learn their expectations, should they become an interim Libyan government, but could not yet properly treat them as a successor regime.

UK and US stabilisation planning

The UK was more forward-leaning in seeking to undertake what it called stabilisation planning with the NTC, although its own formal recognition would come only in late July. Ministerial responsibility was assigned to the international development secretary, Andrew Mitchell, together with a cross-departmental Post-Conflict Coordination Cell. A major role was played by the

Stabilisation Unit, a joint unit of the development, defence and foreign ministries, established in 2007 to apply lessons arising in particular from experiences of Afghanistan and Iraq. The UK would have liked the UN to take an immediate lead in coordinating post-conflict planning with the NTC, which the UN felt politically constrained from doing. Thus, after discussion at the Rome Contact Group meeting of 5 May, the UK itself deployed an 'International Stabilisation Response Team' (ISRT) to Benghazi in late May–early June, in which UK experts were joined by some from Australia, Denmark, Italy, Turkey and the US, with later participation from Canada.[11] The ISRT was described as working in partnership with the NTC's planners, but in fact there was considerable friction on the ground, with Libyan interlocutors suspicious of what they feared to be too assertive an international role.

The ISRT's report set out its analysis of needs across five areas—political settlement, security and justice, basic and social services, economy and infrastructure—during three phases: immediate—actions required in NTC-controlled areas until the establishment of an agreed ceasefire; early—actions required across Libya in the first month after a ceasefire; and interim— actions required after the first month to bridge the gap to longer-term recovery.[12] Interviewed about the report at the end of June, Mitchell said the government had learned the lesson of Iraq about the importance of using existing structures to the maximum possible extent. He said that the US, Britain and the UN would have 'strong input' into a post-Gaddafi political settlement; the EU, NATO and the UN would take the lead on issues of security and justice; Australia, Turkey and the UN would help with basic services; Turkey, the US and the international financial institutions would lead on the economy. But, he said, 'it is incredibly important that the whole of this process is Libyan-owned'.[13] However, his statements about who would be doing what had not been cleared with partners, let alone with the Libyans, and were not well received, and the handover of the report was accepted with some reluctance by the NTC.[14] The ISRT disbanded once the report had been completed, so it was a one-off exercise rather than an analysis or plan that continued to be developed as events unfolded, although there remained a significant presence of UK, US and other conflict or stabilisation advisers in Benghazi, with some interaction among them and with NTC representatives.

In Washington, the White House set up a task force to plan for the situation after Gaddafi—the 'post-Q' task force—headed by the National Security Council's senior director for strategic planning, Derek Chollet.[15] Chollet notes that the US believed that, especially compared with places like Iraq and Afghanistan, Libya had a lot going for it—a relatively small, homogeneous population with a professional class; rich energy supplies; proximity and close ties to Europe; and a vast amount of international support and enthusiasm to help. 'There was reason to hope that, with some concerted yet modest assistance, Libya could lift itself out of the swamp decades of Qaddafi's rule had left.' The US was determined to maintain the 'unique capabilities' approach that defined its role in the military campaign. While the bureaucracy's 'muscle memory' was for the US to go in big, offer the Libyans help on everything, and if necessary be ready to do the job for them, Obama 'remained determined not to allow Libya to morph into a massive American-led effort ... Moreover, outsiders engaging in nation-building is not what the Libyans wanted.'[16]

NTC plans

The NTC was indeed determined to set its own course. As head of its Executive Committee, Mahmoud Jibril presented 'A Roadmap for Libya' to the 5 May Contact Group meeting in Rome. It set out a political process: an interim government would be formed out of the NTC, together with technocrats from the old regime and senior military and security officials; a national congress composed of representatives of each city, town and village would select a committee to draft a constitution, to be approved by the congress and then by referendum; and the process would culminate in parliamentary and presidential elections and the formation of a new government. The roadmap welcomed international assistance to the interim government and proposed that the UN would convene an international conference on the reconstruction of Libya; the

NTC, it said, was preparing a 'Marshall Plan'—a reconstruction plan that would involve qualified Libyans from inside and outside the country. 'We have over 100,000 qualified Libyans in the diaspora who can contribute to the reconstruction and regeneration of their homeland', it claimed. 'Unlike many countries facing similar upheavals, the Libyan situation gives cause for hope because it is a country with wealth, enormous qualified human resources and talents, it possesses the right vision for the future—and its people have the will and determination to see it achieved.'[17]

The NTC had been anxious to show that they had not seized or assumed power. As Peter Bartu writes: 'After forty-two years of Qadhafi, the Libyan opposition, obsessed about legitimate representation, trusted neither themselves nor the outside world, and both feared and embraced their new-found environment in the liberated areas, often leading to stasis and indecision over seemingly mundane issues.'[18] They did not then see themselves as a government, but rapidly had to assume responsibility for quasi-governmental functions in areas liberated from regime control in eastern Libya and elsewhere. The 'Crisis Management Committee' headed by Jibril rapidly expanded beyond its initial responsibility for foreign relations, adding members to an 'Executive Team' to run vital sectors of administration and the economy. Jibril was assisted by 'Support Offices' that had been established by Aref Ali Nayed, who had been an early NTC envoy to Qatar and recruited Libyan expertise from around the world, as well as securing the assistance of the UAE and Qatar in bringing a group of representatives from the west, south and centre of Libya to Benghazi, to broaden the geographical membership of the NTC.[19] Nayed and his team were involved in early initiatives to negotiate the international marketing of oil from eastern Libya and the creation of an international financial mechanism to channel funds through the NTC. These were pursued, including at Contact Group meetings, by the de facto minister for oil and finance Ali Tarhouni, an academic economist from the US. Another well-qualified professional was a former World Bank official, Ahmed Jehani, who took on the portfolio for infrastructure and reconstruction and became a key interlocutor with the international planners.

The engagement of international actors with the NTC was complicated by internal divisions, which they did not always understand, and by the geographical dispersion of Libyan interlocutors. There were tensions between Jibril, who spent little time in Benghazi and undertook constant travel for his very effective external lobbying from his base in Doha, and NTC Chairman Mustafa Abdul Jalil and other members. Interactions about stabilisation and post-conflict scenarios would take place in Benghazi, Dubai, Abu Dhabi and Doha, as well as wherever the Contact Group met, but usually amid uncertainty over the extent to which a collective NTC view was being represented.

The US and UK politicians and planners were strongly conditioned by the need to avoid their intervention being discredited by Libya's capital experiencing the chaos that followed the taking of Baghdad in 2003. After the US expressed concern about the lack of a plan to stabilise Tripoli once it fell to the rebels, the NTC in mid-May established a 'Tripoli Task Force' to work on 'comprehensive planning for stabilising, harmonising, operating, and managing Tripoli in the critical period post-Gaddafi'. Nayed was designated to head the Task Force, which was charged with working closely with international stabilisation teams and experts.[20] He began developing plans for Tripoli with British and French military officers. However, strong tensions arose with an Islamist network led by members of the Muslim Brotherhood, brought into the NTC as representatives of Tripoli when the council was expanded in May. The rival networks could not be reconciled. In early July, Jibril and Nayed dissolved the Tripoli Task Force and established a 'Libya Stabilisation Committee', which Nayed would head from the UAE, to which he was named ambassador. Thereafter, the development of the military strategy to take over Tripoli was in principle separated from the stabilisation planning for the aftermath. But rival plans for the liberation and governance of Tripoli continued to be pursued, one by Jibril and another by the Tripoli Islamist network.[21]

Jehani and Nayed had interacted with the UK-led ISRT in Benghazi, and once the NTC's Stabilisation Planning Team had been established, the UN, UK and US teams responsible for post-conflict or stabilisation planning engaged with it, as well as to some extent with each other. On 12 July, the Libyan Team met in Doha with a mixed US delegation comprising the State Department, USAID and other agencies, ahead of the 15 July meeting of the Contact Group in Istanbul. At the Istanbul meeting, the outline of a Libya Stabilisation Plan was presented to the plenary on behalf of the NTC, and the ISRT findings were discussed in a side meeting. In a short speech to the plenary, I described the UN pre-assessment process, setting out five principles for our approach: national ownership; speed of response; effective coordination of international assistance; understanding of the uniqueness of Libya; and humility, noting that 'the record of the international community in post-conflict transitions displayed at least as many mistakes as successes to learn from'.[22]

The chair's statement welcomed the NTC presentation, noting that the post-conflict process 'will be Libyan-led, with the international community in a supportive role'.[23] The statement reiterated the coordinating role of the UN in leading the international efforts to assist Libyans in the field of post-conflict planning for early recovery and peace-building and encouraged the UN to accelerate its planning. At the end of July, the Libyan Stabilisation Planning Team convened a two-day workshop in Dubai, where it presented its more detailed preliminary plan to representatives of the US, UK, EU and UN. The recognised need for further discussion of the security dimension of the plan was the focus of another such Dubai workshop on 22–23 August, with participants from the US, UK, Canada, Italy, UAE and UN; France and Qatar had also been invited, but were not present.[24]

Meanwhile, events on the ground in western Libya had been moving rapidly towards the fall of Tripoli. Most discussions were dominated by the fears that this would involve heavy fighting and disruption and destruction of essential infrastructure, perhaps through deliberate sabotage during a last stand of the Gaddafi regime. Predictions by Libyans associated with the NTC varied widely in their pessimism or optimism, ensuring that the spectre of Baghdad 2003 weighed heavily on some of the discussions. The Libyan Team drew on the US Institute of Peace and US Army

Peacekeeping and Stability Operations Institute's 'Guiding Principles for Stabilization and Reconstruction', and its late July workshop opened with a US presentation on the experience in Iraq. The UN participant noted that the plans were a mix of strategic objectives and operational/tactical considerations; the main focus was said to be the first six weeks, while sometimes they confused support for the war effort and post-conflict planning. Nayed emphasised that there was to be only one plan: Libya would not accept foreign plans.

Final preparations

Despite the NTC's strongly and consistently expressed opposition to foreign troops, the UN had to consider the possibility that it would be asked to undertake a military deployment. The AU roadmap envisaged a ceasefire with a monitoring mechanism, which the Gaddafi regime stated it would be willing to accept. The UN's Department of Peacekeeping Operations (DPKO) developed a contingency plan for the deployment of up to 200 military observers, the first of whom could be drawn from existing UN operations. This would also require an armed force to guarantee the security of unarmed observers, and when I first briefed the Security Council about the post-conflict planning, on 27 June, I told them that there might thus need to be an interim military protection presence to be deployed almost immediately once the fighting ended, 'despite strong Libyan and international wishes to avoid the necessity for this'.[25] Given the time needed for the UN to generate and deploy troops, such a presence would have to come—if requested by the Libyans and authorised by the council—from some other source, such as a multinational force under a lead nation command. Senior UN officials met the permanent representatives of France, the UK and US in late July to make clear to them that even for a permissive or semi-permissive environment, the UN could not deploy a protection force in less than ninety days; a stabilisation force for a semi-permissive or non-permissive environment could not be a UN peacekeeping operation. If, then, they believed such a force would be necessary, it was up to them to discuss this with the NTC as well as to talk to potential lead nations and troop contributors. Force requirements for a possible protection element to accompany unarmed UN military observers were provided to two governments for them to consider. DPKO also prepared a contingency plan to deploy up to seventy-eight UN police officers after forty-five days and 190 after ninety days. At the Libyan Stabilisation Team's Dubai workshop, even though many then expected a worst-case scenario for Tripoli, Nayed said that Libya would not accept foreign troops, except UN monitors, or perhaps protection of vital infrastructure by countries such as Jordan and Qatar.

The UN's internal pre-assessment process culminated in early August in a Consolidated Report and a series of detailed sub-group reports. No sooner had these been completed than the rebels were closing in on Tripoli, and the prospect of its imminent fall required the UN to be ready to seek a Security Council mandate for a post-conflict mission and get a team on the ground. On 21 August, I put forward proposals for UN post-conflict deployment, pending consultations with the transitional Libyan authorities. These envisaged a political mission for an initial three months, able to offer immediate advice to the authorities while discussing with them what further support they desired; they left open the possibilities of military observers or UN police on the basis of DPKO's contingency plans. Just as the fighting in Tripoli was making clear that the Gaddafi regime was being defeated, I discussed the UN's plans in Doha and Dubai with Jibril, Jehani and Nayed, when Jibril made clear that the NTC would not request any military deployment. I conveyed this to the Contact Group in a briefing reflecting these discussions when it met at the level of political directors in Istanbul on 25 August; Nayed was present to represent the Libyan Stabilisation Team, and the presentation it circulated declared its authority from the NTC to coordinate international assistance. Once Tripoli had fallen, Sarkozy was once more out in front in convening a 'Friends of Libya' meeting in Paris on 1 September, where the NTC was received as the authority that would now govern from Libya's capital. Ban and the UN team met there with Abdul Jalil and Jibril to further discuss expectations of the UN.

The Libya Stabilisation Team was naturally focused on the immediate situation in Tripoli, especially a crisis in the water supply, where it was the UN humanitarian agencies that were able to be of assistance. Meanwhile, Jehani, as NTC minister for infrastructure and reconstruction and chairman of the team, issued invitations to a meeting with donor agencies interested in supporting Libya's stabilisation needs, to follow on from the Paris meeting. This 2 September meeting agreed that needs assessments in Libya would be carried out within the Post-Conflict Needs Assessment Framework agreed by the EU, the UN and the World Bank, avoiding bilateral missions and thus reducing the burden on the new Libyan authorities. This was reaffirmed when the relevant governments and other actors met in New York on 20 September, in a meeting held alongside a high-level event on Libya in the margins of the General Assembly. A few days earlier, the credentials submitted by the NTC had been accepted by the General Assembly on the recommendation of the UN's Credentials Committee. The donor meetings in Paris and New York were co-chaired by Jehani and the UN. Sector co-leads were identified from among UN entities, the World Bank, the IMF and the EU for each of twelve sectors to carry out assessments of transition requirements in partnership with government focal points to be designated by the new authorities. Other multilateral and bilateral actors were invited to participate, but the strong concern was to discourage multiple uncoordinated visits and assessment missions that would overburden the Libyans.

Meanwhile, the UN was determining what form its presence in Libya should take. Ban set this out in a letter to the Security Council on 7 September, proposing the establishment of an integrated UN Support Mission in Libya (UNSMIL). Its mandate, which reflected discussions with the NTC, would include assistance and support for national efforts to, among other things,

(a) restore public security and order and promote the rule of law;
(b) undertake inclusive political dialogue, promote national reconciliation, and embark upon the constitution-making and electoral processes;
(c) extend State authority, including through the strengthening of emerging accountable institutions and the restoration of public services;

(d) protect human rights, particularly for vulnerable groups, and support transitional justice;

(e) take the immediate steps required to initiate economic recovery;

(f) coordinate the support that may be requested from other multilateral and bilateral actors.[26]

I visited Tripoli and Benghazi to continue discussions with Abdul Jalil and key NTC interlocutors regarding the UN role, and elaborated on the proposed approach when I briefed the council on 9 September. An initial three-month mandate would see deployment of staff phased according to the readiness of key interlocutors, as well as security conditions.[27] A formal letter from Jibril endorsed the proposed mandate,[28] which was adopted by the council in its resolution establishing UNSMIL.[29] I was appointed to head UNSMIL as special representative of the secretary-general, and the deployment of mission staff began in mid-September, at a pace determined by security constraints.

On the ground

Events in Libya were, however, rendering it impossible to embark on the agreed approach to post-conflict assessment and support. There was great relief that the fears of prolonged fighting in Tripoli and devastation of infrastructure had not come to pass, putting an end to what little inclination there had been to consider the deployment of foreign troops or police. Nayed and his Stabilisation Team had continued to work with those bringing early external assistance, focusing heavily on utilities, telecoms and fuel. The team was therefore able to contribute to specific stabilisation challenges—including managing the handover of the telecommunications network and opening and managing ports—as well as working with UN agencies to contribute to the management of the water crisis.[30]

There was, however, serious confusion and contestation over authority in the capital, at three interrelated levels: national government, administration of the city, and the command of armed groups. The NTC had been in some disarray since the assassination of its military commander, General Abd al-Fattah Younis, on 29 July: in the resulting uproar and allegations regarding the implication of some of its members, Abdul Jalil had dissolved the Executive Committee. Jibril had been under increasing criticism for his absence from Benghazi, and although he was asked to submit a new list of committee members for NTC approval—and to spend less time outside the country—the committee had not been fully reconstituted.[31] The first senior member of the Executive Committee to take charge in Tripoli was Tarhouni, the holder of the key portfolio of oil and finance and now designated deputy prime minister, who began to function from the seat of government. Jibril was still the external face of the NTC, along with Abdul Jalil, appearing with him at the Paris meeting and briefing the Security Council on 26 September, but he was increasingly criticised in Libya.

The rift with the Islamists became public with an outspoken attack by Ali al-Sallabi, a cleric based in Qatar who had been influential in steering its support to the Islamist armed groups[32] and who now denounced Jibril and his allies on Al Jazeera as 'extreme secularists';[33] his brother, Ismail al-Sallabi, a leading Islamist commander in Benghazi, declared that '[t]he role of the executive committee is no longer required because they are remnants of the old regime. They should all resign starting from the head of the pyramid all the way down.'[34] The previous tension over rival plans between Nayed and those who formed the Tripoli Local Council turned into feuding on the ground, as Nayed took on a high profile, giving briefings on the work of the Stabilisation Team to international actors.[35] This brought him into conflict not only with the Tripoli Local Council but ultimately with Jibril, from whom his authority had flowed. After Jibril accused him of operating as a 'shadow government', Nayed returned to his embassy, having handed over the work of the Stabilisation Team to the respective ministries and announced its closing out in Dubai on 21 September.[36] When the NTC formally endorsed a cabinet on 4 October, Jibril remained prime minister but stated that he would stand down once the country was fully liberated.[37]

Related to these contestations was the struggle to establish authority over the diverse armed groups in the capital. Peter Cole and Umar Khan describe how the unexpectedly rapid fall of Tripoli resulted in an utterly confused and uncoordinated presence of fighters comprising battalions that had been training outside Tripoli for the eventual assault, others sweeping in from Zintan and elsewhere in the Nafusa Mountains and from Misrata, military elements that rose up inside Tripoli, and new militia emerging in city neighbourhoods. When Abdel Hakim Belhaj, the military commander closest to Ali al-Sallabi and Qatar, was presented on Al Jazeera as the head of the Tripoli Military Council and apparent leader of the forces that had taken Gaddafi's compound, resentment was rife among other fighters. Jibril's proposed nomination of a former military officer to head a security committee was rejected, while Ali al-Sallabi's early attempt to shore up support for Belhaj's Tripoli Military Council had only limited success. Tarhouni then attempted to bring all armed groups under the authority of the Executive Committee through formation of a Supreme Security Committee, but this too failed. When Abdul Jalil came to Tripoli to try to resolve the crisis on 11–12 September, the Qatari chief of staff accompanied Belhaj to one meeting and clashed with Jibril. Abdul Jalil took the authority for security away from the Executive Committee and gave it to a new Supreme Security Committee composed of three NTC members of different political backgrounds. The authority of Jibril's Executive Committee was effectively over, and it was soon thereafter that he announced his intention to resign.[38] The influence of the Islamists would be more strongly reflected when the new interim government was formed.

UNSMIL tried to carry forward the agreements of the meetings in Paris and New York regarding post-conflict needs assessment and coordination between the new authorities and the international actors. The high-level meeting in New York had decided that future meetings of the Friends of Libya would be convened by the Libyan government and the UN in Tripoli. At the request of the embassies now reopening in the capital, UNSMIL attempted to convene an initial such meeting with Tarhouni as the acting prime minister, but he made clear at the meeting that the Libyans wanted no such configuration to operate, at least at that juncture. He also told UNSMIL to await the appointment of ministers in the new government before continuing with the plans for post-conflict needs assessments. Jehani meanwhile remained in Benghazi. The NTC was understandably preoccupied with the continuing battles for Bani Walid and Sirte, while Gaddafi's uncertain whereabouts and his defiant radio statements were still an ominous cloud over its victory. On 23 October, after Gaddafi had been killed, the NTC could at last make its Declaration of Liberation and proceed to appoint the interim government. On 31 October, Abdurrahim el-Keib was elected prime minister by the NTC, and when his government was formed, it included none of those with whom the UN and other post-conflict planners had worked over the preceding months—Jibril, Tarhouni, Jehani or Nayed.

Reflections

It is thus far from being the case that no thought was given to the day after. Both the US and the UK had large teams of officials focusing on Libya; western governments had churned out volumes of assessments, estimates, and plans 'the size of a Manhattan phone book'.[39] But there were several major constraints on the planning that was undertaken. Too many of the decision-makers in the western governments assumed that if the kind of initial chaos that followed the fall of Baghdad could be avoided, the subsequent task in a wealthy country with a small population and no sectarian divide would be manageable. This, of course, was a view that went well with their desire not to take any major post-conflict responsibility.

This desire was especially firm on the part of the US. The US approach was set out in a September 2011 State Department note:

> Post-conflict stabilisation in Libya, while clearly a worthy under-taking at the right level of investment, cannot be counted as one of our highest priorities. Strategically for us, Libya does not loom as large as Egypt and Syria ... We should not allow the momentum of our involvement to date in the Libyan revolution to determine our strategy for longer-term assistance ... This means that, for the United States, Libya must not become a state-building exercise.[40]

The note went on to argue that the US should only assist when it had a 'unique' ability to provide a particular service; had a proven track record of success and Congress would provide funds; and Libyans expressly requested the US to do so, 'even if we feel that the Libyan government or its people are making a mistake in not seeking our help'. Having from the outset regarded the European intervening countries as primarily responsible for Libya after the conflict, Obama in his retrospective reflections would express his disappointment with them: he had had more faith in the Europeans, given Libya's proximity, being invested in the follow-up, and noted that Cameron soon stopped paying attention, becoming 'distracted by a range of other things'.[41]

Despite the leading role in the intervention of France and the UK, their political leadership was little more ready to give priority to state-building in Libya. The former UK ambassador describes the reluctance of the western allies as stemming from several factors:

> Firstly, they knew that their electorates supported humanitarian intervention, but had no appetite for occupation or nation building after Iraq and Afghanistan. Secondly, they understood that the Libyans themselves were wary of direct foreign involvement ... Thirdly, they were optimistic that the transitional authorities had a feasible plan and timetable (which broadly suited coalition interests) for establishing an open political system. Moreover, there was no obvious threat from external neighboring or regional powers to subvert this political process. Finally, the allies knew that direct Western interference might prove counter-productive, provoking a hostile political reaction not only in Libya but also in the wider Arab world.[42]

The main focus of the 'stabilisation planning' of the western governments had been short term—often focused on 'the first 100 days'—and the fact that Libya's wealth meant that it was not to be a significant recipient of donor funds limited the attention of bilateral development actors. The UN's pre-assessment process took a longer view and was fairly clear-eyed about the challenges. But the UN fully shared the emphasis on national ownership, which was the consistent mantra of both Libyans and internationals, including at Contact Group and Security Council meetings. The impressive professional qualifications of those who represented the NTC, especially on the international stage, contributed to over-confidence in their eventual ability to govern—an over-confidence that some of them would later admit they shared. While some of the political divisions among them were evident, the NTC's relative success in presenting a united front to the international community, together with the latter's failure to reach out to Libyans more broadly, led to an underestimation of the threat those divisions would come to pose to post-conflict governance. There was insufficient recognition of the full implications of the ways in which Gaddafi's rule had inhibited political and governing experience and had exploited regional and tribal divisions for generations.

The most fatal flaw in planning for the challenges ahead related to security and the proliferation of armed groups. The UN pre-assessment, the ISRT report and other post-conflict analyses all recognised this as a central issue. They described the nature of the security sector under Gaddafi, with a national army that had been kept deliberately weak and a barely functioning Ministry of Defence, and reliance on the family and tribal loyalties of parallel security brigades. They noted that rebel fighters would need to be demobilised or integrated into state security forces and arms and armaments brought under control. The ISRT report said that the most critical early security challenge would be 'ensuring anti-Qadhafi militia do not evolve into armed wings of political factions, but are either merged into new, democratically accountable national security organisations, or disarmed and demobilised'.[43] But the various analyses had little to propose about how this might be addressed, beyond conventional approaches to security sector reform and demobilisation.

The UN pre-assessment noted that a key information gap was the exact composition, organisation and weaponry of the forces on the side of the NTC and their command and control: the UN team had no means of understanding at the time the fast-developing armed groups. Those who might better have done so were the countries deeply involved in arming, training and mentoring the rebel forces, the manner of whose support exacerbated fragmentation, as it avoided 'official' lines of control and went directly to commanders on the ground.[44] There is, however, nothing to indi-

cate that knowledge from these relationships was used systemati-
cally to inform their post-conflict analysis. The UK special forces
who had been alongside the rebels had been focused on victory and
most were withdrawn once it was achieved, so there was little
continuity with the more conventional defence advisory team that
was sent to work with the interim government.

US policy-makers lacked the knowledge of the ground war that
their French and British allies had from their direct participation;
the CIA presence did not engage in military-to-military intelligence. Chollet notes that 'we only later learned the full extent of
what our partners like the French and the Qataris had done'; if the
US had deployed special forces or more weapons, it might have had
'valuable leverage over the various militias after Gaddafi's ouster'.[45]
But the reflections of UK Chief of Defence Staff Richards seem to
recognise that countries that had engaged most closely with the
rebel armed groups failed to derive from their knowledge on the
ground any realistic understanding of the challenge ahead: '[W]e
underestimated the incoherence, even anarchy, of the tribal and
militia patchwork that filled the vacuum left by the Gaddafi
regime.'[46] Asked about the failure to foresee this, he noted:

> What I do remember is that there was a quorum of respectable
> Libyans who were absolutely assuring the Foreign Office and our
> political leaders that this would not happen, that they had a grasp
> over these militias and all we needed to do was to win and they
> would all come to heel. Now we know, with the benefit of hind-
> sight, that that was wishful thinking at best.[47]

There were some whose concern at the possibility that the post-
Gaddafi security situation would be beyond the control of new
political authorities led them to argue during the military campaign
that there should be planning for deployment of a stabilisation or
peacekeeping force, and many more commentators have suggested
in retrospect that this is what should have taken place. NATO's
supreme commander had said at the outset that Libya might need
a stabilisation force; in early June, and again as Tripoli fell,
NATO's planners concluded that Libya would be left in a very
fragile condition following the regime's collapse and wanted to
address security sector reform and stabilisation.[48] But there was no

willingness at a political level to consider a NATO military deployment to Libya when Operation Unified Protector came to an end,
although 'several of its officials were convinced that the country
would have trouble dealing with its imploded security sector
alone'.[49] In late June, the Pentagon held a post-Q tabletop exercise
dubbed 'Island Breeze', playing out scenarios for the fall of Tripoli
and the post-conflict situation, which considered the circumstances
under which international 'boots on the ground' might be advis-
able, but subsequent discussions 'went nowhere'.[50] In retrospect,
White House officials saw it as a downside of the rapid fall of
Tripoli that much of the planning that had been done for post-
conflict stabilisation was significantly less applicable than if the war
had played out as expected: '[T]he speed of the collapse combined
with the stable postcollapse security situation and the rebels' objections to foreign peacekeepers put an end to deliberations about the
possibility of a postwar stabilization force.'[51] As for the UK, the
then national security adviser's testimony is stark:

> None of the European countries were willing to put boots on the
> ground either. The question of deploying Western ground
> forces—either to defeat Gaddafi's forces, or to stabilise the situa-
> tion after his regime collapsed—simply never arose. Libya marked
> the end of a cycle in Western thinking about how to safeguard
> security and protect core values.[52]

Estimates of the required size of a foreign assistance force were
extremely high. One analysis in September 2011 ranged from
6,000 troops for a permissive environment where fighting had
ceased internally to 85,800 for a worst-case scenario, depending
on the burden that could be shouldered by local forces.[53] A later
study of what might have been required in 2011 sketched out three
options: 4,500 to 15,000, including gendarmes or formed police
units, for a force deployed solely to Tripoli; 24,000 to cover the
major coastal cities; or 61,000 for the whole country or possibly
more, if assisting in monitoring, let alone controlling, the country's vast and porous borders.[54] The latter study notes that, after
the Iraq and Afghan wars, 'appetite for post-conflict deployments
was very low in most western capitals', and that when NTC leaders objected to post-conflict peacekeepers, 'discussion in NATO

capitals fizzled'.[55] A more realistic proposal might have been 'hundreds' of military and police advisers, assuming

> that elements loyal to the former regime mostly give up the fight, the rebels stay mostly united, and the population stays calm. At the other end of the spectrum is an international force of several thousand troops, which seems a lot but which in fact is quite modest given Libya's population (6m) and size.[56]

However, other than the UN's contingency plans for ceasefire monitoring, there seems to have been no consideration of possible military roles short of a full-scale stabilisation deployment. Christopher Chivvis suggests that

> [p]ostwar planners were no doubt correct to eschew a major occupation force on the Iraq model, but there is a huge difference between the deployments in Iraq and Afghanistan, where more than 100,000 troops were sent in to fight extended counterinsurgencies, and complete absence of any foreign forces whatsoever in Libya. A more balanced approach could have involved some military footprint without violating the principle of local ownership. This would have increased the chances of stable recovery from the war.[57]

As Libya fell into civil war from 2014, some Libyans would indeed retrospectively wish there had been some foreign security presence, but it is hard to exaggerate the strength and unanimity of Libyan opposition to considering this in any form in 2011, especially after Tripoli had fallen with such limited fighting. All of us who engaged with NTC representatives can testify to this: Benghazi-based advisers conveyed to NATO that the NTC would not tolerate a peacekeeping or mentoring force of any sort, and external forces deployed without their consent could become a target.[58] The memory of the brutality of the Italian occupation during Libya's colonial experience, together with the xenophobia that Gaddafi had successfully cultivated, went deep among Libyans. It has been suggested that the dependence on NATO and the intervening countries was so great that their insistence could have overcome the resistance of the NTC,[59] but this is not a view that has been supported by anyone who interacted with the Libyans in 2011 or by any Libya experts.[60]

In the discussions with the UN, the NTC invited advisory assistance in building a reformed police force but not the deployment of foreign police with executive policing authority. They also envisaged eventual support to programmes for disarmament, demobilisation and reintegration. But neither the UN nor the NTC thought that the UN would have a role in building the national army—a post-conflict role that is usually played by whichever bilateral actors are most acceptable to the government concerned. When noting the need to develop a national army, Jibril explicitly made clear that this would not be a role for the UN. In the Security Council's discussions, no member suggested that UNSMIL should be equipped to play a role in the defence sector.

* * *

With Prime Minister el-Keib's announcement of his ministerial team on 22 November, the UN and other external actors could begin to build again the relationships essential to supporting Libya's post-conflict transition. The period ahead to Libya's first elections in July 2012 would provide reasons for both hope and concern about the prospects for that transition.

5

THE INTERIM GOVERNMENT
AND THE FIRST ELECTION

Prime Minister Abdurrahim el-Keib and the ministers of the interim government took office with immense challenges and significant handicaps. Very few had experience of government, and many had been outside Libya for years, or indeed decades. El-Keib and his deputy prime minister, Mustafa Abushagur, were both distinguished academics who had been Gaddafi opponents in exile since the 1970s and had returned to join the rebels during the conflict. Ministers hardly knew each other, still less had worked together. A major factor in their selection had been the need to strike a balance among the divisions that had emerged within the NTC and the geographical centres of its support. The machinery of government they inherited as they entered the ministries had never been an efficient one, as real power had lain in the capricious decision-making of Gaddafi and his circle, outside the formal structures of government; it was now hollowed out at the top by defections and departures of senior officials—who would in any event not have been trusted by the new ministers—and overstaffed below by an inflated payroll of civil servants of whom little had ever been expected. It derived its authority from the NTC, but there was no clear definition or understanding of the respective roles of the government as executive and the NTC as quasi-legislature.

First priorities

The immediate tasks the government faced were daunting. Many rebel fighters needed medical treatment, some facing permanent disability. Families sought loved ones who had disappeared in Gaddafi's jails or during the conflict, as new grave sites were discovered. Thousands of detainees in the hands of the rebels, including many sub-Saharan African migrants wrongly accused of being mercenaries, needed to be brought within the justice system, either to be released or to have their detention regularised with protection against abuse. The country was awash with arms and munitions, some supplied during the conflict, but far more from the huge stockpiles on which Gaddafi had squandered Libya's wealth to the benefit of eager arms suppliers around the world; unexploded ordnance and mines posed a serious threat along former front lines. Public security needed to be restored or maintained in a climate of paranoia that persisted well beyond the death of Gaddafi and with the threat of reprisals against communities or individuals who had supported him. The future of those who had been—or claimed to have been—revolutionary fighters had to be addressed; meanwhile, there were tensions and clashes between armed groups in Tripoli and elsewhere. It was vital to resume the flow of oil production; in the meantime, only access to Libya's frozen assets could enable urgent public expenditure.

After celebratory visits by Sarkozy and Cameron in mid-September and by Clinton in mid-October, much of the international community seemed more concerned by threats that might spread beyond Libya than with how Libya could best be assisted to address its internal challenges. Inspectors of the Organisation for the Prohibition of Chemical Weapons (OPCW) had been overseeing the destruction of Gaddafi's stockpiles of chemical weapons, until such activity was halted when the conflict began; before it resumed, NTC forces had discovered two previously undeclared depots of chemical weapons materials. Stocks of uranium fissile material ('yellowcake') were also secured by NTC forces, the International Atomic Energy Agency (IAEA) assessing that these did not pose a major proliferation concern or radiological hazard pending export for sale. Of greater concern was the fate of Gaddafi's stocks of man-portable defence systems (MANPADS)—the largest known stockpile outside those countries that produce them. Thousands had been destroyed during the NATO operations, but there were increasing concerns about the looting and likely proliferation of the unknown number that remained, as well as of munitions and mines. At the end of October, the UN Security Council adopted a Russian-initiated resolution highlighting these issues, and at the beginning of December, a further resolution expanded UNSMIL's mandate to include supporting Libyan efforts to address threats of proliferation of arms and related materiel, in particular MANPADS.[1] UNSMIL was indeed already doing this, together with the UN Mine Action Service (UNMAS)—convening international actors, liaising with Libyan authorities and facilitating visits by OPCW and IAEA inspectors. The destruction of MANPADs became a particular priority for US bilateral assistance,[2] but after months of work the scale of the problem appeared to have been over-estimated; meanwhile, the heavy US pressure for access to munition stores, destruction of their contents and control of information upset Libyan sensitivities regarding their sovereignty.

A more widespread problem was the threat of mines and unexploded ordnance and the proliferation of arms and ammunition. Soon after the uprising began, UNMAS had commenced clearance efforts behind the front lines in eastern Libya, establishing important relationships and gaining knowledge of local situations. As its efforts became nationwide, they would have benefitted from fuller information from NATO. As early as the beginning of June 2011, NATO had agreed to inform UNMAS where Operation Unified Protector munitions had been employed in order to facilitate post-conflict clearing operations. But information was provided only after the end of the operation and was limited to specifying 313 locations, together with the weight of the ordnance used and a description of the means of delivery.[3] The reluctance of relevant member states to approve disclosure and declassify information stood in the way of specifying types of missiles or bombs used and failure rates and targets, which could have better enabled rapid deployment of teams to areas of greatest need.[4] Not only could

NATO have been more helpful to those who were trying to deal with the aftermath of its bombing; it could also have offered to support Libyan and UN efforts with its own clean-up operation on the ground, which need not have required armed and uniformed military personnel to which the Libyans were averse.

From the outset of the international intervention, there had been little consideration of its regional implications, other than on the part of the AU and Libya's neighbours; now, the return of armed fighters from Gaddafi's forces to their countries of origin and the flow of weapons across Libya's borders, as well as the unemployment of returning migrant workers, added to concern about a growing crisis in the Sahel. The UN was joined by the AU in a December assessment mission to Mali, Niger, Chad and Mauritania to look into the impact of the Libyan crisis on the Sahel region.[5] While some of the region's problems were directly related to the fall of the Gaddafi regime, the mission's interlocutors emphasised that most were longstanding. The coup that ousted Mali's President Amadou Toumani Touré in March 2012 exposed how inadequate international attention to the longstanding and intensifying crisis of northern Mali had been in particular, and gave rise to another international military intervention with troops from France, the Economic Community of West African States and eventually the UN. The new focus of the UN Security Council on the Sahel provided further opportunities for squabbling over how far the Libyan intervention bore major responsibility for its problems.[6]

The broader willingness to assist Libya's recovery was constrained by the loss of interest as attention turned to ongoing crises in the Arab world, particularly Syria; by the very limited allocation of donor funding to an oil-rich country; and by wariness regarding the security situation for foreign nationals. A higher priority for many governments was to secure an affirmation of Gaddafi-era contracts or a share of the future business opportunities that Libya seemed to promise, sometimes explicitly to those that had supported the NTC during the conflict.[7] The government itself was slow to formulate requests for assistance, to sign off on formal agreements where support had been agreed in principle or to deliver the funding that it had promised to accompany external technical advice.

After the long hiatus between the 2 September Paris donor meeting and the late November appointment of ministers, the government showed little enthusiasm for proceeding with the intended post-conflict needs assessment missions and even less for multiple bilateral visits. UNSMIL attempted to pursue its mandate to coordinate support from bilateral and multilateral actors by convening, with Deputy Prime Minister Abushagur, a late January 2012 workshop on the coordination of international assistance, with participation of international partners including the World Bank and the EU. The workshop addressed public administration; anti-corruption, transparency and public financial management; social services delivery; transitional justice and rule of law; civil society and media strengthening; and strategic communications. The deputy prime minister assumed responsibility for a future coordination structure, and thereafter the UN worked with his office and with the minister of planning to try to align external support with the government's priorities. In general, the government was resistant to having foreign advisers embedded in its ministries, but a senior UN public administration adviser, and later a former assistant secretary to the Canadian cabinet as a UN consultant, as well as an EU adviser, worked in the Office of the Prime Minister to develop its capacity to coordinate the machinery of government.

To meet its budgetary needs, the government pressed for the release of assets that had been frozen under UN and other sanctions. Executive Committee Chairman Mahmoud Jibril had made the case when he addressed the Security Council on 26 September. The sanctions resolution, he said, had sought to deprive the Gaddafi regime of its funds, assets and authority, but now the ones being deprived of those assets and wealth were the Libyan people: it was imperative to lift the freeze fully so that the reconstruction process could begin.[8] The Executive Committee's minister for infrastructure and reconstruction, Ahmed Jehani, had discussed with the World Bank and the IMF a possible framework according to which the unfreezing of assets should be managed in a gradual way: he proposed a trust fund to hold unfrozen cash and assets to be managed by the Libyan authorities with the World Bank and IMF as trustees, ensuring fiscal prudence in the programme of the interim government.[9] But the government did not proceed with this proposal: facing a budget deficit while oil production recovered, Chairman Mustafa Abdul Jalil and Prime Minister el-Keib emphasised that liquid funds were urgently needed, while individual Libyans contrasted the knowledge that the country had great wealth with their inability to draw fully from their own bank accounts. Briefing the Security Council in late November, I conveyed their sense of urgency, and in mid-December, the council agreed to the de-listing of the Central Bank of Libya and the Libyan Foreign Bank, enabling the government to assume management of these funds. The assets of the Libyan Investment Authority and the Libya Africa Investment Portfolio remained frozen until the new authorities could replace their officials appointed by the Gaddafi regime.

The political roadmap

When Secretary-General Ban Ki-moon visited Tripoli on 2 November, foremost among the requests for UN support—as in many previous UN discussions with the NTC, commencing in Benghazi—was enabling them to meet the electoral timetable to which they had committed themselves. From the outset, the NTC and the government had very limited confidence in their own authority: they were well aware that they had public acceptance only on an interim basis. The NTC had never fully led the uprising militarily, nor established a presence in much of the country; as one western battalion commander said: 'The NTC performed well in terms of building international recognition for us and in terms of acquiring funds. But it was never a government for us here in Libya.'[10]

Acceptance of the legitimacy of its leadership had encountered three sets of challenges: regional divisions, the Islamists' mistrust of those they deemed secularists, and the tensions between leaders who had had careers under Gaddafi and those rebels who had been powerless or persecuted under the former regime.[11] El-Keib's government had wider political support than Jibril's Executive Committee, with representation from more regions, including the new power centres of Zintan and Misrata, and members not seen as tainted by prior positions under Gaddafi.[12] But it too understood that its legitimacy was highly conditional. The NTC and the government faced a strong demand that they must make possible the early election required by the Constitutional Declaration adopted by the NTC in August 2011 and then give way to a new congress and government.

This Constitutional Declaration had been the outcome of an intense and sometimes divisive debate among the then rebels. The roadmap that Jibril had presented to the Contact Group in May had envisaged a national congress composed of representatives of each city, town and village, which would select a committee to draft a constitution, to be approved by the congress and by referendum; only thereafter would the process culminate in parliamentary and presidential elections. This had been subjected to immediate criticism, which continued amid vigorous debate in Benghazi after the brief roadmap had been developed into a more detailed 'Constitutional Covenant'.[13] The main focus of contention was its Article 30, which set out the process according to which the expanded but unelected NTC would appoint the constituent body to draft the constitution, and only after its adoption would be replaced by an elected body. The Muslim Brotherhood's insistence on an earlier election was assumed to reflect self-interested confidence in its own organisational strength, but it was not only Islamist voices that were raised against the NTC—even if expanded—prolonging its authority. As multiple proposals were drafted and debated, many other groups and civil society actors argued for elections ahead of the drafting of a constitution; this became the sequence set out in a revised Article 30 when the NTC voted to adopt the Constitutional Declaration on 3 August. The process of consultation and decision-making around its adoption continued to be criticised, but the NTC had made a decision by which it would be bound—in its own mind and by public expectations—when the fighting ended.

This NTC decision regarding the electoral and constitutional process was not significantly influenced by the international community, and the UN had no role in advising on it. Members of the Contact Group had welcomed the roadmap that Jibril had presented to them and were still assuming at its Istanbul meeting in mid-July that this represented the NTC's position when in fact it was by then being hotly contested in Benghazi; Jibril's position had US sympathy, but there was no intervention by any external actors in what was an entirely Libyan debate. Although different proposals featured different sequences of steps in the political process, they all embodied similarly brief periods before the holding of the first election.

The 23 October Declaration of Liberation started the clock running on the timetable set out in the Constitutional Declaration. The NTC met the first undertaking, that within thirty days it would relocate to Tripoli and establish an interim government. It was then required to adopt electoral legislation and establish an electoral management body within ninety days of the declaration. The elections for the national congress, which would give democratic legitimacy to a new government and to the drafting of a new constitution, were to be held within 240 days. After the new constitution had been adopted by the national congress and put to a popular referendum, Libya would proceed to its first elections according to that constitution.

Preparing for the election

In November, the NTC appointed an Electoral Committee from among its members, balanced among regions and different perspectives: its chairperson was a lawyer from Tobruk in the east, Othman al-Mgairhi, one of the founding NTC members, and it included a leading member of the Muslim Brotherhood from Tripoli, Alamin Belhaj. The committee was charged with studying what was needed for the electoral process, carrying out consultations, drafting the legislation and preparing for the NTC to appoint an election commission. They worked on two laws: a relatively straightforward one to establish the election commission, and a more complex one to define the electoral process. The key choices that had to be made concerned the electoral system—would it be proportional or majoritarian?—and the allocation of constituencies, which was highly controversial among Libya's regions and cities.

Both these issues were left unanswered when on 2 January 2012, with the ninety-day deadline of 21 January looming, the committee published a draft law. The limited time available allowed for only inadequate consultations, although these included some public meetings as well as online responses. The most contentious issue was how to balance a politically acceptable representation of Libya's historic regions—the former Tripolitania in western Libya, Cyrenaica in the east and Fezzan in the south—with the distribution of its population: the draft kept the issue open by referring only to constituencies being determined by both population and geographic criteria. With an estimated two-thirds of Libya's 6.5 million people living in the west, eastern representatives were hostile to a formula based on population. Amid mounting criticism in Benghazi of the NTC's performance, three public discussions heard heated calls for 'equality between regions', and there was violent protest when the NTC met to finalise the law, delaying a final decision.[14] When the NTC did adopt its law on the electoral process, it still left the issue unresolved.

Also contentious was the extent to which the election should be based on political parties. Parties had been outlawed from Libyan political life since King Idris al-Senussi had banned them in 1952, until the NTC adopted legislation ending their criminalisation. But some felt that an election based on premature recognition of parties would favour those already most organised underground—most obviously, the Muslim Brotherhood. Others argued that localised elections without parties would leave tribal loyalties as the dominant factor and favour old power structures.[15] A compromise was reached in the adoption of a parallel electoral system, with eighty members to be elected from proportional representation lists of political 'entities' and 120 as individuals on a majoritarian basis. After debate, the NTC concluded that the timescale did not allow for a law providing for the proper long-term registration of political parties, so the acceptance of lists of candidates from emerging political or other groupings—referred to as 'entities' as they were not yet registered parties—was left to the election commission.

The law establishing the High National Election Commission (HNEC) was less contentious, and its members were sworn in on 12 February. But the Electoral Committee and the NTC still had to negotiate the constituencies, and only in mid-March was this resolved. Of the 200 GNC seats, 100 were allocated to the western region, including Tripoli; sixty to the eastern region, including Benghazi; and forty to the south and centre. Further disputes about relative representation extended down to the level of individual cities and towns, with each jealously comparing the number of seats it had been allocated with those of its neighbours and rivals. The committee negotiated these claims through horse-trading over seat allocations and boundaries among NTC members and other community representatives, and by modifying the parallel system to accommodate their concerns. The outcome was a division of the country into seventy-two constituencies for the majoritarian race (with a total of 120 seats); most of these constituencies would return a single member, others more than one. For the proportional race (eighty seats), in contrast, the country was divided into twenty constituencies. In the effort to squeeze out extra seats to meet local demands, these two electoral maps were overlaid in such a way that not every voter would participate in both races. Throughout the Election Committee's deliberations, the UN made available expert advice on the implications of the alternatives it was considering but respected the need for decisions of high political sensitivity to be negotiated among Libyans. The outcome was not one that any electoral expert would have recommended, and it was criticised for its complexity and for not fully respecting the principle of equality of suffrage by according each voter and vote equal weight.[16] But the Libyan negotiators were aware of these implications: the understandable priority for the NTC was the accommodation of as many community concerns as possible. Nevertheless, resentment at the rejection of eastern claims for equality of regions persisted, as well as some grumbling at perceived underrepresentation elsewhere.

There was considerable debate regarding measures to promote representation of women. The NTC rejected the Electoral Committee's initial proposal of a 10 per cent quota. For a while it seemed that there might be no special measures, which would have meant very little if any representation of women. Secretary-General Ban wrote to the NTC advocating special measures, and the UN worked with women's and other civil society groups in support of this, explaining how different measures would operate. Eventually, the NTC decided to require that women candidates should alternate with men on the lists put forward in the proportional race by political entities, and that an entity entering lists in multiple constituencies should alternate men and women at the head of its lists.

The HNEC faced a formidable set of challenges: members from different regions and cities who had never worked together; no electoral experience or useful precedents; and no offices, staff or internal regulations setting out how it was to function. Moreover, Libya's new civil society, emerging political parties, media and population at large were unfamiliar with electoral issues and suspicious of the intentions of the new leaders. The HNEC would have to undertake a completely new registration of electors, since what records did exist could not be relied upon, and to organise an election in less than five months—and much less than that by the time the NTC decided on the final constituency allocation. All this had to be accomplished in a highly uncertain security environment.

Despite early internal tensions, the HNEC addressed these issues with vigour and determination, as well as some trepidation, and opened voter registration on 1 May at over 1,500 registration centres. Voter education had hardly begun, and early registration was slow, especially of women. Soon, however, public scepticism was overtaken by enthusiasm, and the registration period was extended for a third week, by the end of which 2.87 million of an estimated 3.2 to 3.5 million eligible voters were registered, and the proportion of women among those registered had risen to 45 per cent. Meanwhile, candidates came forward with equal enthusiasm: 2,501 independent candidates and 142 political entities with 1,207 candidates on their lists registered in the allotted timeframe. Women comprised 45 per cent of the candidates in the proportional representation race, as a result of the requirement to alternate male and female candidates on the lists of entities, but only 3 per cent in the majoritarian race.

Public confidence grew in the intention of the NTC and the government to proceed with the election, and the HNEC, under the chairmanship of Nuri Elabbar, was showing itself capable of doing so. The success of locally organised elections for city councils in Misrata in February and Benghazi in May had a significant impact in increasing positive expectations. The NTC's target election day date of 19 June, however, proved unrealistic. Before ballot papers could be printed, candidates had to be vetted by the 'High Commission for the Application of Standards on Integrity and Patriotism', established to exclude from public office those who had been closely associated with the Gaddafi regime and its abuses: 242 candidates were initially disqualified, of whom eighty-two had appeals upheld in the courts, leaving 150 excluded.[17] Political entities and candidates needed at least a minimum period to advertise themselves to voters and to campaign. In the face of great reluctance on the part of Abdul Jalil to envisage any postponement beyond the 240-day deadline of 19 June, the HNEC's recommendation of an election date of 7 July was accepted by the NTC.

The fragmented security sector

With the election arrangements largely in the hands of the NTC and the HNEC, the government's greatest challenge was the security situation and the future of the armed groups. The end of the fighting left Libya with hundreds of armed groups, styling themselves as *kata'ib* (singular *katiba*),[18] giving varying degrees of allegiance to the NTC but with no single chain of command even within individual cities and towns.[19] A detailed account of the emergence of armed groups in Misrata enumerates 236 revolutionary battalions in the city that experienced the most prolonged fighting; despite this large number, a high level of coordination was achieved under the Misratan Union of Revolutionaries and the Misrata Military Council.[20] Some of the armed groups—notably from Misrata, the Nafusa Mountains and Benghazi—could rightly call themselves 'revolutionaries' (*thuwwar*), having fought to take or defend control of their localities against regime armed forces; of these, some remained in place as the local protectors of their communities, while others joined the battles in Tripoli, Bani Walid and Sirte. Others saw little or no fighting but emerged to fill the security vacuum in their localities. Such groups included many that emerged in Tripoli during the fall of the capital, remnants of the army that defected in the east and largely sat out the fighting, and others in western towns that had stayed neutral or loyal to Gaddafi, transferring their allegiance only once the success of the revolution was assured. Lastly, groups that were little more than armed gangs formed opportunistically, especially in the large metropolis of Tripoli, to take advantage of immediate and later rewards to 'revolutionaries', or in the worst cases to engage in personal vengeance, hostage-taking for ransom or other crime. Local military councils brought together the more responsible leadership of the armed groups and linked them to local civilian authorities. The complexity of this diverse spectrum and the tensions among them were increased by the ideological divide that emerged between some who preferred a managed transition with the participation of elements of the former regime's security forces, and those revolutionaries—particularly Misratans, civilian fighters from the east and former members of the Libyan Islamic Fighting Group (LIFG)—who wanted to exclude these elements.[21]

The immediate security situation compelled substantial dependence by the new authorities on the battalions. Even after the remnants of Gaddafi's forces were defeated in Sirte in mid-October, concern at potential destabilisation by Gaddafi loyalists, perhaps planned or encouraged by those who had taken refuge in neighbouring countries, continued long after his death. Vital installations and stockpiles of weapons throughout the country had come to be guarded by the battalions. The new authorities began by pressing local military councils to reduce the checkpoints and visible armed presence, especially of heavy weapons, in the cities; equipping and deploying what police were at their disposal; and negotiating—sometimes with difficulty—the handover of security at key state facilities to security elements under a greater degree of authority of the government, which initially often meant the more disciplined battalions. Although the Libyan police had not attracted the public hatred reserved for Gaddafi's parallel internal security apparatus and were largely welcomed back on to the streets, they had lost roughly 40 per cent of their workforce and had little reach outside Tripoli;[22] they could not impose their authority over armed groups, or intervene as local fighting erupted. Even on the most optimistic view, their development into a well-trained, robust police force, able to tackle crime in cities awash with weapons, and into which thousands of criminals had been released from prisons by the Gaddafi regime, could only be a lengthy process.

A first initiative to address the future of the members of armed groups was launched before the interim government was formed, when in October the NTC established a 'Warriors Affairs Commission' (WAC). The WAC embarked on what became the most comprehensive registration of those who claimed to have been fighters, which included interviews and use of social security numbers to avoid duplication. Eventually, it processed over 200,000 potential applicants through nationwide branch offices and ultimately determined 162,702 to be eligible beneficiaries, not including those who were already members of official state security agencies, and began developing and implementing awareness, counselling, education and reintegration programmes.[23] As the aim was to take care of all those who participated in the revolution plus those actively participating in ongoing operations, it did not seek to define strictly what constituted *thuwwar*. In Misrata alone, the 236 battalions registered with the Misratan Union of Revolutionaries accounted for almost 40,000 fighters.[24] In the Nafusa Mountains, Zintan had up to 6,000 fighters in eight battalions, followed by Nalut with 5,000 in six battalions, and other significant forces existed in Jadu, Al Zawiya and Zuwara.[25] The eastern battalions that had formed in Benghazi, including the February 17 Battalion, were also substantial. As noted, the overall numbers greatly increased with those who participated in the Tripoli uprising as well as those who participated in locally raised armed groups to ensure security, and others who joined after the fighting was effectively over—many simply for the benefits.

While the comprehensive registration by the WAC was getting under way, the interim government announced that it would develop plans for the future of 75,000 revolutionaries through the Ministries of Interior, Defence and Labour, each to be responsible for integrating 25,000 into the police, armed forces or civilian life. The ministries began to undertake their own registration exercises, without awaiting referrals from the WAC, whose initial analysis was that 15 per cent would opt for the police and 15 per cent for the army, with the majority seeking education or vocational training, employment or self-employment. The Misratan Union of Revolutionaries expected 80 per cent of the Misratan revolutionaries to return to civilian life.[26] But the NTC had started making salary payments to battalions in the east during the fighting, and there was heavy pressure to put armed groups throughout the country on the payroll.[27] When the pressure led to a decision to make payments to revolutionary fighters nationwide, they were made through military councils and battalion commanders, not as direct payments to individuals. The payments provided a disincentive to demobilisation, especially for those who had no other employment opportunities, and an incentive to inflate claims of eligible numbers, while the confusion of overlapping registration exercises allowed for duplication and corruption. Soon after his appointment, el-Keib had to pacify an angry crowd of armed fighters at the Finance Ministry demanding back pay and jobs.[28] Later government attempts to suspend payroll payments while procedures were put in place to properly regulate the disbursement of funds led to lethal disturbances and intimidation at the Prime Minister's Office.[29]

The new minister of interior, Fawzi Abd al-Aal, a former prosecutor from Misrata, had been a member of the three-person Supreme Security Committee (SSC) appointed by the NTC in September to try to establish a single command over the competing armed groups in Tripoli.[30] With public security requirements clearly far exceeding the numbers and capabilities of the police officers who had returned to work, he brought SSC members under his ministry's authority and undertook further recruitment. His decree gave the SSC not only immediate law and order responsibilities but also authority to investigate elements of the former regime and other intelligence functions. In practice, the ministry—even the SSC's central headquarters—had only limited authority over the local SSC branches. Relations between the Libyan police and the SSC were tense, and coordination at the local level was mostly very poor. The initial recruitment target of 25,000 was quickly exceeded, and by August 2012, 149,000 had registered with the SSC; the ministry suspected that as many as 60 per cent were double-registered with other formations or did not show up for work. While some SSC members carried out security functions in a disciplined manner, including during the election, others on the payroll abused their status: SSC units were accused of beatings and arbitrary detention and of being implicated in the destruction of Sufi shrines by Salafists in August 2012.[31]

While the weaknesses of the Ministry of Interior and command levels of the Libyan police posed difficulties for any attempted integration of members of armed groups as police, the challenge for integration into a national army was far greater. The regular army had been deliberately neglected by Gaddafi, who relied on his parallel security brigades.[32] The latter had been destroyed by the end of the conflict, while the regular armed forces had split between those who defected, either as units in the east or to join revolutionary battalions as individuals, and the units that remained intact and loyal to the regime in the west and south.[33] The new minister of defence, the former head of Zintan's military council, Usama al-Juwayli, inherited no defence ministry, while the authority of the Chief of General Staff of the Armed Forces Yusuf al-Manqoush, appointed by the NTC in January 2012 after a difficult negotiation, was immediately contested in a weak and divided officer corps. The army had a profusion of officers, many of them elderly, and few soldiers fit to fight: Juwayli estimated that it included fifty-five major generals, 537 brigadiers and 1,350 colonels, with some officers in their seventies, 'because salaries were good and pensions poor'.[34]

The clearest vision for the integration of revolutionary fighters into a new national army was put forward in December 2011 to the government and the international community by Salem Joha, a former military officer who had headed the Misratan Union of Revolutionaries in the defence of the city. He described his proposal as the result of extensive dialogue among revolutionary leaders in Misrata and throughout the country, and a starting point for national dialogue. It proposed dividing the transition period into two phases: a pre-election phase, in which the objective would be to achieve stability and the demilitarisation of civilian areas; and a post-election phase focusing on the development of integrated and representative armed forces. In the pre-election phase, revolutionary battalions would be assigned to military bases in each city and their weapons inventoried, with heavy and excess weapons transferred to central depots managed by the Ministry of Defence. Individuals could choose to become part of the transitional military force, or to return to civilian life. Pre-revolutionary military personnel would be vetted, and those who had not fought against the revolution and wished to remain in the military would be assigned to the base in their hometown. Military weapons would be banned from civilian areas, except when authorised by the Ministry of Defence for emergency response. In phase two, following the elections, military forces would be redistributed throughout the country, and the military at each base would be composed at all levels of personnel from across Libya, instead of groups from one specific region.[35]

The interim government was almost immediately faced with the outbreak of local conflicts in western and southern Libya,[36] some of which demanded intervention far beyond any capacity of the national army. Manqoush deployed what regular troops he could, but they were clearly inadequate on their own to impose and maintain ceasefires, and battalions that felt some responsibility—or community loyalty—towards each situation did not wait for orders before moving to intervene themselves. Battalions formed themselves into larger fighting entities in western Libya, Benghazi and Misrata and conducted nationwide conferences to formulate proposals to the government. The major coalitions of battalions proposed the formalisation of the ad-hoc deployments that they had already undertaken into the 'Libya Shield Forces' (LSF), presenting this to el-Keib and Manqoush at a conference in

Misrata. In June 2012, the NTC formally created the LSF as a temporary reserve force, nominally under the command of the chief of staff, in parallel to the army.[37] The problem of how to deal with the remaining armed groups resisting state authority—especially those occupying public property in Tripoli—remained unresolved. In July 2012, the NTC established a small National Mobile Force under the armed forces chief,[38] but this could make little impact on the problem.

The pursuit of an effective strategy towards the security sector and the integration or demobilisation of former fighters would have been a challenge of great complexity and political difficulty for any government faced with the legacy of the Gaddafi regime and the proliferation of armed groups during the conflict. But its prospects were further diminished by the failure of those with key responsibilities to work together. Relations between Defence Minister Juwayli and Chief of Staff Manqoush were poor and had been ill-defined by the NTC's decisions;[39] Juwayli accorded legitimacy and funding to battalions not under the command of Manqoush. Both were critical of the exercise of responsibility for border security that had been given to Deputy Defence Minister al-Siddiq al-Mabrouk al-Ghithi, a former member of the LIFG, who also funded forces with a separate chain of command.[40] The relationship between the Ministries of Defence and Interior over border security was ill-defined and tense. Interior Minister al-Aal had little control over Deputy Interior Minister Omar al-Khadrawi, a Muslim Brother, who oversaw the SSC.[41] Neither of the security ministries, nor the Ministry of Labour, worked happily with the WAC, which answered directly to the prime minister with its relationship with the ministries undefined; its head, Mustafa al-Saqizli, had been a senior officer in Benghazi's February 17 Battalion, seen as Islamist. The distribution of posts to the different cities and factions was perhaps unavoidable, but it added to the difficulty of a coordinated strategy.[42]

The NTC had made clear its desire for international assistance in the development of the Libyan police, and this had been reflected in the UN's planning and early deployment. A small team of UN police advisers was soon embedded in the Ministry of the Interior;

the UK too made policing a priority, fielding two UK advisers. The international advisers encountered much confusion on the Libyan side caused by poor control and coordination within the Ministry of Interior and uncertainty over the postings and empowerment of senior officers. Several countries offered their own police advisory or training presence, or training in their own facilities. Results were mixed, at best. The largest out-of-country training of *thuwwar* as police, in Jordan, revealed the poor preparation and unrealistic expectations of the Libyans, some of whom were repatriated after unruly behaviour. The deficiencies of decision-making within the Ministry of Interior, its lack of coordination with other ministries and the dangers emerging from the creation of the SSC became increasingly apparent. But only a new government, with a stronger mandate and a longer timeframe, could address these issues, which required a vision, structure and long-term strategy for the Libyan police as part of a coordinated approach to the security sector. The international community too would need to offer a strategic and coordinated approach, and not merely isolated training packages.

Under Gaddafi, controls over trafficking of goods and persons across Libya's land borders of over 2,700 miles had been limited, capricious and often corrupt, but not entirely ineffective. The impact of the conflict on border and cross-border communities, especially in the south, was the wholesale replacement of state authority by local armed groups and ad-hoc authorities. This eliminated what controls had existed and gave rise to new competition and conflict over opportunities for trafficking.[43] The ready availability of arms and ammunition brought new possibilities for lucrative smuggling. As the conflict was ending, the NTC, with the assistance of foreign military advisers, drew up plans for border security, but these were never harmonised into a single plan and remained on paper, pending the formation of the interim government and beyond. Meanwhile, the government became increasingly concerned by its incapacity to cope with an influx of irregular migrants, detained in conditions they recognised as wholly unsatisfactory.

Border control had been a particular interest of the EU and Italy before the conflict, in view of their strong concerns over migration, and the EU asked to take the international lead. However, it was May 2012 before the EU's border management assessment reported, and implementation awaited the new government. Meanwhile, in addition to bilateral discussions and agreements with neighbouring countries, the government convened a Regional Ministerial Meeting on Border Security in March, which attracted strong participation from all of Libya's neighbours, plus Mali, Mauritania and Morocco; but there was little follow-up beyond whatever contribution it made to bilateral discussions.

The UN had not been asked to play a role in the defence sector and expected the Libyans to request this from bilateral actors, most likely those that had assisted the revolutionary battalions on the ground. The degree of coordination among the 'Four Amigos'—France, Qatar, the UAE and the UK—regarding the ground war did not survive into a coordinated approach to the defence needs of the new Libya: the conflicting affinities of Qatar and the UAE had contributed to the Libyans' own tensions before the fall of Tripoli,[44] while France and the UK had competing interests in the prospect of arms sales. Qatar attempted to take the lead by convening a meeting of some thirteen countries in Doha in late October 2011, which it said would constitute a new international coalition to oversee 'military training, collecting weapons, and integrating the rebels in newly established military institutions'.[45] This proved to be acceptable neither to the Libyans nor to international actors. But in the absence of international coordination, Chief of Staff Manqoush became increasingly frustrated by his dealings with bilateral actors seeking to be preferred partners.

The UN's engagement across the security sector enabled UNSMIL to discuss the urgent need to address its fragmentation with the Office of the Prime Minister. UNSMIL persuaded and then assisted the Prime Minister's Office to organise an inter-ministerial retreat in February 2012 to promote coordination and strategic policy-making among Libyan security sector actors. The Ministries of Interior, Justice and Defence presented plans and requirements regarding public security, including police and other law enforcement matters, border security and management, defence architecture and weapons control, with the prime minister and deputy prime minister addressing the need for a national security framework and coordination in inter-ministerial decision-making.

Proposals from the retreat regarding the defence sector included the establishment of a group of Libyan and international experts to provide the minister of defence and chief of staff with experiences, lessons and best practices on the reorganisation or transformation of defence forces in other contexts; and an information-sharing group of bilateral and multilateral partners interested in providing support to the military. Manqoush, with Juwayli's agreement, asked the UN to assist his office in such efforts. Accepting a US proposal that an expert group should consolidate its expertise in a defence white paper as a framework for reconstituting the armed forces, Manqoush nominated planners from his office and asked the UN to join in coordinating the group, with experts initially from six countries he selected: France, Jordan, Turkey, the UAE, the UK and the US. The UN facilitated two strategic planning workshops where participation included the deputy prime minister, the minister of defence, the chief of staff, the deputy interior minister, senior defence staff and representatives of other ministries. An eventual white paper was intended to lay out the principal military tasks, doctrine and vision, civilian democratic oversight, overall command and control issues, and basic structure of the armed forces, including their relationship with the Ministry of Defence and the future parliament. Recognising the demands for an enhanced UN role, UNSMIL had recruited a former senior Australian general, who arrived at the beginning of July, to head its own security sector advisory and coordination division. The UK meanwhile had fielded a ten-person defence advisory team and was the only country to have an embedded civilian adviser in the Ministry of Defence.[46] The work on a white paper would be intensified by UNSMIL after the election and change of government, with assistance from the Geneva Centre for Security Sector Governance.

Governmental coordination of the security sector, however, remained weak, and relations among the key Libyan actors were tense—sometimes featuring public criticism of each other—to the end of the interim government. To address this, UNSMIL presented proposals for a national security coordination committee, as well as further mechanisms for much-needed coordination in relation to arms and ammunition management, and to demo-bilisation, disarmament and reintegration. But such decisions were unlikely to be taken and implemented by a government that by that point was approaching the July election and its own end. The UN therefore prepared a set of initiatives ready to recommend to the incoming government,[47] which it hoped would have a stronger mandate to address the security sector and its multiple, fragmented actors, including the armed groups, with the legitimacy flowing from an election in which security was the foremost concern of voters.

The election of the General National Congress (GNC)

Despite the achievements of the HNEC's technical preparations, the NTC feared threats to the security of the election, especially as a consequence of disaffection in eastern Libya. The NTC had moved to Tripoli as promised, as had most international representatives, although UNSMIL maintained a small but effective presence in Benghazi. Ministerial appointments to the interim government were weighted more to the west, compared with the initial dominance of the NTC by easterners. The NTC's decision on the distribution of seats among the regions continued to be resented in the east; it was rejected, as indeed was the very authority of the NTC, when at the beginning of March a 'Barqa Conference' (Barqa being eastern Libya's historical name) refused to recognise the NTC's Constitutional Declaration and argued for a return to Libya's original 1951 federal constitution. Although there was a strong backlash in support of the unity of the country, including in the east and from both liberal and Islamist groups, Abdul Jalil was so concerned that the NTC quickly amended the Constitutional Declaration to provide Libya's three regions with equal representation on a sixty-member constitutional commission. The Barqa Council leaders, having excluded themselves from entering the political process through the election, now called for a boycott of the poll in favour of a referendum on federalism and threatened violence if the poll went ahead. Just days before the poll, Abdul

Jalil persuaded a meeting of the NTC—which the Supreme Court would find in February 2013 lacked the necessary quorum—to make the further concession that this constitution-making body should be directly elected, twenty members by each region, and take decisions only by a majority of two-thirds plus one.[48]

The NTC's concessions, and the efforts of many including the UN to dissuade those threatening violence, may have reduced the attempts at disruption but did not fully avert them. Armed adherents of the Barqa Council set up roadblocks on the traditional boundary between Barqa and Tripolitania, shut down oil export terminals, stormed HNEC offices in Benghazi and Tobruk, and set on fire a key warehouse storing election materials in a third eastern city, Ajdabiya. A young election worker lost his life when a helicopter transporting electoral materials was shot at. But HNEC staff defied the threats as they replaced materials to overcome the sabotage, and public revulsion strengthened the determination and courage of voters and electoral staff when further attacks on polling stations in Benghazi and elsewhere in the east were attempted on election day. Disruption was overcome to enable votes to be cast by the end of the day, and the few deaths that occurred in clashes that day were of persons attempting sabotage.

Security fears were not limited to eastern Libya. There had been recent fighting in the Nafusa Mountains between the Zintan and Mashashiya tribes, causing fresh displacement of would-be voters, and in Kufra in the south. But all situations were sufficiently stabilised for polling to take place on 7 July, except for two polling centres in Kufra. There, concerted efforts by the HNEC and the UN led the Tabu leadership to agree to enable voting on 10 and 11 July. This further indicated the HNEC's commitment to an inclusive election, which had led it to put in place special voting arrangements for internally displaced Tawerghas, Tuaregs and Mashashiyas.

In all, over 1.7 million Libyans cast their votes—some 62 per cent of those registered. They did so in a well-ordered process that did credit to HNEC's training of its nearly 40,000 staff. Over 25,000 domestic observers and agents were accredited, as well as 190 international observers from ten organisations: their assessments were overwhelmingly positive, notwithstanding rec-

ommendations for improvements for future electoral processes.[49]
The transparency HNEC had displayed continued during the count,
which was inevitably lengthy as a result of the complexity of the
mixed electoral system. The campaign period had gone smoothly,
with no conflicts between candidates or their supporters, very few
allegations of misconduct, a spirit of goodwill among political entities, and general observance of the voluntary code of conduct that
the UN had helped to facilitate; there were no significant disputes
regarding the results. Many observers had expected that the Justice
and Construction Party, established by the Muslim Brotherhood,
would benefit from years of covert organisation and emulate the
successes of similar parties in Tunisia and Egypt. But this expectation was confounded when it received only just over 10 per cent
of the vote and seventeen of the eighty proportional representation
seats, while the National Forces Alliance headed by Jibril garnered
48 per cent of the vote and thirty-nine seats. The allegiances or
alliances of the 120 individuals elected in local constituencies
would only gradually emerge when the GNC began to vote.
Thirty-three women were elected among the 200 members,
thirty-two on the lists of political entities and just one as an individual candidate, making clear that the special measures had been
essential for achieving representation of women.

On 8 August 2012, the NTC ceased to exist, as Chairman Abdul
Jalil symbolically transferred power to the oldest member of the
GNC. The interim government remained as caretaker until a new
prime minister would be elected by the GNC and form a government. A peaceful transfer of power followed from an election seen
as 'a remarkable democratic experiment in a state that had had no
experience in any sort of participatory politics or civic action for
over four decades'.[50]

Human rights, rule of law and transitional justice

The new Libya faced a heavy legacy of human rights violations. The
uprising had been ignited in February 2011 by a planned demon-
stration by the relatives of the victims of the worst single massacre
by the Gaddafi regime, when over 1,200 inmates were killed in

Abu Salim prison in June 1996. On top of the decades of arbitrary detention, torture, summary and extrajudicial executions and unresolved disappearances, the 2011 conflict added new crimes against humanity, war crimes and other violations of human rights and international humanitarian law. Terrible evidence soon emerged of the crimes of the Gaddafi regime, both over many years and during the fighting in Tripoli in late August 2011, when some of its remaining political prisoners were massacred. Several mass graves were discovered, while survivors emerged to testify to years of detention, torture and mistreatment, and relatives tried to discover the fate of their loved ones. Although many of the worst crimes during the conflict were on the side of Gaddafi loyalists, it became clear that the revolutionaries too had committed serious abuses, especially during the final fighting in Sirte.[51]

The most urgent demand was to determine the fate of the missing, as relatives sought the exhumation of remains long before proper arrangements for identification were possible. The NTC established a National Commission for the Search for and Identification of Missing Persons, and the interim government later subsumed this responsibility in the mandate of a new Ministry for the Affairs of Families of Martyrs and Missing Persons.

There was a strong public demand for bringing to justice the worst perpetrators of past abuses and insistence that this take place in Libya, reflected in almost universal opposition to conceding to possible decisions of the ICC that Saif al-Islam Gaddafi or Abdullah al-Senussi, once captured, should be handed over to it. A strong basis for the Libyan objections was that the ICC's jurisdiction extended only to international crimes during the conflict, and not to the many charges that might emerge from investigations into the entire period of the Gaddafi regime, which in the case of Senussi were likely to include the Abu Salim massacre itself. The NTC had adopted the language of 'transitional justice' and was in a hurry to enact a transitional justice law, but there was little appetite for debate about how its objective of national reconciliation could best be combined with the need for truth and justice.[52]

Meanwhile, the present as well as the past required attention to human rights protection and justice. The victorious battalions took into their custody the last of Gaddafi's fighters and others who were alleged to be his loyalists, making little distinction between those who had merely fought on the side of the regime and direct participants in violations of human rights or humanitarian law. Among those detained, amid exaggerated accusations of mercenaries having fought for Gaddafi, were many sub-Saharan Africans, many of them legal or illegal migrant workers rounded up in the aftermath of the fighting. Some of the prisoners were brutalised when first detained, and UNSMIL's visits and reports of non-governmental organisations made it increasingly clear that torture and ill-treatment, sometimes resulting in deaths in custody, were continuing, particularly where detainees were interrogated to extract confessions or information about other alleged perpetrators.

The government committed itself to transferring detainees out of the hands of the battalions into the custody of the state, and began efforts in that direction. It faced acute shortages of physical facilities—many prisons had been destroyed—and even more of judicial police, the personnel who managed Libyan prisons. Some battalions did their best to provide decent conditions and treatment, seeing themselves as fulfilling a responsibility they wanted the state to assume as soon as possible. Others suspected that those they regarded as guilty would be released if handed over, or were continuing efforts to track down more of those they held responsible for atrocities. Some of the Misratan revolutionaries, in particular, persisted in interrogating under torture detainees from Tawergha, the dark-skinned community south of Misrata from where Gaddafi's 32nd Brigade had carried out its offensive against that city, whom the Misratans accused of committing rape and other atrocities and had driven out of their town;[53] suspects continued to be hunted down across Libya and abducted outside the law. In Tripoli, too, alleged fighters and regime loyalists were sometimes newly seized and held in secret detention centres, and reports of torture came also from battalion-run centres in Al Zawiyah and Zintan.

These abuses were detailed in the March 2012 report of the UN Human Rights Council-mandated International Commission of Inquiry[54] and investigated and denounced by international human rights organisations.[55] The UN tried to mobilise international support to help overcome the bottlenecks the state faced in transferring prisoners to its own custody by accelerating the training of additional judicial police and contributing international expertise to develop the capacity of state prosecutors to screen detainees. With the evidence of UNSMIL's visits to places of detention, it pressed the authorities to carry out their own inspections and investigate custodial deaths and torture, even while the state lacked the immediate capacity to take all prisoners into its own custody. Despite strong representations to the highest levels of the interim government, supported by public statements, including reports and briefings to the Security Council,[56] the lack of action by the government was disappointing, although around 3,300 prisoners were transferred from illegal detention to state custody. It was international and local pressure, as members of local councils became concerned for the reputation of their communities and some emerging human rights non-governmental organisations began to monitor detention and speak out bravely, that led to some mitigation of treatment and a handful of releases. At the same time, the residual conflicts between communities that flared up in different parts of the country created conditions for new human rights violations.

All these challenges required a functioning judicial system, which was essential to reconciliation—not just as a matter of theory or principle, but as a very practical matter of how to resolve local conflicts, where—for example, in Bani Walid—communities that had no confidence in state detention and impartial justice would refuse to surrender accused persons. However, the judicial system under the former regime had been characterised by politicisation, corruption, inefficiency and poor training. It lacked independence, and parallel institutions and contradictory legislative and regulatory frameworks were prevalent. Many judges and lawyers had played leading roles in the NTC and the revolution and had a strong commitment to judicial reform. But the courts only slowly became functional again as staff returned to work, and insecurity remained a constraint, with prosecutors and judges facing threats and intimidation from members of armed groups.

UNSMIL sought to assist the Office of the Prosecutor-General to develop an overall strategy for the investigation and prosecution of past crimes that would focus on the most senior former regime members and on serious crimes. Such a strategy would both promote the early release of persons against whom there was no evidence or who were not accused of serious crimes and promote fair trials for those who ought to be tried.

There was little immediate prospect that justice would extend to human rights violations by the revolutionaries themselves. The NTC passed laws containing provisions for amnesty, although their language was open to different interpretations, as it depended on whether acts were deemed 'to promote or protect the revolution'. In any event, prosecution or even effective investigation remained highly unlikely. The most promising prospect of translating the revulsion against Gaddafi's crimes into a culture of human rights protection lay in the emergence of new civil society organisations that began to engage in human rights monitoring and demanding accountability. Ministers no longer denied or justified ongoing violations and generally authorised access to places of detention, but their personal human rights orientation gave rise to little effective government action.

Beyond detention and possible prosecution, controversy raged around what acts or form of association with the previous regime should justify exclusion from public office, including government posts, membership of the security forces and candidacy for election. The NTC had understood—and had had impressed upon it by the countries that played post-conflict roles in Iraq—the potential consequences of any policy similar to de-Baathification. The standards applied in 2012 by its High Commission on Integrity and Patriotism were ill-defined. Some former members of the regime were not to be excluded if their allegiance to the revolution prior to 11 March 2011 was unequivocally established. Other regime members—such as Revolutionary Guard officers, Revolutionary Committee members, those who 'glorify the ideology of the former regime and the Green Book', former regime business partners and those implicated in torture in prisons—were forbidden from holding office regardless of when they pledged such allegiance.[57]

Decisions were subject to appeal to the courts. However, both the criteria and due process in their application remained matters for much future debate, as those who regarded themselves as true revolutionaries sought to widen the exclusion of those linked to the Gaddafi regime.

Reflections

The apparent success of the July election gave rise to a surge of optimism among Libyans and external actors. It was a considerable organisational achievement by an Election Commission created out of nothing, led and staffed by Libyans, with the support of a relatively small UN-led advisory team. The armed groups had mainly provided security for a fair process, without engaging in intimidation to influence the outcome. Those who feared a possible victory of Islamist parties were reassured by the Islamists' weak performance. Contrary to initial public scepticism about the NTC's commitment to holding the election and transferring power, it had—whatever its failings—fulfilled the key responsibility of a transitional authority: the peaceful and democratic transfer of power in a country that, while fractious, remained united. The interim government too had played its part in support of the electoral authorities.

El-Keib's assessment

As Prime Minister el-Keib left office, he prepared an analysis of the challenges his interim government had faced and its achievements,[58] which he presented to the Libyan public on TV; it was based on reports from individual ministries that were conveyed to his successor, Ali Zeidan. He maintained that the situation was a lot better than it had been a year ago:

> Our cities and villages have started to become free of vehicles filled with heavy arms roaming the streets and all the Libyan territory has been liberated. In addition to that, life has returned to normal: our children have returned to schools, institutes and universities, the economic situation is changing for the better, the services are

in constant improvement and, most importantly, the elections were a success that surprised the whole world and were a major step in order to transition from revolution to state.

Noting the legacy of the systematic destruction of the state over four decades and inheritance of projects characterised by a frightening level of corruption, he described the restoration of services, resumption of oil and gas production, economic and development performance, and implementation of the budget. He also addressed aspects of the security situation in some detail. Among the difficulties he described the government as facing were the collapse of security and military agencies, the proliferation of arms and the release of criminal prisoners. The government's efforts were hampered, he said, by 'overlapping competences' with the NTC; tensions that erupted between some revolutionaries and Gaddafi regime supporters, triggering tribal and regional disputes requiring government intervention; and the legitimisation of many security agencies before the formation of the government that were very difficult to dismantle or reform.

He noted that many had accused the government of being weak in its response to the challenges of the security situation but dismissed the accusation as 'invalid and untrue'—its decision to avoid the use of force as much as it could was 'a fundamental and strategic option':

> The Government worked to resolve tribal disputes, demands, sit-ins and attacks on its headquarters using wisdom and quiet discussion. It succeeded in preventing confrontations with the citizens and avoided using force, not as a sign of weakness, as some people claim, but in a way to understand the nature of the phase and its requirements, in order to avoid sliding into an unknown future and in support of the culture of dialogue as the way to achieve the main objective of holding elections on time successfully for the sake of the country's unity.

The government, he said, had never regarded the real revolutionaries as a problem but rather as part of the solution, including as a supporting force for the government in achieving security. He recognised, however, that implementing a decision of the preceding minister of defence to grant the revolutionaries payments for a period of eight months had seen a lot of fraud, forcing the suspension of payments for the purpose of auditing.

Looking to the future:

> The circumstances of the transitional period demanded dealing with many of the threats gently and quietly in order to preserve national unity and to reach the goals of the revolution, in particular holding the elections. Now that the elections have succeeded, the people have their legitimate candidates and the state started to take shape, raising the degree of firmness, imposing the prestige of the state and extending its full control over the entire Libyan territory have become a firm and unequivocal requirement.

The separation between legislative and executive functions must be clear, he said, and the government given sufficient authority. The institutional capacities of the state had collapsed: rebuilding and using them at the same time placed a double burden on the senior leadership. As for security:

> It is necessary to keep on communicating seriously and sincerely with the real revolutionaries based on respect and appreciation, to raise their competencies and actively involve them in the building of the state and establishment of its power by enabling them to join the army and the Ministry of Interior as individuals and collecting heavy and medium weapons and placing them under state control … We wouldn't be surprised if young real revolutionaries would accept the surrender of arms once they make sure that the revolution is oriented towards its goals and that they have an opportunity to participate in nation-building. That's what we've worked on and what we expect to happen soon, God willing.

Optimism and collapse

Leading Libya experts, while recognising the difficulties of the task ahead, were mostly positive. Lisa Anderson wrote:

> If the new spheres of fairly harmonious public debate implied by the creation of political parties and independent news outlets with a broad appeal come to reflect a measure of shared values and reinforce countrywide identities, then there is reason to think that the General National Congress might be able to manage the task with which it has been entrusted—transition to constitutional

democratic governance that instills renewed trust, hope, and confidence in a population that today is aggrieved, angry, and fearful. It is a tall order, of course, particularly since 40 years of turmoil have led Libyans not only to distrust their government, but also each other ... if the right balance is struck between forming a 'center' capable of governing while devolving enough authority to harness the energy of the 'periphery' and counter its centrifugal tendencies, then there is no reason why Libya should not become the envy of the Arab World—a successful postauthoritarian state.[59]

Diederik Vandewalle concluded that

[t]he tasks ahead for the Libyan government are as daunting as they are numerous ... But the larger picture of the transition should still inspire hope. Just a year after the fall of a dictatorship that deprived Libyans of any political role, a modern state has, against all odds, started to emerge.[60]

Such optimism was short-lived. The international community was shocked by the death of Ambassador Chris Stevens in the September jihadist attack on the US compound in Benghazi, and increasing targeting of foreign representatives further inhibited the engagement of those seeking to support the transition: the US in particular became even less active as 'whatever limited willingness there was to accept risks evaporated'.[61] Most Libyans too were dismayed, but the authorities failed to harness the revulsion against the extremist militia held responsible so as to bring about their continuing marginalisation. Assassinations of former military officers deepened the divisions in the east. The difficulties of building and sustaining national political coalitions were displayed in the struggles to elect a new prime minister and approve ministers, and in the performance thereafter of the GNC and the government of Prime Minister Ali Zeidan. Libya's divisions were driven deeper by the adoption of a Political Isolation Law excluding not only those, like Jibril, who despite recent associations with the Gaddafi regime were among the earliest representatives of the revolution but even some of Gaddafi's longest-standing opponents, such as the GNC's first president, Muhammad al-Magarief.[62] Rather than demobilising, armed groups dug in to protect their political and economic interests. Pessimism grew as Libya slid towards full-scale civil war, which—together with the efforts of the UN and other external actors to avert it—lies beyond the scope of this account.[63]

It is thus necessary to ask in what ways the seeds of Libya's later collapse lay in the period of the interim government, and whether the international engagement during that period could have prevented or mitigated it. Was the July 2012 election held too soon? What more could have been done, by whom, to begin the demobilisation and reintegration of members of armed groups, and the development of state security forces under government authority? Should the UN's role have been more prescriptive?

The early election

Well before the Arab uprisings of 2011, there was a literature critiquing the early holding of post-conflict elections as likely to be premature for the lasting success of political transitions, and there were some early voices arguing for caution about rushing to elections in Libya.[64] The case for delay can include allowing time for the emergence of a credible independent electoral management body and legal system, for the formation of political parties and for the strengthening of civil society and a free media. Some maintain that the security sector should be addressed before elections are held, and that in Libya this should have meant the prior demobilisation of armed groups. My successor as head of UNSMIL, Tarek Mitri, believes that the July 2012 election was held prematurely and asks:

> How can elections be held in a jungle of arms and in the absence of institutions, a judiciary and a national consensus on the priorities of proper state-building? In other words, the election made the power struggle take precedence over the state-building process. Building the state should have preceded the struggle for power.[65]

It has been implied that the international community pushed Libya towards an early election. But the decision to set a short timeline for the first election was, as already described, taken by Libyans without international pressure or significant advice in August 2011. Thereafter, the overwhelming insistence of Libyans would have brushed aside any external pressure to substantially prolong the timetable they had set. An election can be delayed if in the meantime the transitional government is well accepted; as a subsequent UN analysis of the timing of post-conflict elections notes, 'any discussion about timing should take into account … how the legitimacy required to govern would be established and maintained other than by an electoral process'.[66] Libyans' limited acceptance of the authority of the NTC and the interim government was temporary and highly conditional on their commitment to deliver the election on time and not to prolong their own existence. This applied in particular to the willingness of the battalions to consider giving up their arms and demobilise. As the International Crisis Group perceived in December 2011, armed groups were unlikely to fully surrender arms and demobilise men before they had confidence in the political process and a legitimate central authority had come into being, meaning at a minimum not before elections for a constituent assembly had been held.[67] The alternative of a coerced pre-election disarmament and demobilisation would have required a substantial international military presence and would have set the external actors who deployed it against the wishes, and probably the resistance, of most of Libya; no Libyan leadership was willing to consider it. An election was a necessary condition for fully tackling the security sector, although a far from sufficient one, as time would soon show.

The electoral system adopted in Libya in 2012 has been criticised as 'creating a deficit in the representativeness of its fledgling political institutions' and resulting 'in fractious bodies that frequently deadlock'.[68] Many of the 120 out of 200 GNC members who were elected by a simple first-past-the-post majority represented only a minority of voters in their constituencies, with nearly one-third of those seats going to candidates who secured less than 10 per cent of the vote. A better system, it is argued, would have been the 'instant-runoff rule' (or single-transferable vote in multi-member constituencies), yielding representatives accountable to a much broader swathe of the electorate. The NTC's Electoral Committee had discussed the single-transferable vote system, which is used for national-level elections in only three countries,[69] but rejected it due to its complexity. They prioritised geographical representation of localities, favouring individual candidates over parties or groups.[70] This did contribute to the difficulty of forming cohesive alliances, but it is far from clear that the undoubted fractiousness of the GNC was the consequence of the voting system.

The security sector

While the limited authority of the NTC and interim government constrained what could be done about the security sector during their stewardship, developments during this period bequeathed a challenge that would prove beyond their successors' ability to address. In retrospect, it has been suggested that 'the euphoria of victory may have provided the first transitional government with a better opportunity for rapid disarmament than was afforded the elected government that finally took the reins a year later, by which time the situation on the ground was already starting to sour'.[71] But neither the NTC, the government, nor the battalions saw this as a possibility, and they received no concerted push or assistance from the external actors that had created their victory. The manner in which members of armed groups were put on the government payroll was a fundamental misstep, yet some support was essential for those who would otherwise be unemployed while still armed. As the International Crisis Group observed, quoting battalion commanders, in principle there was little dispute about the need to unite the security forces and bring them under the authority of a single credible authority.[72] But there were radically differing views about how that should be achieved. Where unit loyalties had been forged by combat and there was community accountability, incorporation into state forces as formed units was more realistic than the incorporation of individual *thuwwar* argued for by conventional military voices. The development of what came to be referred to as a hybrid security sector, with a state army and police force alongside parallel armed groups employed by the state, is now seen almost entirely negatively, but it was to some extent inevitable. The weakness of the army and police was an inheritance from Gaddafi's own hybrid security sector, in which he relied on parallel forces. Some reliance on the battalions was necessary, and their formation into the SSC and Libya Shield Forces could be seen as bringing them under a degree of state authority.

Thus I told the Security Council that 'it is positive that the SSC goes some way towards providing a unified command and control of the brigades and limits their fragmentation'.[73] This was over-optimistic. But as Frederic Wehrey puts it, these formations developed 'an arsonist-and-fireman approach to Libya's security', justifying their utility on the basis of their ability to handle neighbourhood security and quell outbreaks of communal fighting but 'worsening instability by involvement in criminal activity or fighting as partisans in the conflicts they were meant to subdue'.[74] Nevertheless, as the responsibility was about to pass from the NTC and interim government to the elected GNC and a new government, Wehrey too was 'guardedly optimistic about Libya's transition':

> The glaring shortfalls in the transition are the lack of development in the security sector and the continued activity of powerful militias. It's tempting on the surface to see the situation on the ground as chaotic and alarming with armed men roving the streets. But it's not all bad news, in many cases the militias actually maintain a degree of discipline, provide pre-election security, and work with the government to police their own areas—so things are being kept under control at least for now. The question is how these militias will react to the election results and the subsequent distribution of power among tribes and towns.[75]

As for the international engagement, if the UN had foreseen that it would be asked to take on an unfamiliar coordinating role in the defence sector, it could have been better prepared: it had been thrust into a convening role before its senior defence adviser arrived at the beginning of July. The general mood of external actors was not to intervene too forcefully; the International Crisis Group cited a French official in agreeing that 'foreign actors are right to proceed gingerly and to be sensitive to local concerns about heavy-handed outside involvement and mindful of the impossibility of quick movement towards militia disarmament or demobilisation'.[76] The UK, which was the most forward-leaning actor in the defence sector, did not initially favour a UN lead in this area, but its own efforts were limited: the senior British military representative records that 'the nervousness of many officials in Whitehall about becoming fixed in Libya whilst Afghanistan was still running hot led to many missed opportunities'; its operations in the east were closed down for budgetary reasons in March 2012, and a proposed strategy became 'a list of pet projects loosely strung together.'[77] Multiple offers of training did not address the central issues and reflected conventional approaches to armed forces development: 'At their core, these assumptions placed too much faith in top-down, national level SSR [security sector reform], devised and executed from the metropole of Tripoli while ignoring the local realities and the disparate post-revolutionary paths of Libya's towns and regions.'[78] Neither the UN nor any other international actor was equipped for close engagement with the battalions, which was discouraged by the interim government. The UN did prepare to put immediate proposals to the new government, and intensified coordination and recognition of the centrality of the issues would be reflected in particular in an Inter-Ministerial Conference in Paris in February 2013; these gave rise to more training initiatives, but to no greater success.[79]

It has taken years of failure for more realistic approaches to a unique situation to be advocated. It is now argued that instead of attempting to pursue a form of centralised security, assuming the existence of a unitary state and a coherent bureaucracy, the need is for a 'decentralised post-conflict model of security provision', gradually defragmenting the armed factions and 'creating a decentralised, but reasonably well-regulated, security structure, a strong central backstop capability, broad ethnic and territorial representation in reconstituted central security forces at all ranks, and the co-optation of armed group leaders into national politics'.[80] This would require 'the diplomatic muscle of a quorum of sponsoring foreign states that act in relative alignment', instead of initiatives that were 'typically either partisan or limited in nature'.

Too light a footprint?

There had been an overwhelming consensus that the Libyans' insistence on national ownership should be respected in the international post-conflict engagement. The UN's light footprint approach had been unanimously endorsed in the Security Council and approved by UN-watchers.[81] In retrospect, however, many Libyans accuse the international community of abandonment in the early period following the fall of the Gaddafi regime, and external actors too conclude that there should have been a more assertive international role. For some, this goes to the extent of arguing that a military peacekeeping or stabilisation mission should have been imposed on Libya, despite the overwhelming strength of local opposition.[82] Others criticise the UN, to whom they assigned the leading post-conflict role, for not performing this as assertively as they believe should have been done. UK Foreign Secretary Hague told a parliamentary committee that '[o]n reflection, the UN programme was not prescriptive enough … The UN programme was very strong in some areas, such as holding elections, and weaker in other areas, such as policing, which turned out to be crucial.'[83]

It was not policing that was crucial, but the broader failure to understand the armed groups and tackle the full security sector. Here the greatest responsibility lay with the governments that had supported, armed and directed the rebel battalions and who were needed to provide a strong coordinated 'diplomatic quorum'; they made no effort to do so, and it was far beyond the capacity of the UN to create this.

The UK ambassador to Libya during the period of the interim government testified that

> it would have been more helpful if the UN had been more prescriptive in identifying the priorities for a Libyan Government or helping that Government to identify those priorities, and then accessing and leveraging out of the international community the sort of assistance that would have helped a Libyan Government to do the things it needed to do, rather than the posture that I think UNSMIL were happier with, which was, 'We will absorb, wait and listen to what the Libyan Government says it needs and then react.' The phrase I heard over and over again in the first month or two of that transitional Government was, 'We need help in knowing what help we need.' That was a private comment. There was a public positioning that was slightly more nationalistic, but at heart, I think that was what they were looking for. We, the international community, with the UN leading it, needed to be responsive to it.[84]

More could perhaps have been done to support the institutional development that was so needed, even in the period of the interim government; the UN contributed to this in the Office of the Prime Minister and some ministries, but this was limited by resistance to embedded foreign advisers. Embedded advice was outstandingly successful in one context: the members and staff of the HNEC formed a strong working relationship with UN technical electoral advisers, which perhaps was more possible in a new institutional setting than in the established ministries encumbered by the legacies of the previous regime. But the critical failure of the period lay not in general institutional development, but in the security sector.

The unfreezing of Libyan assets in December placed the government under immediate pressure to be generous with payments to the revolutionaries, and it went on to increase salaries and family allowances and give hand-outs on the anniversary of the revolution and the celebration of Eid. The interim government, and international complicity in the unconditional unfreezing, have been criticised for this.[85] But any attempt through the Security Council to control the use of the assets would have been hugely resented in the context of late 2011.

A divided Libya

There remains the question of whether the external actors could have promoted political dialogue that would have limited the consequences of Libya's internal divisions. From Sarkozy's premature recognition of the NTC as the legitimate representative of the Libyan people, through the Contact Group meetings of 2011, little consideration was given to how a genuinely inclusive and representative leadership might be encouraged and greater cooperation achieved before and after an election. More engagement with commanders of armed groups might have helped promote greater inclusivity; so might greater support to municipal leaderships, although some of these were also divided and dysfunctional. But in 2011–12, Libyans did not seem open to international facilitation of national dialogue, and even when the need became more widely recognised in a later period, UN efforts were met with little enthusiasm or success. From the earliest days of diplomatic engagement in post-conflict Libya, key foreign governments contributed to exacerbating divisions rather than overcoming them—an unhappy feature of Libya's return to conflict that would only widen and intensify in the years ahead.

6

REFLECTIONS AND REASSESSMENT

Today, there are many who suggest that it would have been better if there had been no military intervention in Libya. I find that ahistorical: in the context of the Arab Spring, and with the commitments made after Rwanda and Bosnia, it is not conceivable that the world would have stood by as it watched on its television screens Gaddafi brutally retaking control of Benghazi and the east. If it had, it is unlikely that Libya would have avoided prolonged civil war. As Wolfram Lacher writes:

> The debate over whether intervention was justified would do well to take the imponderables facing decision-makers in March 2011 as its starting point, rather than the current chaos in Libya. It is a debate that all too often ignores the unknowns of the counterfactual scenario as well, particularly the trajectory the uprising would have taken without an intervention.[1]

But the lack of strategic foresight of those who intervened, especially the French and UK decision-makers, now seems astounding. The prospects of mediation leading to a managed transition faced an immense obstacle in the person of Gaddafi, but a more united international community might have achieved it. The external actors who drove the ground war, outside the framework of international law and with no accountability to the UN or domestically, bore a major share of the responsibility for the legacy of a proliferation of armed groups that it was beyond Libya's interim government to address. This was not an area of post-conflict support that could be left largely to the UN. A heavy international stabilisation mission was never a realistic possibility—nor, in my view, a desirable one. But those who led the intervention stood aside from their responsibility to address effectively the central aspect of the legacy of the conflict, and before long external actors would add to the problem rather than to any solution. The election that Libyans demanded, and succeeded admirably in organising, was a necessary condition for a government to have the legitimacy to address the security sector, but the actual government that emerged from that election would soon show that it was not a sufficient condition.

Reflecting on my own responsibility requires me to assess whether, within the context set by the intervening governments, the UN could have made a better contribution to the first stage of Libya's post-Gaddafi transition—one that would have averted, or at least mitigated, later conflict and collapse.

When I became special adviser on post-conflict planning at UN headquarters in April 2011, my terms of reference were to consult with various parts of the UN system and prepare the overall vision, concept and guidance for design of a future UN mission in Libya. This was an unprecedented approach to mission planning, which usually began in earnest only when the political context became known and the UN could send a 'technical assessment mission' to the country concerned. Moreover, while I worked from the Department of Political Affairs as the lead department, I was given system-wide authority as special adviser to the secretary-general. I asked for a deputy from the UN Development Group and with colleagues designed a process that would draw on all relevant parts of the system—UN agencies, funds and programmes as well as the Secretariat—and the World Bank.[2]

I termed this a 'pre-assessment' and not a planning process, with three considerations in mind. The first was national ownership. As I put it when I first briefed the Security Council:

> The future of Libya is to be determined by the people of Libya, and the United Nations is committed to helping them to realise their wishes and aspirations. On the one hand, to be ready to respond

promptly to requests they may make requires preparation, and the international community must be conscious of the failures which may occur in the critical early period after a conflict ends if such preparation has not taken place, and the delivery of assistance then requested is too slow. On the other hand, interaction with a full range of Libyan stakeholders regarding their needs and wishes for international support is not possible prior to a political agreement on the authorities which will be responsible for the transition in a reunited nation. It is inappropriate to attempt to draw up an international plan which does not have Libyan ownership, or for international actors to make premature assumptions as to where Libya will choose to look for whatever assistance it decides it requires.[3]

Second, I was respecting the UN's agreement with the World Bank and the EU, which would imply an eventual in-country joint assessment mission in partnership with the host government. But third, I was also trying to hold back the various parts of the UN system from staking their claims to ownership of areas of future action, which characteristically overlap and give rise to competing—sometimes excessive—bids for staffing and budgets. I insisted that we were working together to establish a common understanding of what might need to be done and be requested of the UN, while discouraging any premature debate over which part of the system should be resourced to do it.

Two issues of external engagement seemed to me to be tricky. We could and did make good use of academic expertise in advancing our understanding of Libya, but of course needed and wanted to consult and learn from Libyans, especially as regards their wishes and expectations about the UN role. The member states committed to support for the NTC and regime change, especially France, the UK and the US—the Security Council's P3—would have been happy to see the UN undertaking planning in a close relationship with the NTC, treating it as a post-Gaddafi government in waiting. But this was not the perspective of some other members of the council, and the mediation of Special Envoy Al-Khatib, as well as that of the AU, envisaged the possibility of a transitional power-sharing executive. It seemed to me right to consult the NTC with full respect and as closely as possible, but not to treat it as already having the legitimacy of a successor government. This I was able to do during visits to Benghazi in May, June and July 2011, where more continuous contacts with the NTC and a wider circle of Libyans were sustained by UN political officers; at Contact Group meetings in Rome, Abu Dhabi and Istanbul; and through interaction with members of the NTC's Executive Committee in Cairo, Doha and Abu Dhabi.

An issue that might have involved similar sensitivities was that of briefings to the Contact Group and the Security Council. I was surprised—and not entirely comfortable—that the secretary-general had so fully associated the UN with the Contact Group that it was referred to as being a member, when permanent Security Council members Russia and China did not participate, some countries including South Africa were present only as 'observers', and the AU chose to attend only as an 'invitee'. Its successive communiqués went far beyond the position of the Security Council, where the significant abstentions on Resolution 1973 were being reflected in vocal criticism of the way the military action was developing, while the Contact Group praised the NATO operation and declared that Gaddafi must leave power. I attended Contact Group meetings with the UN delegation, briefing the plenary for the first time in Istanbul in mid-July. Meanwhile, the Security Council had been made aware of my role in briefings by Under-Secretary-General for Political Affairs Lynn Pascoe, and I first briefed the council myself in consultations—that is, not in public—on 27 June. Despite the angry exchanges that now characterised council consultations about the intervention, the accounts of my role and activities were heard without controversy. But in view of the strong criticisms of NATO's Operation Unified Protector and interpretation of Resolution 1973, I was surprised that Russia, in particular, was not more openly critical of the UN's membership of the Contact Group.

The most difficult aspect of the UN's contingency planning was the possibility of a call for the deployment of military peacekeepers and/or an executive police force. At the UN, there was an overwhelming consensus that blue helmets could not undertake 'peace enforcement'—the Brahimi report had observed more than a decade before that enforcement action had consistently been entrusted not to UN peacekeepers but to coalitions of willing states,[4] and the High-Level Independent Panel on Peace Operations established by Secretary-General Ban in 2014 similarly warned that 'extreme caution must guide any call for a United Nations peace-keeping operation to undertake enforcement tasks'.[5] It was also well understood that the deployment of peacekeepers through UN processes would always take time, so in a crisis situation would need to be preceded by a coalition of the willing, as in East Timor in 1999, or by a regional or sub-regional organisation, as in several African contexts, including Mali in 2012–13. One suggestion early in the Libyan crisis was to follow the precedent of the rapid deploy-ment to Lebanon in 2006 of European contingents to help end the war between Israel and Hizbollah, under the UN but using their own logistical mechanisms.[6] Since the P3 were the member states that had dominated the Security Council's consideration of Libya and led the intervention, the responsibility for developing any such coalition option was theirs, as the Secretariat made clear to them. But there was absolutely no inclination on the part of these or any member states to contemplate this.

There was however a UN responsibility to have contingency plans for the possibility that mediation might achieve a ceasefire. The Department of Peacekeeping Operations advised that its maxi-mum initial capability would be to redeploy some 200 military observers into Libya from other missions, and that this would also require a small armed force for their protection that could not be promptly fielded by the UN itself. As noted above, when there was no negotiated ceasefire and Tripoli fell without prolonged fighting, these contingency plans for military observers were not pursued.[7] Decisive in this were the strong antipathy of almost all Libyan inter-locutors to any foreign 'boots on the ground' once the support of Arab and western special forces had delivered victory over Gaddafi, and the unanimous disinclination of the leaders of NATO countries or other intervening governments to encourage any consideration of such a possibility. I was not myself unhappy about this: like most Libyans, I was conscious of the failings of the stabilisation operations in Iraq and Afghanistan and did not believe that Libya would be well-served by any substantial foreign military presence.

Beyond the military dimension, my own scepticism about the uncertain effectiveness and the unintended consequences of large multidimensional peace operations inclined me towards a more general preference for 'light footprint' missions.[8] After my role in designing and managing the UN mission in Nepal, I had reflected on 'the ability of a relatively light mission to make a contribution to peace process implementation no less successful than that of many far larger operations'.[9] This had found support in the analysis of critics of what had become a heavy international footprint in Afghanistan.[10] Thus Rory Stewart wrote that: 'Sitting in the British Parliament at the time, I was worried that the West might respond to Libya by lurching from a fatal inertness to a still more terrible activity', but he was later relieved that 'the moderate, incremental approach in Libya' avoided the 'over-interventions' of incompetent state-building in Iraq and Afghanistan.[11] For my part, while I was in no doubt that Libya was an utterly different context from either Nepal or Afghanistan, I felt confirmed in my own bias towards a light footprint by Libyans' justified suspicions of external actors and foreign presence.

That said, Libya was more friendly to a UN role than perhaps any other country in the region because of a history long-forgotten inside the UN but well remembered by politically conscious Libyans. I was unaware of it myself, until I set out upon my practice at the outset of any involvement in a country new to me: reading its history. I thus learned of the remarkable role of the UN commissioner, Adrian Pelt, in steering Libya from the General Assembly resolution of November 1949, which finally resolved post-war divisions in deciding that Libya's three provinces should become a single independent sovereign state, to the adoption of its first constitution and proclamation of independence by King Idris al-Senussi on 24 December 1951. I was fascinated by Pelt's own 888-page account of that story.[12] In its description of the disagreements among Cyrenaica, Tripolitania and the Fezzan during debates about the composition of bodies that drafted the constitution, and ultimately about its federal character, it foreshadows tensions we would encounter in 2012. I enjoyed Pelt's sage observations as he describes establishing the Libyan mission at a time when the Secretariat had only four years' experience in mission management,[13] while his resistance to potentially damaging cuts in the mission budget by the Advisory Committee on Administrative and Budgetary Questions (ACABQ) has an entirely familiar ring today.[14] Once in Libya, I would quote his belief that 'the guiding principle to follow ... should be encouragement of the Libyan people in formulating their own wishes and making their own plans without undue interference from himself, the Administering Powers, or the Council, thereby inducing them to take the responsibility for their own future'.[15] His concluding reflections address the way in which trust, which he says is more likely to be placed in an international body than in a colonial power, should be retained:

> Experience shows beyond doubt that the mere fact of being international is not enough to command this trust: it has to be earned, no matter who is involved. It must be earned by the disinterestedness and impartiality of the policies pursued and processes used, and, last but not least, by the conduct of the staff chosen to carry them out.[16]

The high regard of Libyans for the manner in which Pelt played his role was reflected in special ceremonies when he returned to Tripoli and Benghazi in 1953, with streets being named after him in both cities. He continued to be consulted by King Idris as the latter contemplated a change from a monarchy to a republican system and from a federal to a unitary constitution in 1955, and again in the 1960s.[17] When I arrived in one town during my series of visits to engage with local officials and civil society, my hosts played me a newsreel of Pelt in Libya in 1950—a video I had been playing to my team, in order to bring to life the UN's history.[18] Finding myself compared to Pelt was embarrassingly inappropriate, but it was an indication of respect for the UN that—despite Gaddafi—had lasted six decades.

As the UN's internal learning process continued, I set out in my briefing to the Contact Group's 15 July meeting in Istanbul the principles that I believed should govern international post-conflict preparation: national ownership, speed of response and rapid delivery, effective coordination of international assistance, and an understanding of Libya's unique context. The mantra of national ownership was far from being mine alone: it featured in all international discussions, in the Contact Group as much as in the Security Council. In stressing effective coordination, I was influenced by what had happened elsewhere as external actors rushed in as conflicts ended, with multiple visiting missions overburdening new transitional authorities, and the UN system itself often failing to provide multidimensional support as 'One UN' in an integrated manner. I concluded by adding—as a final principle—'humility', noting that the international community's record in post-conflict transitions displays at least as many mistakes as successes to learn from.[19] I was conscious of saying this to an audience that included ministers from the countries most heavily engaged in the international post-conflict operations in Afghanistan and Iraq.

It was fortunate timing that the pre-assessment process had culminated in its series of reports in early August, shortly before the fall of Tripoli. I was then asked to put forward proposals for what in UN terms would be a special political mission,[20] and to discuss these with the NTC, confirming previous consultations about the possible UN role. These were reflected in the mandate recommended by the secretary-general to the Security Council, and supported in the NTC's request.[21] Despite the sharp divisions in the council regarding the military intervention, there were no disagreements about the mandate or proposals for the mission: Russia and the other critics of the intervention wanted the next stage of international involvement with Libya brought back from the Contact Group and NATO into a UN framework.

It was on my proposal that the secretary-general requested an initial three-month mandate, stating that this was intended to allow for in-country engagement in further defining the needs and wishes of Libya for UN support, while delivering urgent advice and assistance. In fact, I initially proposed that in its first mandate the mission should be explicitly named an 'advance mission'. The initial three months was already expiring as the interim government came into office, so was extended to six. UNSMIL would then experience the difficulty of getting the budgetary committee, the ACABQ, to understand and accept a two-stage process, rather than to treat second-stage proposals as staffing and budgetary increases that it was conditioned to resist. An important advantage of the pre-assessment process was that a number of those who had worked on it and thus become informed about Libya were immediately deployed with me and became core staff members of UNSMIL; my deputy in the process became the UNDP country director.

Once on the ground, the quality of my interaction, and that of the UN overall, with Libya's transitional leaders was very positive: they were readily accessible and open in our discussions. There was continuity throughout more than a year in conversations with NTC Chairman Abdul Jalil, from our first meetings in Benghazi until he handed over to the elected GNC. But the changes in those with executive authority[22] meant that the UN had only just over six months of working with the interim government of Prime Minister el-Keib before the election. El-Keib, Deputy Prime Minister Abushagur and the team of ministers were equally accessible during this period. UNSMIL used its access, above all, to press for the government to prioritise a coordinated approach to the security sector, but with little success.[23] Meanwhile, after a bumpy start, the UN relationship with the HNEC was particularly close, with an embedded team of electoral technical advisers working effectively and largely harmoniously with its members and staff, to the credit of both.

Could we have done more during this period to avert Libya's subsequent collapse into civil war if the UN and I had been more 'prescriptive', as the UK argued later, and to some extent urged on us at the time; or by a heavier mission footprint, which was not argued at any stage by any of the members of the Security Council? I doubt it. In addition to the security sector, we pressed particularly hard on human rights issues, especially the prolonged detention and ill-treatment of suspected Gaddafi loyalists, sub-Saharan Africans and refugees attempting to transit Libya. But in so many respects we were pressing ministers who had no levers to pull in their ministries, and the UN's early efforts to promote the development of institutional capacity could only assist the beginning of an inevitably long process. Our proposals for the configuration of UNSMIL beyond its first six months were still for a relatively light footprint mission: 136 international staff and twenty-two national officers.

In retrospect, there are a few ways in which I might have proposed a somewhat larger footprint. If I had anticipated the role that UNSMIL would be asked to play in the defence sector, I would have included in the initial core team the senior defence adviser, who joined UNSMIL at the beginning of July 2012 to head a Security Sector Advisory and Coordination Division. I would also have planned a greater capacity—which would have needed to be more political than military—to interact with the revolutionary battalions. UNSMIL maintained a small but effective office in Benghazi, at a time when the east quickly felt downgraded in the priority of the overall international presence, but engaged with the south only through visits; a standing presence in the southern city of Sabha and a greater capacity to maintain contacts with more municipalities throughout the country would have been valuable, to the extent that security conditions permitted this at the time. I had envisaged that the World Bank would carry forward the issues of economic reform on which it had led in our pre-assessment process, together with the IMF, as indeed they sought to do, but I failed to follow through on an intention to have a senior economic adviser in UNSMIL to link us to the leading international and national actors on the economy. UNSMIL would have benefitted from an earlier understanding of Libya's political economy and what would become leading drivers of later conflict.

I have no second thoughts regarding the impossibility and undesirability of seeking to impose a large military stabilisation mission on Libya. My own view is particularly well expressed by Marc Lynch:

> Even had it been possible, the idea that a stabilization force would have made the difference misses the many ways in which such an international military deployment could have gone wrong, without solving any of the deeper problems. An international force would have confronted the same array of heavily armed militias, forcing it to tread carefully. Its presence could have disincentivized rather than facilitated the creation of national security forces. It could easily have become a target for nationalist mobilization and Islamist attacks. And once established as a vital guarantor of stability on the ground, it would have been virtually impossible to withdraw.[24]

As for election timing, once the Constitutional Declaration had been adopted in August 2011, it would have been futile to attempt to persuade the NTC to plan for a substantially longer period before the first election, and to expect the NTC and the interim government to address the security sector in the meantime. Moreover, it would have been mistaken: there was no way that a longer transitional government would have been effective, or even survived, without electoral legitimacy. When de facto Prime Minister Jibril expressed to me in mid-October his alarm at what he regarded as a rapidly deteriorating security situation, especially the behaviour of the armed groups in Tripoli, he urged that the Constitutional Declaration's timeline to the election should be shortened, not delayed. In mid-May 2012, representatives of an association of revolutionary battalions did call for a delay of some months in the election, seeking the addition of their representatives to the NTC and amendments to the electoral law. But my only uncomfortable meeting with NTC Chairman Abdul Jalil was when I had to tell him that the UN agreed with the HNEC that it was not technically feasible for election day to be sooner than 7 July, three weeks after the NTC's commitment to hold it on 19 June in strict accordance with the Constitutional Declaration. Abdul Jalil's sense of urgency came not just from his desire to hold to the NTC's promise but also from his fear that the situation in eastern Libya was unravelling so rapidly as to threaten the election if delayed.

Some have suggested that a national dialogue should have taken place to agree on fully inclusive transitional authorities and mitigate the divisions that would follow the election.[25] Such an alternative path would have had to begin at the outset of the Contact Group's approach to the NTC. But Sarkozy's recognition of the NTC as the legitimate representative of the Libyan people had preceded even the London Conference that initiated the Contact Group. At the time, others criticised Sarkozy's decision as highly premature: German Foreign Minister Guido Westerwelle said that 'before taking such steps, one should really know with whom one is dealing', and Netherlands Prime Minister Mark Rutte called it 'a crazy move'.[26] Although other governments set their own pace for such recognition, one-by-one they followed suit; Norway was in a clear minority in the Contact Group in advising caution in the light of the limited representative character of the NTC.[27] Once on the ground, the UN was in no position to press Libyan factions into a national dialogue ahead of a delayed electoral process. Any such initiative would have required the combined weight of all the countries that supported the uprising: none of them advocated it.

In retrospect, many of us in the international community underestimated two factors that would be the most divisive as Libya began to tear itself apart: the conflict between Islamist and other political groups and battalions; and the rivalries of external actors, especially Qatar and the UAE, being played out in Libya. Libya's two main Islamist opposition groups, the Muslim Brotherhood and the former LIFG, were, as Mary Fitzgerald puts it, 'almost neutralised on the eve of the revolution due to decades of repression followed by tentative reconciliation' with Gaddafi.[28] Those who had fought as jihadis in Afghanistan were quick to disassociate themselves from al-Qaeda. When they joined the uprising and increasingly asserted themselves politically and among armed groups, the Islamists nonetheless worked within the framework of the NTC and the roadmap of its Constitutional Declaration. The members of the Brotherhood whom I met as members of the NTC, of the first three-person Supreme Security Committee and of the Electoral Committee that the NTC established, and later as leaders of the Brotherhood-dominated Justice and Construction Party, were reasonable interlocutors with the UN as they negotiated compromises with other NTC representatives.

The sort of accommodation of different viewpoints that was being achieved nearby in Tunisia thus seemed possible. The short election campaign was conducted in a largely positive spirit, with armed groups of different allegiances providing security rather than intervening to affect the outcome. The victory of Jibril's National Forces Alliance over the Justice and Construction Party in the proportional race, and the failure of the al-Watan Party—which was formed by former Tripoli Military Council head Abdel Hakim Belhaj and seen as supported by Qatar—to win even a single seat, seemed to confirm that Islamist parties had only limited public support. One post-election assessment concluded that 'if the LIFG and Brotherhood members continue their quest to enter mainstream Libyan politics, it appears likely that they will reach out to more liberal actors like the National Forces Alliance against the destabilizing role of the Salafists and freelance jihadists'.[29]

There were, however, increasingly ominous signs of such a destabilising role in the growing number of assassinations of those with previous links to the Gaddafi regime, the emergence of Ansar al-Sharia militia in Benghazi and Derna, and Salafist attacks on Sufi shrines in Tripoli. When a small IED was thrown at my vehicle in Benghazi in April, we did not know that this would be the beginning of a spate of escalating attacks on foreign targets, including on the UK ambassador's vehicle, and on compounds of the US and the International Committee of the Red Cross, nor did we know who was responsible.[30] It was with the death of Ambassador Stevens and three fellow Americans in the September attack on US premises in Benghazi that the seriousness of the jihadist threat became more fully apparent, and even then the popular revulsion that drove the armed group responsible out of Benghazi seemed to offer hope of Libyan resistance to extremism.

I was much less fully aware then than I am today of the roles that Qatar and UAE had played in arming and mentoring different armed groups, and of their developing rivalry. My own discussions with the two governments in Doha and Abu Dhabi seemed constructive. Qatar was on the defensive in the light of public criticism after it overplayed its hand in the taking of Tripoli. In October 2011, Oil and Finance Minister Tarhouni said at a press conference that it was time to 'publicly declare that anyone who wants to come to our house has to knock on our front door first';[31] he was more explicit on a later US visit, saying

> I think what they have done is basically support the Muslim Brotherhood, and I think that's an infringement on the sovereignty of the country. They have brought armaments, and they have given them to people that we don't know—I think paid money to just about everybody. They intervened in committees that have control over security issues.[32]

Qatar was rebuffed when it sought to play a major role in the post-conflict security sector and received more suspicion than gratitude for its post-war investment in a military control room at Tripoli's Mitiga Airport. But Richard Northern and Jason Pack note that during the uprising Qatar connected itself to secularists, non-militia-aligned Islamists, Cyrenaican Islamist militiamen and Tripolitanian militiamen with jihadist backgrounds, in addition to hosting Mahmoud Jibril and providing logistical and financial support to the NTC leadership. On their analysis, it was the disbursement of its assistance through different and uncoordinated elements of Libyan society that had a destabilising influence: '[T]he disparate networks of Qatari patronage have tended to aid peripheral elements in undermining the center's agenda.'[33]

The role of the UAE was less evident and did not attract public controversy, although the Zintani defence minister was closely advised by a UAE military officer. The seeds of the major role it would play in later conflicts were not apparent, at least to me.

Libyan politics and society presented a difficult context for the UN to pursue our goal of promoting the empowerment of women, despite the ways in which they had empowered themselves through their roles in the uprising. As the prominent lawyer Salwa Bughaighis—who would be brutally murdered after casting her vote in the 2014 election—said:

> We were Benghazi's decision-makers. We took to the streets in our thousands. We ran the civil society institutions and the media, and protected the revolution from collapsing into chaos while men went to the front. And after the revolution, they came and said thank you very much, it's not your business now.[34]

When Secretary-General Ban met with the NTC during his one-day visit to Tripoli in October 2011, he noted that there was only one woman among some forty members around the table—at which one NTC member observed that this was one more than among the sizeable UN delegation. The only other senior UN official whose visit I encouraged was Michelle Bachelet, as executive director of UN Women. UNSMIL regularly sought engagement with women's groups, supporting their most significant victory: the adoption of special measures in the electoral law to ensure representation of women in the GNC.[35]

The most inspiring aspect of my involvement with Libya was experiencing the energy of a nascent civil society, liberated by the end of the repression of the Gaddafi regime—an inspiration I shared with others but felt especially strongly because of my own civil society background. An area of UNSMIL's work dear to my heart was the training and support that our human rights team offered to committed but inexperienced human rights defenders. We were able to achieve little or nothing in terms of accountability, but we saw brave activists develop increasing capacity to stand against ongoing human rights violations, as they would continue to do, sometimes paying for their courage with their lives.

Lessons for the United Nations

At the UN, aspects of this early engagement with Libya were regarded positively. Some are reflected in the 2015 analysis and recommendations of the High-Level Independent Panel on Peace Operations, of which I was a member. The panel recommended that as a matter of future practice, a full-time senior leader of a mission planning process should be appointed, ideally a senior member of the future mission leadership team or intended special representative of the secretary-general, and supported by an integrated planning team. It also recommended that a two-stage mandating process should be undertaken, to avoid template missions and help design more effective, situation-specific missions; such an approach, it said, can ensure an initial UN presence while providing time for consultations with the host government, civil society and partners.[36] The engagement of all relevant elements of the UN system, and of the World Bank, in the pre-assessment process was welcomed and contributed to better integration on the ground. UN and other international electoral assistance was well coordinated, in line with UNSMIL's explicit mandate from the Security Council to coordinate support from other multilateral and bilateral actors. The Security Sector Advisory and Coordination Division was innovative in bringing together the UN's capacity to support Libyan efforts across six functional areas: security sector architecture and coordination; disarmament, demobilisation and reintegration; arms and ammunition management; border security and management; defence reform and development; and police reform and development.

In the defence sector, the UN has never been expected to be a leading actor and cannot substitute for the role of bilateral actors. UNSMIL could, however, have been better resourced to play a coordinating role in the sector if we had foreseen the expectations that would emerge, initially neither requested by Libyans nor proposed by Security Council member states.[37] There was a post-conflict abdication of responsibility by the intervening states, and the UN should be wary of allowing itself to appear to accept a greater role than governments enable it to play.

Lessons for international intervention

In assessing the potential consequences of intervention and the forms it may take, the need for strategic thinking, building on a strong information base, is obvious. The immediacy of the crisis in Libya, amid the wider turmoil of the Arab Spring, made this difficult, but its absence among the intervening countries was inexcusable, as was their lack of attention to the concerns of African neighbours. Libya is also far from being the only context to make clear that the prospects of a managed transition are greater if international actors are able to align their mediation efforts, pressures and inducements.

The absence of effective accountability once a mandate of limited clarity had been given threatens any future UN Security Council authorisation of intervention involving use of force, essential for its legitimacy. This accountability deficit applied not only to NATO's Operation Unified Protector[38] but also to the supplies of weapons in breach of council sanctions and the secret deployments of special forces. In this respect too, the Libya experience does not stand alone. As Jonathan Eyal writes:

> Unfortunately, the handling of the legal framework for the Libya operation mirrors Western behaviour in previous interventions, from the Bosnia operation in 1995, to the Kosovo war in 1999 and the invasion of Iraq in 2003. In every one of these occasions:

- A handful of Western governments used a UN Security Council resolution which lacked full backing, supposedly on behalf of the 'international community'
- In every single case, the aim was to persuade Russia to abstain, rather than veto a resolution, on the calculation that, once this was accomplished, China would be too embarrassed to be in a minority of one to torpedo the same resolution
- At every stage, this was accomplished by fudging the real extent of the operation being contemplated
- The scope of the operation then grew and was invariably translated into 'regime change'
- Weapons were provided to local combatants, in violation of existing provisions
- Resolutions were reinterpreted unilaterally, to suit whatever purposes were required
- And, in every single case, once a resolution passed in the UN, Western governments precluded any further debate over its interpretation and application.[39]

One can argue about the finer points regarding each intervention in this analysis, but the burden of the charge is hard to escape.

It is for this reason that the Libya experience has done such damage to the limited international consensus there was around the doctrine of 'responsibility to protect', on which there is a substantial literature.[40] I have not explored this, in part because I am unconvinced that R2P played as significant a role in Libya decision-making as either its supporters or detractors suggest. I have argued that the experiences of Rwanda and Srebrenica had a major influence on western politicians regarding Libya, and I believe that they would have powerfully influenced their decisions even if they had not in the meantime led to the formulation of R2P.

The International Commission on Intervention and State Sovereignty, which gave birth to the formulation of R2P, emphasised the 'paramount importance' of a post-intervention strategy, saying:

The responsibility to protect implies the responsibility not just to prevent and react, but to follow through and rebuild. This means that if military action is taken—because of a breakdown or abdication of a state's own capacity and authority in discharging its 'responsibility to protect'—there should be a genuine commitment to helping to build a durable peace, and promoting good governance and sustainable development.[41]

Karin Wester concludes that in the case of Libya, this need 'seemed to have been either underestimated or effectively neglected'.[42] This need was both underestimated and neglected on the part of France and the UK in particular, while the US stood back, regarding it as primarily a European responsibility.

Libya's past and future

Reflecting on Libya's history, it was not possible for there to have been a smooth path to a modern democratic state in a country that had never known any period of sustained institutional development and that displays the distortions of an oil-rich economy. Libya had successively experienced being ruled as separate provinces of the Ottoman Empire; then, a degree of unification during a particularly brutal Italian colonisation; then, a battleground for the wars of others, giving rise to three separate military administrations; then, a weak monarchy; and then, forty years of a leader explicitly hostile to the development of the institutions of a modern state. Libya's fragmentation, Lacher writes, was not simply due to the breakdown of the state monopoly on violence in 2011: '[L]ocalism preceded the dispersal of the state's arsenals and the inflows of weapons from foreign states backing the rebels.'[43] And international efforts, as Jacob Mundy says, vastly underestimated two key things: '[F]irst, the socio-political networks of support underwriting the Jamahiriyyah's durability; and, second, the implacable anger that would be directed towards those networks once the revolution seized power.'[44]

The decade since Gaddafi was ousted has thus seen more conflict and division, exacerbated by the countries that have supported and armed contending factions. In 2011–12, I hoped to be able to believe in what the British Libyan writer Hisham Matar describes as 'the possibility of a different reality, one that we had all glimpsed during the short window of hope between the revolution and the devastation of the civil war that followed':[45]

> We didn't know it then, but this was a precious window when justice, democracy and the rule of law were within reach. Soon, in

the absence of a strong army and police force, armed groups would rule the day, seeking only to advance their power. Political factions would become entrenched, and, amidst the squabble, foreign militias and governments would violently enter, seeking their opportunity. The dead would mount. Universities and schools would close. Hospitals would become only partially operative. The situation would get so grim that the unimaginable would happen: people would come to long for the days of Qaddafi.[46]

'The calamity that followed the fall of Qaddafi', Matar concludes, 'is more true to the nature of his dictatorship than to the ideals of the revolution.'[47] But there remain many Libyans who stay true to those ideals, and the UN must continue to work to ensure that they have another opportunity to put them into practice.

NOTES

INTRODUCTION

1. Philip Gordon, 'The Middle East Is Falling Apart', Politico Magazine, 4 June 2015, https://www.politico.com/magazine/story/2015/06/america-not-to-blame-for-middle-east-falling-apart-118611
2. See 'Amnesty International Report 1989', London: Amnesty International, 1990, pp. 269–71, https://www.amnesty.org/en/documents/pol10/0002/1989/en
3. Described in Ian Martin, *Self-Determination in East Timor: The United Nations, the Ballot, and International Intervention*, Boulder, CO: Lynne Rienner, 2001.
4. These are extremely well described and analysed in Peter Cole and Brian McQuinn (eds), *The Libyan Revolution and Its Aftermath*, London: Hurst, 2015; especially in chapters by Peter Bartu, 'The Corridor of Uncertainty: The National Transitional Council's Battle for Recognition and Relevance'; Peter Cole with Umar Khan, 'The Fall of Tripoli'; and in Part 2: Sub-National Identities and Narratives.

1. THE CASE FOR INTERVENTION AND THE SECURITY COUNCIL MANDATE

1. See interviews in Karin Wester, *Intervention in Libya: The Responsibility to Protect in North Africa*, Cambridge: Cambridge University Press, 2020, pp. 94–5.
2. On the weeks before 17 February, see Alison Pargeter, *Libya: The Rise and Fall of Qaddafi*, New Haven: Yale University Press, 2012, pp. 216–19; Rob Weighill and Florence Gaub, *The Cauldron: NATO's Campaign in Libya*, London: Hurst, 2018, pp. 10–16; Ethan Chorin, *Exit the Colonel: The Hidden History of the Libyan Revolution*, London: Saqi Books, 2012, pp. 188–92.
3. Details of the relationship with the UK and US were exposed by documents found after the fall of Tripoli. See Human Rights Watch, 'US/UK: Documents Reveal Libya Rendition Details', 8 September 2011, https://www.hrw.org/news/2011/09/08/us/uk-documents-reveal-libya-rendition-details; and 'Delivered into Enemy Hands: US-Led Abuse and Rendition of Opponents to Gaddafi's

Libya', 5 September 2012, https://www.hrw.org/report/2012/09/05/delivered-enemy-hands/us-led-abuse-and-rendition-opponents-gaddafis-libya

4. Frederic Wehrey, *The Burning Shores: Inside the Battle for the New Libya*, New York: Farrar, Straus and Giroux, 2018, p. 22.

5. Pargeter, *Libya*, p. 8.

6. The atmosphere and unfolding of the uprising, as well as its background, are well described in Lindsey Hilsum, *Sandstorm: Libya from Gaddafi to Revolution*, London: Faber & Faber, 2012. A good factual overview is in Anthony Bell and David Witter, 'The Libyan Revolution, Part I: The Roots of Rebellion', Washington, DC: Institute for the Study of War, September 2011, https://www.jstor.org/stable/resrep07869?seq=7#metadata_info_tab_contents. There is a detailed description of the first five days in Benghazi in Chorin, *Exit the Colonel*, pp. 192–200. See also Weighill and Gaub, *Cauldron*, pp. 10–18. The early uprisings and regime response in Tripoli, Misrata and the Nafusa Mountains are described in relevant chapters in Peter Cole and Brian McQuinn (eds), *The Libyan Revolution and Its Aftermath*, London: Hurst, 2015: Peter Cole with Umar Khan, 'The Fall of Tripoli: Part 1'; Brian McQuinn, 'History's Warriors: The Emergence of Revolutionary Battalions in Misrata'; Wolfram Lacher and Ahmed Labnouj, 'Factionalism Resurgent: The War in the Jabal Nafusa'.

7. United Nations, Human Rights Council, 'Report of the International Commission of Inquiry on Libya', 2 March 2012, A/HRC/19/68, pp. 51–6, https://www.refworld.org/docid/4ffd19532.html

8. Human Rights Watch, 'Libya: Security Forces Kill 84 Over Three Days', 18 February 2011, https://www.hrw.org/news/2011/02/18/libya-security-forces-kill-84-over-three-days; 'Libya: Governments Should Demand End to Unlawful Killings', 20 February 2011, https://www.hrw.org/news/2011/02/20/libya-governments-should-demand-end-unlawful-killings; 'Libya: Commanders Should Face Justice for Killings', 22 February 2011, https://www.hrw.org/news/2011/02/22/libya-commanders-should-face-justice-killings. See also descriptions of shootings in Tripoli in Cole with Khan, 'Fall of Tripoli: Part 1', pp. 58–60.

9. Cole with Khan, 'Fall of Tripoli: Part 1', p. 60.

10. Amnesty International, 'The Battle for Libya: Killings, Disappearances and Torture', September 2011, p. 35, https://www.amnesty.org/en/documents/mde19/025/2011/en

11. International Criminal Court, Office of the Prosecutor, 'First Report of the Prosecutor of the International Criminal Court to the UN Security Council Pursuant to UNSCR 1970 (2011)', 4 May 2011, https://www.icc-cpi.int/NR/rdonlyres/A077E5F8-29B6-4A78-9EAB-A179A105738E/0/UNSCLibyaReportEng04052011.pdf

12. International Criminal Court, Pre-Trial Chamber 1, Decision on the 'Prosecutor's Application Pursuant to Article 58 as to Muammar Mohammed

Abu Minya GADDAFI, Saif Al-Islam GADDAFI and Abdullah AL-SENUSSI', ICC-01/11, 27 June 2011.

13. For a first-hand account by a journalist who witnessed the firing on predominantly unarmed civilians in Al Zawiyah, see Alex Crawford, *Colonel Gaddafi's Hat*, London: Collins, 2012, pp. 24–48.

14. Amnesty International, 'Battle for Libya', p. 34.

15. 'BBC Team's Libya Ordeal in Their Own Words', BBC, 9 March 2011, https://www.bbc.co.uk/news/world-africa-12695138

16. Amnesty International, 'Battle for Libya', p. 59.

17. For a detailed account of Saif's response and dynamics within the Gaddafi family, see Pargeter, *Libya*, pp. 226–30. See also Philippe Sands, 'The Accomplice', *Vanity Fair*, 22 August 2011.

18. Peter Beaumont, 'Saif Gaddafi: His Father's Son, or the Would-be Face of Libyan Reform?', *Guardian*, 7 April 2011.

19. Quoted in Weighill and Gaub, *Cauldron*, p. 42.

20. Adel Al Taraifi, 'Mustafa Abdel-Jalil on Libya's Revolution', *Asharq Al-Awsat*, 21 October 2013.

21. The BBC and other media reported Gaddafi as calling the rebels 'cockroaches' as well as 'rats': 'Libya Protests: Defiant Gaddafi Refuses to Quit', BBC, 22 February 2011, https://www.bbc.co.uk/news/world-middle-east-125 44624. This has entered much of the literature, with explicit comparisons to the use of 'cockroaches' in the hate speech inciting genocide in Rwanda. But this seems to have been a mistranslation.

22. Hilsum, *Sandstorm*, p. 187.

23. David Cameron, *For the Record*, London: William Collins, 2019, p. 274; Anthony Seldon and Peter Snowdon, *Cameron at Ten: The Inside Story 2010–2015*, London: William Collins, 2015, pp. 98–9.

24. UK House of Commons, Foreign Affairs Select Committee, 'Libya: Examination of Intervention and Collapse and the UK's Future Policy Options', correspondence, https://www.parliament.uk/business/committees/committees-a-z/commons-select/foreign-affairs-committee/inquiries1/parliament-2015/libya-policy/publications

25. Ed Pilkington, blog, 'Libya Erupts as Gaddafi Clings On—Live Updates' at 3.51 p.m., and 'UN Ambassadors Clash over Condemnation of Gaddafi', *Guardian*, 22 and 23 February 2011.

26. Wester, *Intervention in Libya*, pp. 108–10, where she quotes a later interview with Dabbashi, describing his considerations, and pp. 120–2. Shalgam's speech is at UN Security Council, S/PV.6490, 25 February 2011, pp. 4–5.

27. Ban Ki-moon, *Resolved: Uniting Nations in a Divided World*, New York: Columbia University Press, 2021, p. 161.

28. Ruben Reike, 'Libya and the Prevention of Atrocity Crimes', in Serena K. Sharma and Jennifer M. Welsh (eds), *The Responsibility to Protect: Overcoming*

the Challenges of Atrocity Prevention, Oxford: Oxford University Press, 2015, pp. 338–9, based on his interviews with diplomats at the UN.

29. Samantha Power, *The Education of an Idealist*, London: William Collins, 2019, p. 291.

30. On the formation of the NTC, see Peter Bartu, 'The Corridor of Uncertainty: The National Transitional Council's Battle for Recognition and Relevance', in Cole and McQuinn, *Libyan Revolution and Its Aftermath*, pp. 35–9. Jibril would come to be referred to externally as prime minister.

31. Josh Rogin, 'Over 200 Arab Groups Call for Libya No-Fly Zone', *Foreign Policy*, 25 February 2011.

32. Weighill and Gaub, *Cauldron*, p. 45.

33. David Roberts, 'Behind Qatar's Intervention in Libya', *Foreign Affairs*, 28 September 2011; Lina Khatib, 'Qatar's Foreign Policy: The Limits of Pragmatism', *International Affairs*, 89:2 (2013); Kristian Coates Ulrichsen, *Qatar and the Arab Spring*, London: Hurst, 2014; Ulrichsen, 'Qatar's Intervention in Libya', in Dag Henriksen and Ann Karin Larssen (eds), *Political Rationale and International Consequences of the War in Libya*, Oxford: Oxford University Press, 2016, pp. 122–4.

34. Ulrichsen, *Qatar and the Arab Spring*, p. 111.

35. Ban Ki-moon describes Gaddafi's behaviour at the Arab League summit in Doha in March 2009: Ban, *Resolved*, p. 157.

36. 'Foreign Ministers Call on the Security Council to Impose an Air Embargo on Libya', France 24 (Arabic), 13 March 2011, https://www.france24.com/ar/20110312-arab-libya-meeting-support-no-fly-zone-kadhafi-crisis-opposition

37. 'Washington Welcomes the Arab League's Call to Impose an Air Embargo on Libya', Al Arabiya, 12 March 2011, https://www.alarabiya.net/articles/2011/03/12/141180.html

38. 'Arabs Call for the Imposition of an Air Embargo on Libya and "Practically" Recognise the Transitional Council', People's Daily Online (Arabic), 13 March 2011, http://arabic.people.com.cn/31662/7317740.html

39. Paul Taylor, 'Special Report: The West's Unwanted War in Libya', Reuters, 1 April 2011, https://www.reuters.com/article/us-libya-decisions-4-idUS-TRE73011H20110401. See also Weighill and Gaub, *Cauldron*, p. 50.

40. Ambassador Richard Northern and Jason Pack, 'The Role of Outside Actors', in Jason Pack (ed.), *The 2011 Libyan Uprisings and the Struggle for the Post-Qadhafi Future*, London: Palgrave Macmillan, 2013, p. 117.

41. Cameron, *For the Record*, p. 278.

42. For a careful analysis of the position of the Arab League from 22 February to 12 March, including 'regional hesitation', see Lucie Kröning, 'The Arab League and the Arab Spring', master's thesis, Institut d'études politiques de Paris, 2013.

43. Diaa Hadid, 'Arab League Asks UN for No-Fly Zone over Libya', Associated Press, 12 March 2011.

44. 'Report of the Bahrain Independent Commission of Inquiry', final revision of 10 December 2011, paragraphs 501, 527, 1580, 1690–713.

45. African Union, 'Communique of the 265th Meeting of the Peace and Security Council', PSC/PR/COMM.2(CCLXV), 10 March 2011, https://oau-aec-au-documents.uwazi.io/en/document/fa0mtdhxp76uzfyddxbn75jyvi?page=1

46. Sarkozy's meeting with NTC representatives is described in Bernard-Henri Lévy, *La guerre sans l'aimer: Journal d'un écrivain au cœur du printemps libyen*, Paris: Grasset, 2011, pp. 104–8.

47. 'West Casts Military Net around Libya', *Financial Times*, 1 March 2011.

48. 'Italy Rules Out Military Action on Libya', Reuters, 16 March 2011, https://www.reuters.com/article/libya-italy-idUSRMEGEE7HU20110316

49. Cameron, *For the Record*, p. 277.

50. General David Richards, *Taking Command*, London: Headline, 2014, pp. 314–15.

51. Cameron, *For the Record*, pp. 276, 278.

52. 'Diplomatiquement ensuite, la No Fly Zone servira de paravent au Français pour parvenir à leur vrai dessein: des frappes cibleés que Nicolas Sarkozy et son entourage considèrent seules à même de faire plier Kadhafi'; Jean-Christophe Notin, *La vérité sur notre guerre en Libye*, Paris: Fayard, 2012, pp. 62, 72, 104–5.

53. Lévy, *La guerre sans l'aimer*, pp. 105–8.

54. Susan Rice, *Tough Love: My Story of the Things Worth Fighting For*, New York: Simon & Schuster, 2019, p. 281.

55. Gérard Araud, *Passeport diplomatique: Quarante ans au Quai d'Orsay*, Paris: Grasset, 2019, p. 234.

56. Barack Obama, *A Promised Land*, New York: Viking, 2020, pp. 654–5.

57. Ibid., pp. 651, 658.

58. Ibid., pp. 656–60; Robert M. Gates, *Duty: Memoirs of a Secretary at War*, New York: Knopf, 2014, pp. 510–23; Hillary Rodham Clinton, *Hard Choices*, New York: Simon & Schuster, 2014, pp. 363–77; Rice, *Tough Love*, pp. 278, 291–4; William J. Burns, *The Back Channel: A Memoir of American Diplomacy and the Case for Its Renewal*, London: Hurst, 2019, pp. 313–22; Ben Rhodes, *The World As It Is: Inside the Obama Whitehouse*, London: Bodley Head, 2018, pp. 109–24; Derek Chollet, *The Long Game: How Obama Defied Washington and Redefined America's Role in the World*, New York: Public Affairs, 2016, pp. 96–116; Power, *Education of an Idealist*, pp. 289–311. See also: Michael Lewis, 'Obama's Way', *Vanity Fair*, October 2012; James Mann, *The Obamians: The Struggle Inside the White House to Redefine American Power*, New York: Viking, 2012, pp. 281–301; David E. Sanger, *Confront and Conceal: Obama's Secret Wars and Surprising Use of American Power*, New York: Broadway, 2013, pp. 337–56; Kim Ghattas, *The Secretary: A Journey with Hillary Clinton from Beirut to the Heart of American Power*, New York: Henry Holt, 2013, pp. 254–73; Jeffrey Goldberg, 'The Obama Doctrine', *The Atlantic*, April 2016, pp. 80–1.

59. Gates, *Duty*, pp. 511–12. Six arguments against military intervention in Libya made by Gates in public, including testimony to Congress, are set out in

Christopher S. Chivvis, *Toppling Qaddafi: Libya and the Limits of Liberal Intervention*, New York: Cambridge University Press, 2014, pp. 44–7.

60. Clinton, *Hard Choices*, pp. 369–70; Ghattas, *Secretary*, pp. 261–3. See also Jo Becker and Scott Shane, 'Clinton, "Smart Power" and a Dictator's Fall', *New York Times*, 28 February 2016, which includes Libyan participants' account of the meeting.

61. Power, *Education of an Idealist*, pp. 296–302.

62. Obama, *Promised Land*, p. 656.

63. Ibid., pp. 657–8.

64. Ibid., p. 659; Rice, *Tough Love*, pp. 281–3.

65. Gates, *Duty*, p. 519.

66. Ibid., p. 522.

67. For a fuller quotation, see Rice, *Tough Love*, pp. 283–4.

68. Araud, *Passeport diplomatique*, pp. 234–5; Rice, *Tough Love*, p. 284.

69. Michael McFaul, *From Cold War to Hot Peace: The Inside Story of Russia and America*, London: Allen Lane, 2018, pp. 222–7.

70. Lewis, 'Obama's Way'.

71. Lévy, *La guerre sans l'aimer*, p. 127.

72. Obama, *Promised Land*, p. 660.

73. See Ann Karin Larssen, 'Russia: The Principle of Non-Intervention and the Libya Case', in Henriksen and Larssen, *Political Rationale*, pp. 74–82. Larssen argues against 'the Medvedev effect'.

74. See Steven Lee Myers, *The New Tsar: The Rise and Reign of Vladimir Putin*, London: Simon & Schuster, 2015, pp. 381–5.

75. Dmitry Gorenburg, 'Russia's Conflicts on Libya', Atlantic Sentinel, 31 March 2011, https://atlanticsentinel.com/2011/03/russias-conflicts-in-libya

76. 'Statement by Dmitry Medvedev on the Situation in Libya', 21 March 2011, http://en.kremlin.ru/events/president/news/10701

77. 'Declaration by the State Duma on the Situation in Libya, 23 March 2011, Annex to the Letter Dated 29 March 2011 from the Permanent Representative of the Russian Federation to the United Nations Addressed to the Secretary-General and the President of the Security Council', A/65/803-S/2011/209, https://digitallibrary.un.org/record/700322?ln=en

78. Obama, *Promised Land*, pp. 667–8.

79. For consideration of China's Libya decision-making, see Courtney J. Fung, *China and Intervention at the UN Security Council: Reconciling Status*, Oxford: Oxford University Press, 2019, pp. 88–107; Sheng Ding, 'The Political Rationale of China's Deliberately Limited Role in the Libyan Civil War', in Henriksen and Larssen, *Political Rationale*, pp. 86–101; and Rosemary Foot, *China, the UN, and Human Protection: Beliefs, Power, Image*, Oxford: Oxford University Press, 2020, pp. 144–7.

80. For an account of South Africa's decision-making, see Eusebius McKaiser, 'Looking an International Relations Gift Horse in the Mouth: SA's Response to

the Libyan Crisis', 2011 Ruth First Memorial Lecture, Johannesburg, 17 August 2011, https://www.politicsweb.co.za/news-and-analysis/sas-response-to-the-libyan-crisis-an-analysis

81. Hardeep Singh Puri, *Perilous Interventions: The Security Council and the Politics of Chaos*, New Delhi: HarperCollins, 2016, p. 90.
82. Explanations of vote are in UN Security Council, S/PV.6498, 17 March 2011, https://undocs.org/en/S/PV.6498
83. Puri, *Perilous Interventions*, pp. 86–7.
84. See Dapo Akande, 'What Does UN Security Council Resolution 1973 Permit?', EJIL:Talk!, 23 March 2011, https://www.ejiltalk.org/what-does-un-security-council-resolution-1973-permit
85. See Weighill and Gaub, *Cauldron*, p. 60.
86. Michael Tomasky, 'Gaddafi's Speech', *Guardian*, 17 March 2011; 'Gaddafi Tells Benghazi His Army Is Coming Tonight', Reuters, 17 March 2011, https://www.reuters.com/article/-libya-gaddafi-address-idAFLDE72G2CH20110317; David D. Kirkpatrick and Kareem Fahim, 'Qaddafi Warns of Assault on Benghazi as U.N. Vote Nears', *New York Times*, 17 March 2011.
87. 'Secretary-General's Remarks to Meeting on Libya', Paris, 19 March 2011, https://www.un.org/sg/en/content/sg/statement/2011-03-19/secretary-generals-remarks-meeting-libya
88. Hilsum, *Sandstorm*, p. 200.
89. Hugh Roberts, 'Who Said Gaddafi Had to Go?', *London Review of Books*, 17 November 2011; Alan Kuperman, 'Obama's Libya Debacle', *Foreign Affairs*, March/April 2015; UK House of Commons, Foreign Affairs Select Committee, 'Libya: Examination of Intervention and Collapse and the UK's Future Policy Options', oral evidence, Q. 1, 13 Oct 2015, George Joffé, visiting professor, King's College, London, and Alison Pargeter, analyst, http://data.parliament.uk/writtenevidence/committeeevidence.svc/evidencedocument/foreign-affairs-committee/libya-examination-of-intervention-and-collapse-and-the-uks-future-policy-options/oral/22980.html
90. February reports said they had been ordered to bomb protesters in Benghazi, but on their return to Tripoli they said they had been ordered to bombard 'a village': John Hooper and Ian Black, 'Libya Defectors: Pilots Told to Bomb Protesters Flee to Malta', *Guardian*, 21 February 2011; Miriam Dalli, 'Defected Libyan Pilots Receive Heroes' Welcome in Tripoli', *Malta Today*, 18 September 2011.
91. Weighill and Gaub, *Cauldron*, pp. 21–3.
92. Rice, *Tough Love*, pp. 282, 284
93. Ben Smith, 'WH: Avoiding "Srebrenica on Steroids"', Politico, 23 March 2011, https://www.politico.com/blogs/ben-smith/2011/03/wh-avoiding-srebrenica-on-steroids-034430
94. 'D'emblée le chef de l'État est décidé à ne pas laisser un nouveau Rwanda ou

un nouveau Srebrenica aux portes de la France.' Notin, *La vérité sur notre guerre en Libye*, p. 57.

95. UK House of Commons, Foreign Affairs Select Committee, 'Libya: Examination of Intervention and Collapse and the UK's Future Policy Options', oral evidence, 19 January 2016, Q. 333, http://data.parliament. uk/writtenevidence/committeeevidence.svc/evidencedocument/foreign-affairs-committee/libya-examination-of-intervention-and-collapse-and-the-uks-future-policy-options/oral/27184.html

96. Jonas Gahr Støre, 'Did We Know What We Were Doing When We Sent F-16s to Libya in March 2011?', *Aftenposten*, 24 September 2015.

97. President Paul Kagame, 'Africa: Rwandans Know Why Gaddafi Must Be Stopped', *The Times*, 24 March 2011.

98. 'Libya: Red Cross Pulls Out of Benghazi Fearing Attack', BBC, 16 March 2011, https://www.bbc.co.uk/news/world-africa-12767759

99. White House, Office of the Press Secretary, 'Remarks by the President in Address to the Nation on Libya', 28 March 2011.

100. Nelly Lahoud, 'What the Jihadis Left Behind', *London Review of Books*, 23 January 2020.

101. Nelly Lahoud, 'Bin Laden's Catastrophic Success', *Foreign Affairs*, September/October 2021.

102. On the limited understanding in France and the UK, see François Heisbourg, 'The War in Libya: The Political Rationale for France', and Christina J. M. Goulter, 'The UK Political Rationale for Intervention and Its Consequences', in Henriksen and Larssen, *Political Rationale*, pp. 25–6, 48–9. For a critique of the 'evidence base' for UK decision-making, see UK House of Commons, Foreign Affairs Select Committee, 'Libya: Examination of Intervention and Collapse and the UK's Future Policy Options', 6 September 2016, paragraphs 24–30. For the lack of understanding of Libya in NATO, see Florence Gaub, 'The North Atlantic Treaty Organisation and Libya: Reviewing Operation Unified Protector', US Army War College, 2013, pp. 15–18, https://www.jstor.org/stable/resrep11532?seq=1#metadata_info_tab_contents

103. Alex de Waal, 'African Roles in the Libyan Conflict of 2011', *International Affairs*, 89(2) (March 2013), p. 370. See also Idriss Déby Itno, 'Si la Libye implose, les conséquences seront incalculables pour la région', *Jeune Afrique*, 6 April 2011.

2. ALL NECESSARY MEASURES: NATO'S OPERATION UNIFIED PROTECTOR AND THE GROUND WAR

1. For accounts of operations before the transition to NATO, see Christopher S. Chivvis, *Toppling Qaddafi: Libya and the Limits of Liberal Intervention*, New York: Cambridge University Press, 2014, pp. 79–90; Anders Nygren, 'Executing

Strategy from the Air', pp. 111–17, and Christian Wollert, 'Naval Assets: Not Just a Tool for War', pp. 137–41, in Kjell Engelbrekt, Marcus Mohlin and Charlotte Wagnsson (eds), *The NATO Intervention in Libya: Lessons Learned from the Campaign*, New York: Routledge, 2014.

2. Hillary Rodham Clinton, *Hard Choices*, New York: Simon & Schuster, 2014, pp. 358–60. On the deployment of GCC Peninsula Shield Forces to Bahrain, see Chapter 1.

3. Susan Rice, *Tough Love: My Story of the Things Worth Fighting For*, New York: Simon & Schuster, 2019, pp. 281–3, quoted more fully above, Chapter 1.

4. See Karin Wester, *Intervention in Libya: The Responsibility to Protect in North Africa*, Cambridge: Cambridge University Press, 2020, p. 206.

5. General David Richards, *Taking Command*, London: Headline, 2014, p. 316.

6. Wester, *Intervention in Libya*, p. 207.

7. Jo Becker and Scott Shane, 'Clinton, "Smart Power" and a Dictator's Fall', *New York Times*, 28 February 2016.

8. Rob Weighill and Florence Gaub, *The Cauldron: NATO's Campaign in Libya*, London: Hurst, 2018, p. 112. 'Technical vehicle' refers to a light improvised fighting vehicle, typically an open-backed civilian pickup truck or four-wheel drive vehicle, with mounted weaponry.

9. Wester, *Intervention in Libya*, pp. 202–3.

10. See Chapter 1.

11. BRICS is the acronym coined to associate five countries—Brazil, Russia, India, China and South Africa—that have held annual summit meetings since 2009.

12. Statements by the BRICS are summarised in Wester, *Intervention in Libya*, pp. 201–5.

13. Thabo Mbeki, 'The UN Security Council Made Absolutely Sure That It Ignored the Continent's Views on What Had to Be Done to Help Libya', *The Star*, 5 April 2011.

14. Quoted by Deborah C. Kidwell, 'The U.S. Experience: Operational', in Karl P. Mueller (ed.), *Precision and Purpose: Airpower in the Libyan Civil War*, Santa Monica: Rand, 2015, p. 134.

15. David Cameron, *For the Record*, London: William Collins, 2019, p. 281.

16. Ian Traynor, 'Turkey and France Clash Over Libya Air Campaign', *Guardian*, 24 March 2011.

17. For fuller accounts of the debate over the transition to NATO, see Chivvis, *Toppling Qaddafi*, pp. 71–9; Weighill and Gaub, *Cauldron*, pp. 74–8; Clinton, *Hard Choices*, pp. 372–7; Wester, *Intervention in Libya*, pp. 207–9; Camille Grand, 'The French Experience: Sarkozy's War?', in Mueller, *Precision and Purpose*, pp. 188–9; Jean-Christophe Notin, *La vérité sur notre guerre en Libye*, Paris: Fayard, 2012, pp. 221–32.

18. On NATO's planning and the transition to Operation Unified Protector, see Weighill and Gaub, *Cauldron*, pp. 79–88; and Wester, *Intervention in Libya*, pp. 213–7. Weighill and Gaub's *The Cauldron* is a particularly authoritative inside

account of the entire course of Operation Unified Protector, which I have relied on heavily throughout this section, since co-author Weighill was head of joint plans and then director of operations at NATO's Joint Force Command in Naples. Other valuable accounts are in Engelbrekt, Mohlin and Wagnsson, *NATO Intervention in Libya*, and Mueller, *Precision and Purpose*.

19. Jeffrey H. Michaels, 'Able But Not Willing: A Critical Assessment of NATO's Libya Intervention', in Engelbrekt, Mohlin and Wagnsson, *NATO Intervention in Libya*, p. 24; Weighill and Gaub, *Cauldron*, p. 79; Notin, *La vérité sur notre guerre en Libye*, pp. 231–2.

20. Quoted in Weighill and Gaub, *Cauldron*, p. 90.

21. Ibid., p. 83.

22. Quoted in Wester, *Intervention in Libya*, p. 197.

23. 'Se mettre du côté des rebelles pour aller libérer des villes n'appartient pas à notre mandate.' Quoted in Notin, *La vérité sur notre guerre en Libye*, p. 236.

24. Quoted in Weighill and Gaub, *Cauldron*, p. 94.

25. Quoted in ibid., p. 101.

26. White House, Office of the Press Secretary, 'Remarks by the President in Address to the Nation on Libya', 28 March 2011, https://obamawhitehouse.archives.gov/the-press-office/2011/03/28/remarks-President-address-nation-libya

27. The Contact Group met at ministerial level in Doha on 13 April, Rome on 5 May, Abu Dhabi on 9 June and Istanbul on 15 July. Members of the Contact Group as of the London meeting are listed in Chivvis, *Toppling Qaddafi*, Appendix D, pp. 223–4.

28. Weighill and Gaub, *Cauldron*, pp. 93–4.

29. Mark Hosenball, 'Obama Authorizes Secret Help for Libya Rebels', Reuters, 30 March 2011, https://www.reuters.com/article/us-libya-usa-order-idUS-TRE72T6H220110330

30. UK House of Commons, 'Official Report', 30 March 2011, column 350, https://publications.parliament.uk/pa/cm201011/cmhansrd/cm110330/debtext/110330-0001.htm

31. Bruce R. Nardulli, 'The Arab States' Experiences', in Mueller, *Precision and Purpose*, pp. 359–60. For a summary of positions at the Doha Contact Group meeting, see Weighill and Gaub, *Cauldron*, p. 133.

32. NATO, 'Statement on Libya following the Working Lunch of NATO Ministers of Foreign Affairs with Non-NATO Contributors to Operation Unified Protector', 14 April 2011, https://www.nato.int/cps/en/natohq/official_texts_72544.htm

33. White House, Office of the Press Secretary, 'Joint Op-Ed by President Obama, Prime Minister Cameron and President Sarkozy: "Libya's Pathway to Peace"', 14 April 2011.

34. For example, in the London *Times* and *Daily Telegraph*.

35. Matthew D'Ancona, *In It Together: The Inside Story of the Coalition Government*, London: Viking, 2013, pp. 176–7.

36. Weighill and Gaub, *Cauldron*, pp. 99–100.
37. Chivvis, *Toppling Qaddafi*, p. 113.
38. Weighill and Gaub, *Cauldron*, pp. 161–2, where they describe the full process for authorisation of targets. For a further detailed description and defence of targeting during Operation Unified Protector, see NATO, 'Response Letter to the International Commission of Inquiry on Libya', 23 January 2012, published as Annex II to UN Human Rights Council, 'Report of the International Commission of Inquiry on Libya', 2 March 2012, A/HRC/19/68, https://www.refworld.org/docid/4ffd19532.html
39. Christopher S. Chivvis, 'Strategic and Political Overview of the Intervention', in Mueller, *Precision and Purpose*, p. 30.
40. Quoted in Wester, *Intervention in Libya*, p. 220.
41. Notin, *La vérité sur notre guerre en Libye*, p. 289.
42. Weighill and Gaub, *Cauldron*, p. 150.
43. Ibid., p. 161.
44. Ibid., p. 126.
45. Con Coughlin, 'Nato Must Target Gaddafi Regime, Says Armed Forces Chief Gen Sir David Richards', *Daily Telegraph*, 14 May 2011.
46. Frederic Wehrey, 'NATO's Intervention', in Peter Cole and Brian McQuinn (eds), *The Libyan Revolution and Its Aftermath*, London: Hurst, 2015, p. 111; Weighill and Gaub, *Cauldron*, pp. 131–2.
47. Weighill and Gaub, *Cauldron*, p. 161.
48. UNESCO press release, 'Director-General Deplores NATO Strike on Libyan State Television Facilities', 8 August 2011, http://www.unesco.org/new/en/media-services/single-view/news/director_general_deplores_nato_strike_on_libyan_state_televi
49. NATO statement, 'NATO Strikes Libyan State TV Satellite Facility', 30 July 2011, https://www.nato.int/cps/en/natohq/news_76776.htm
50. Quoted in Chivvis, *Toppling Qaddafi*, p. 101; Anthony Bell and David Witter, 'The Libyan Revolution, Part 3: Stalemate & Siege', Washington, DC: Institute for the Study of War, October 2011, p. 22, https://www.understandingwar.org/report/libyan-revolution-part-3-stalemate-siege
51. Interviews by Frederic Wehrey: see Wehrey, 'The Hidden Story of Airpower in Libya (and What It Means for Syria)', *Foreign Policy*, 11 February 2013, and Wehrey, 'NATO's Intervention', pp. 105–25.
52. Weighill and Gaub, *Cauldron*, p. 123; Wehrey, 'NATO's Intervention', pp. 122–3.
53. Weighill and Gaub, *Cauldron*, pp. 159–60.
54. The operation of red-card holders is described in Weighill and Gaub, *Cauldron*, pp. 161–3; and by Kidwell, 'U.S. Experience', p. 143.
55. Christina Goulter, 'The British Experience: Operation Ellamy', in Mueller, *Precision and Purpose*, p. 166; General Charles Bouchard, 'Liberating Libya: A Commander's Perspective', in Atlantic Council, 'Coalition Building and the

Future of NATO Operations', 14 February 2012, https://www.atlanticcoun-cil.org/commentary/transcript/coalition-building-and-the-future-of-nato-operations-2-14-2012-transcript

56. Robert Egnell, 'The Swedish Experience: Overcoming the Non-NATO-Member Conundrum', in Mueller, *Precision and Purpose*, pp. 331–6, where he describes the domestic political debate.

57. Norway Libya Commission, 'Evaluering av Norsk Deltakelse i Libya Operas-jonene i 2011', 2018, pp. 62, 113, 155, https://www.regjeringen.no/global-assets/departementene/fd/dokumenter/rapporter-og-regelverk/libya-rap-porten.pdf. See also Chivvis, *Toppling Qaddafi*, pp. 135–6, summarising interviews with Norwegian officials.

58. Cameron, *For the Record*, p. 283.

59. Richards, *Taking Command*, p. 318. The UK government's National Security Committee (Libya) met on sixty-two occasions during the campaign: Prime Minister's Office, 'Libya Crisis: National Security Adviser's View of Central Coordination and Lessons Learned', 29 April 2013, pp. 19, 31, https://www.gov.uk/government/publications/libya-crisis-national-security-advisers-view-of-central-coordination-and-lessons-learned

60. Ambassador Richard Northern and Jason Pack, 'The Role of Outside Actors', in Jason Pack (ed.), *The 2011 Libyan Uprisings and the Struggle for the Post-Qadhafi Future*, London: Palgrave Macmillan, 2013, p. 119.

61. Robert M. Gates, *Duty: Memoirs of a Secretary at War*, New York: Knopf, 2014, p. 522.

62. Weighill and Gaub, *Cauldron*, p. 163; Chivvis, *Toppling Qaddafi*, pp. 121–2, 126–9. For a detailed account of France's assessment of the risks of the use of helicopters, and overcoming the reservations of NATO, see Notin, *La vérité sur notre guerre en Libye*, pp. 368–80.

63. Notin, *La vérité sur notre guerre en Libye*, p. 436.

64. Grand, 'French Experience', p. 189.

65. Weighill and Gaub, *Cauldron*, pp. 147, 186–7.

66. 'Et ce sont, chez eux, les Anglais, des discussions interminables pour savoir s'ils sont, ou non, dans l'épure de la resolution. Moyennant quoi, en bas, les cibles n'attendent pas le rapport d'avocat pour aller se mettre à l'abri.' Bernard-Henri Lévy, *La guerre sans l'aimer: Journal d'un écrivain au cœur du printemps libyen*, Paris: Grasset, 2011, p. 455.

67. Norway Libya Commission, 'Evaluering av Norsk Deltakelse i Libya Operasjonene i 2011', p. 99.

68. Weighill and Gaub, *Cauldron*, p. 218.

69. UK House of Commons Library, International Affairs and Defence Section, 'Interpretation of Security Council Resolution 1973 on Libya', 6 April 2011, https://researchbriefings.files.parliament.uk/documents/SN05916/SN05916.pdf

70. Mark Urban, 'Inside Story of the UK's Secret Mission to Beat Gaddafi', BBC, 19 January 2012, https://www.bbc.co.uk/news/magazine-16573516

71. Lindsey Hilsum, *Sandstorm: Libya in the Time of Revolution*, London: Faber & Faber, 2012, pp. 190–1.

72. Goulter, 'British Experience', p. 163; telephone conversation, broadcast on Libyan state TV, between Richard Northern, British ambassador to Libya, and a spokesman for Libyan former justice minister, YouTube, 7 March 2011, https://www.youtube.com/watch?v=4SY1-B0gi28

73. Stratfor, 'Egypt's Crude Stake in Libya's Unrest', *The Australian*, 1 March 2011; Charles Levinson and Matthew Rosenberg, 'Egypt Said to Arm Libya Rebels', *Wall Street Journal*, 17 March 2011; email to Hillary Clinton, 'Egypt Special Forces Now in Libya', 1 March, Hillary Clinton Archive, WikiLeaks, https://wikileaks.org/clinton-emails/emailid/12744

74. 'Note by the President of the Security Council, Annexing Letter Dated 17 February 2012 from the Panel of Experts Established Pursuant to Resolution 1973 (2011) Addressed to the President of the Security Council', 20 March 2012, S/2012/163, paragraphs 77, 80, 83, https://digitallibrary.un.org/record/724030?ln=en

75. UK Ministry of Defence, 'UK Military Liaison Advisory Team to Be Sent to Libya', 19 April 2011, https://www.gov.uk/government/news/uk-military-liaison-advisory-team-to-be-sent-to-libya

76. UK House of Commons Defence Committee, 'Operations in Libya', Ninth Report of Session 2010–12, vol. I, Ev 5, Q. 28–9, evidence taken 27 April 2011, report published 25 January 2012, https://publications.parliament.uk/pa/cm201012/cmselect/cmdfence/950/950vw.pdf

77. Gregory Alegi, 'The Italian Experience: Pivotal and Underestimated', in Mueller, *Precision and Purpose*, p. 226.

78. Quoted in Michaels, 'Able But Not Willing', p. 32.

79. Wehrey, 'NATO's Intervention', p. 111.

80. Weighill and Gaub, *Cauldron*, p. 124.

81. Notin, *La vérité sur notre guerre en Libye*, pp. 339, 458.

82. Wehrey, 'NATO's Intervention', p. 119.

83. Notin, *La vérité sur notre guerre en Libye*, pp. 424–5.

84. Weighill and Gaub, *Cauldron*, p. 193.

85. Ibid., p. 213, quoting a Brussels interview.

86. Florence Gaub, 'The North Atlantic Treaty Organization and Libya: Reviewing Operation Unified Protector', US Army War College, 2013, pp. 18, 21, https://press.armywarcollege.edu/monographs/323

87. Weighill and Gaub, *Cauldron*, pp. 121–2; Mark Muller Stuart, *Storm in the Desert: Britain's Intervention in Libya and the Arab Spring*, Edinburgh: Birlinn, 2017, pp. 121–3; Bell and Witter, 'Libyan Revolution: Part 3', pp. 23–4.

88. Peter Cole with Umar Khan, 'The Fall of Tripoli: Part 1', in Cole and McQuinn, *Libyan Revolution*, p. 65.

89. Sam Dagher, Charles Levinson and Margaret Coker, 'Tiny Kingdom's Huge Role in Libya Draws Concern', *Wall Street Journal*, 17 October 2011. For supplies smuggled from Sudan, see Cole with Khan, 'Fall of Tripoli: Part 1', pp. 69–70, 76.

90. Cole with Khan, 'Fall of Tripoli: Part 1', p. 72.

91. Wolfram Lacher and Ahmed Labnouj, 'Factionalism Resurgent: The War in the Jabal Nafusa', in Cole and McQuinn, *Libyan Revolution*, p. 273.

92. Cole with Khan, 'Fall of Tripoli: Part 1', pp. 74–7.

93. See for example Notin, *La vérité sur notre guerre en Libye*, p. 471.

94. Kirit Radia, 'Libya Rebels: US to Send Gadhafi Opponents $25 Million in Aid', ABC News, 20 April 2011, https://abcnews.go.com/Politics/libya-rebels-us-send-libyan-rebels-25-million/story?id=13418779; Samia Nakhoul, 'The Secret Plan to Take Tripoli', Reuters, 6 September 2011, https://www.reuters.com/article/us-libya-endgame-idUSTRE7853C520110906

95. Becker and Shane, 'Clinton, "Smart Power" and a Dictator's Fall'.

96. Cole with Khan, 'Fall of Tripoli: Part 1', pp. 65, 75–6.

97. Sarkozy's meeting with Younis is described in Lévy, *La guerre sans l'aimer*, pp. 249–59.

98. 'France Providing Weapons to Libya Rebels: *Le Figaro*', Reuters, 29 June 2011, https://www.reuters.com/article/ozatp-libya-france-weapons-20110629-idAFJOE75S0B020110629

99. Notin, *La vérité sur notre guerre en Libye*, pp. 389–93, 439–40.

100. BBC, 'Libya Conflict: France Air-Dropped Arms to Rebels', 29 June 2011, https://www.bbc.co.uk/news/world-africa-13955751

101. 'Note by the President of the Security Council, Annexing Letter Dated 17 February 2012 from the Panel of Experts Established Pursuant to Resolution 1973 (2011) Addressed to the President of the Security Council', 20 March 2012, paragraph 78.

102. Sarkozy's meeting with the Misrata delegation is described in Lévy, *La guerre sans l'aimer*, pp. 502–9. See also Notin, *La vérité sur notre guerre en Libye*, p. 453; Bell and Witter, 'Libyan Revolution: Part 3', pp. 28–9.

103. Dagher, Levinson and Coker, 'Tiny Kingdom's Huge Role in Libya Draws Concern'.

104. 'Note by the President of the Security Council, Annexing Letter Dated 17 February 2012 from the Panel of Experts Established Pursuant to Resolution 1973 (2011) Addressed to the President of the Security Council', 20 March 2012, paragraphs 91–102 and Annex V.

105. 'Letter Dated 4 March 2016 from the Panel of Experts on Libya Established Pursuant to Resolution 1973 (2011) Addressed to the President of the Security Council', 9 March 2016, S/2016/209, Annex 30, https://digitallibrary.un.org/record/822636?ln=en

106. 'Note by the President of the Security Council, Annexing Letter Dated 15 February 2013 from the Panel of Experts Established Pursuant to Resolution 1973 (2011) Addressed to the President of the Security Council', 9 March

2013, S/2013/99, paragraph 60, https://digitallibrary.un.org/record/7475 41?ln=en

107. 'Deconfliction' means ensuring that an authorised flight does not come into conflict with the NATO operation. Ibid., paragraphs 94–5.
108. Hilsum, *Sandstorm*, pp. 208–9.
109. 'Bashir Says Sudan Armed Libyan Rebels', Sudan Tribune, 27 October 2011, https://sudantribune.com/Bashir-says-Sudan-armed-Libyan,40547
110. Alex de Waal, 'African Roles in the Libyan Conflict', *International Affairs*, 89:2 (March 2013), pp. 375–8.
111. For an early account of the role of special forces, based on an extensive analysis of open source material, including media reports, individual sightings, videos and photographs to the time of writing, see Mark Phillips, 'The Ground Offensive: The Role of Special Forces', in Royal United Services Institute (RUSI), 'Accidental Heroes: Britain, France and the Libya Operation', September 2011, pp. 10–12, https://www.wired-gov.net/wg/wg-news-1. nsf/0/5F7E73AEF0357468802579140035B620?OpenDocument. See also the description of their various roles in Marcus Mohlin, 'Cloak and Dagger in Libya: The Libyan *Thuwar* and the Role of the Allied Special Forces', in Engelbrekt, Mohlin and Wagnsson, *NATO Intervention in Libya*, pp. 195–220.
112. Wehrey, 'NATO's Intervention', pp. 118–19. See also Wehrey, 'Hidden Story of Airpower in Libya'; and Wehrey, 'Libyan Experience', pp. 43–68.
113. Wehrey, 'Libyan Experience', p. 45. He details the special forces' role in ending the siege and planning the offensive out of Misrata on pp. 63–6.
114. Lévy, *La guerre sans l'aimer*, p. 256.
115. Richards, *Taking Command*, p. 316.
116. D'Ancona, *In It Together*, pp. 178–9.
117. Cameron, *For the Record*, p. 284.
118. The tensions are described in detail in Cole with Khan, 'Fall of Tripoli: Part 1', pp. 71–9.
119. Wehrey, 'NATO's Intervention', pp. 114–15.
120. Cole with Khan, 'Fall of Tripoli: Part 1'; and Lacher and Labnouj, 'Factionalism Resurgent', pp. 77, 273–4.
121. Urban, 'Inside Story of the UK's Secret Mission to Beat Gaddafi'.
122. Rupert Wieloch, *Belfast to Benghazi: Untold Challenges of War*, Cirencester: Mereo Books, 2016, pp. 244, 255–6.
123. Notin, *La vérité sur notre guerre en Libye*, pp. 472–3.
124. Quoted in Wehrey, 'NATO's Intervention', p. 120.
125. Julian Borger and Martin Chulov, 'Al Jazeera Footage Captures "Western Troops on the Ground" in Libya', *Guardian*, 30 May 2011.
126. Cole with Khan, 'Fall of Tripoli: Part 1' and 'The Fall of Tripoli: Part 2', in Cole and McQuinn, *Libyan Revolution*, pp. 55–104.
127. See Chapter 4.
128. Wehrey, 'NATO's Intervention', p. 119.
129. Ibid.

130. Goulter, 'British Experience', p. 173.
131. Richards, *Taking Command*, p. 317.
132. 'Factbox: U.S. Stepped Up Pace of Libya Air Strikes; Pentagon', Reuters, 22 August 2011, https://www.reuters.com/article/us-libya-usa-strikes-idUSTRE77L76C20110822; Karen DeYoung and Greg Miller, 'Allies Guided Rebel "Pincer" Assault on Tripoli', *Washington Post*, 22 August 2011; Kareem Fahim and Mark Mazzetti, 'Rebels' Assault on Tripoli Began with Careful Work Inside', *New York Times*, 22 August 2011.
133. Wehrey, 'NATO's Intervention', p. 117.
134. The taking of Tripoli and the involvement of special forces is detailed in Cole with Khan, 'Fall of Tripoli: Part 2', pp. 86–93.
135. UN Department of Public Information, 'After Much Wrangling, General Assembly Seats National Transitional Council of Libya as Country's Representative for Sixty-Sixth Session', 16 September 2011, https://www.un.org/press/en/2011/ga11137.doc.htm
136. UN Security Council, S/PV.6622, 26 September 2011, https://undocs.org/en/S/PV.6622
137. NATO, 'Press Briefing on Libya', 22 September 2011, https://www.nato.int/cps/en/natohq/opinions_78388.htm?selectedLocale=en
138. Weighill and Gaub, *Cauldron*, p. 207.
139. NATO, 'Press Briefing on Libya', 18 October 2011, https://www.nato.int/cps/en/natohq/opinions_79613.htm?selectedLocale=uk
140. Weighill and Gaub, *Cauldron*, p. 115.
141. Quoted in Wehrey, 'NATO's Intervention', p. 111.
142. Weighill and Gaub, *Cauldron*, p. 226.
143. Human Rights Watch, 'Libya: Apparent Execution of 53 Gaddafi Supporters', 24 October 2011, https://www.hrw.org/news/2011/10/24/libya-apparent-execution-53-gaddafi-supporters
144. Andrew Gilligan, 'Gaddafi's Ghost Town after the Loyalists Retreat', *Daily Telegraph*, 11 September 2011; Amnesty International, 'Tawarghas Must Be Protected from Reprisals and Arbitrary Arrest in Libya', 7 September 2011, https://www.amnesty.org/en/latest/news/2011/09/tawarghas-must-be-protected-reprisals-and-arbitrary-arrest-libya; Human Rights Watch, 'Libya: Militias Terrorizing Residents of "Loyalist" Town', 30 October 2011, https://www.hrw.org/news/2011/10/30/libya-militias-terrorizing-residents-loyalist-town
145. International Crisis Group, 'Holding Libya Together: Security Challenges after Qadhafi', 14 December 2011, p. 28, https://www.crisisgroup.org/middle-east-north-africa/north-africa/libya/holding-libya-together-security-challenges-after-qadhafi; Wolfram Lacher, *Libya's Fragmentation: Structure and Process in Violent Conflict*, London: I.B. Tauris, 2020, p. 24.
146. Thomas Harding, Gordon Rayner and Damien McElroy, 'Libya: SAS Leads Hunt for Gaddafi', *Daily Telegraph*, 24 August 2011.

147. Quoted in Weighill and Gaub, *Cauldron*, p. 213.

148. Quoted in Notin, *La vérité sur notre guerre en Libye*, p. 485.

149. Weighill and Gaub, *Cauldron*, pp. 231–2. See also Notin, *La vérité sur notre guerre en Libye*, pp. 503–7.

150. NATO, 'Press Briefing on Libya', 18 October 2011.

151. Quoted in Wester, *Intervention in Libya*, pp. 236–7.

152. The most detailed investigation of the killing of Gaddafi is in Andrei Netto, *Bringing Down Gaddafi: On the Ground with the Libyan Rebels*, New York: St. Martin's Press, 2014, pp. 1–5, 277–80.

153. NATO, 'Monthly Press Briefing by NATO Secretary General Anders Fogh Rasmussen', 3 November 2011, https://www.nato.int/cps/en/natohq/news_80248.htm

154. UN Department of Public Information, 'Press Conference by Secretary-General Ban Ki-moon at United Nations Headquarters', 14 December 2011, SG/SM/14021, https://www.un.org/press/en/2011/sgsm14021.doc.htm

155. UN Security Council, 7 March 2012, S/PV.6731, https://undocs.org/en/S/PV.6731

156. Weighill and Gaub, *Cauldron*, p. 240.

157. UN Human Rights Council, 'Report of the International Commission of Inquiry on Libya', 2 March 2012, paragraphs 83–9, 122, 130.

158. Amnesty International, 'Libya: The Forgotten Victims of NATO Strikes', March 2012, https://www.amnesty.org/en/documents/mde19/003/2012/en

159. Human Rights Watch, 'Unacknowledged Deaths: Civilian Casualties in NATO's Air Campaign in Libya', 13 May 2012, https://www.hrw.org/report/2012/05/13/unacknowledged-deaths/civilian-casualties-natos-air-campaign-libya#:~:text=The%20numbers%20were%20inflated%20and,1%2C108%20civilians%20and%20wounded%206%2C362

160. Joe Dyke, 'NATO Killed Civilians in Libya: It's Time to Admit It', *Foreign Policy*, 20 March 2021.

161. NATO, 'Response Letter to the International Commission of Inquiry on Libya', 23 January 2012, published as Annex II to UN Human Rights Council, 'Report of the International Commission of Inquiry on Libya'.

162. See C. J. Chivers and Eric Schmitt, 'In Strikes on Libya by NATO, an Unspoken Civilian Toll', *New York Times*, 17 December 2011.

163. M. Cherif Bassiouni (ed.), *Libya: From Repression to Revolution; A Record of Armed Conflicts and International Law Violations, 2011–2013*, Leiden: Martinus Nijhoff, 2013, pp. 267–8.

164. Amnesty International, 'Revenge Killings and Reckless Firing in Opposition-Held Eastern Libya', 13 May 2011, https://www.amnesty.org/en/latest/campaigns/2011/05/revenge-killings-and-reckless-firing-in-opposition-held-eastern-libya. See also Human Rights Watch, 'Libya: Opposition Arbitrarily Detaining Suspected Gaddafi Loyalists', 5 June 2011, https://www.hrw.org/

news/2011/06/05/libya-opposition-arbitrarily-detaining-suspected-gaddafi-loyalists

165. Amnesty International, 'Revenge Killings and Reckless Firing'.
166. See Marieke I. Wierda, 'The Local Impact of a Global Court', PhD thesis, Leiden University, 2019, pp. 258–9.
167. See Human Rights Watch, 'The Murder Brigades of Misrata', 28 October 2011, https://www.hrw.org/news/2011/10/28/murder-brigades-misrata
168. Wierda, 'Local Impact of a Global Court', p. 258.
169. UN Department of Public Information, 'Press Conference by Secretary-General Ban Ki-moon at United Nations Headquarters', 14 December 2011, SG/SM/14021.
170. Bouchard, 'Liberating Libya'.
171. Norway Libya Commission, 'Evaluering av Norsk Deltakelse i Libya Operasjonene i 2011', p. 61.
172. UK House of Commons, Foreign Affairs Select Committee, 'Libya: Examination of Intervention and Collapse and the UK's Future Policy Options', oral evidence, Q. 317, 19 January 2016, http://data.parliament.uk/writtenevidence/committeeevidence.svc/evidencedocument/foreign-affairs-committee/libya-examination-of-intervention-and-collapse-and-the-uks-future-policy-options/oral/27184.html
173. Sasha Swire, *Diary of an MP's Wife: Inside and Outside Power*, London: Little, Brown, 2020, p. 69.
174. Corbett Daly, 'Clinton on Qaddafi: "We Came, We Saw, He Died"', CBS News, 20 October 2011, https://www.cbsnews.com/news/clinton-on-qaddafi-we-came-we-saw-he-died
175. Leon Panetta, *Worthy Fights: A Memoir of Leadership in War and Peace*, New York: Penguin, 2015, p. 354.
176. 'L'objectif qui était le nôtre, c'est-à-dire accompagner les forces du CNT dans la libération de leur territoire, est maintenant attaint.' Quoted in Notin, *La vérité sur notre guerre en Libye*, p. 510.
177. Geir Ulfstein and Hege Fosund Christiansen, 'The Legality of the NATO Bombing in Libya', *International and Comparative Law Quarterly*, 62:1 (January 2013), pp. 159–71. See also the analysis in Bassiouni, *Libya*, pp. 223–30.
178. Richards, *Taking Command*, pp. 315–17; and UK House of Commons, Foreign Affairs Select Committee, 'Libya: Examination of Intervention and Collapse and the UK's Future Policy Options', oral evidence, 19 January 2016, Q. 330, http://data.parliament.uk/writtenevidence/committeeevidence.svc/evidencedocument/foreign-affairs-committee/libya-examination-of-intervention-and-collse-and-the-uks-future-policy-options/oral/27184.html
179. 'sont allés arracher la victoire avec leurs tripes'. Quoted in Notin, *La vérité sur notre guerre en Libye*, p. 526.
180. 'Qatar Admits It Had Boots on the Ground in Libya', Al-Arabiya, 26 October 2011, https://english.alarabiya.net/articles/2011%2F10%2F26%2F173833

181. Ibid.
182. Nardulli, 'Arab States' Experiences', pp. 365–6.
183. Phillips, 'Ground Offensive', p. 11.
184. Ibid., p. 12.
185. Alegi, 'Italian Experience', p. 226.
186. Gianandrea Gaiani, 'Tra le forze speciali in Libia 40 uomini del Col Moschin', *Il Sole 24 ORE*, 15 October 2011.
187. US House of Representatives, 'Report of the Select Committee on the Events Surrounding the 2012. Terrorist Attack in Benghazi', III-20, https://archives-benghazi-republicans-oversight.house.gov/sites/republicans.benghazi.house.gov/files/documents/Part%20III_Redacted.pdf
188. Mohlin, 'Cloak and Dagger in Libya', p. 198.
189. Wehrey, 'NATO's Intervention', pp. 117, 119; Frederic Wehrey, *The Burning Shores: Inside the Battle for the New Libya*, New York: Farrar, Straus and Giroux, 2018, p. 56.
190. 'At the end of the war, NATO had had 3,000 media engagements (including Rasmussen appearing on Russia Today) and forty press conferences, not counting press releases (translated into Arabic) and videos.' Weighill and Gaub, *Cauldron*, p. 91.
191. 'a des collaborateurs, nous avons des observateurs, parce que nous avons besoin de renseignements, mais il n'y a pas de forces spéciales'. Quoted in Notin, *La vérité sur notre guerre en Libye*, p. 395.
192. Quoted in Emily O'Brien and Andrew Sinclair, 'The Libyan War: A Diplomatic History February–August 2011', New York University, Center on International Cooperation, August 2011, p. 20, https://reliefweb.int/report/libya/libyan-war-diplomatic-history-february-august-2011
193. See the discussion in Mohlin, 'Cloak and Dagger in Libya', pp. 214–15.

3. A NEGOTIATED TRANSITION?

1. See Chapter 1.
2. 'Letter Dated 2 March 2011 from the Secretary of the General People's Committee of Foreign Liaison and International Cooperation of the Libyan Arab Jamahirya Addressed to the President of the Security Council', circulated 4 March 2011; revised version dated 3 March 2011, circulated 7 March 2011.
3. On the emergence of the NTC and its evolution during the conflict, see Peter Bartu, 'The Corridor of Uncertainty: The National Transitional Council's Battle for Recognition and Relevance', in Peter Cole and Brian McQuinn (eds), *The Libyan Revolution and Its Aftermath*, London: Hurst, 2015, pp. 31–54.
4. When first established on 5 March, this was called a Crisis Management Committee, later Executive Team, then Executive Committee.
5. Bartu, 'Corridor of Uncertainty', p. 31.
6. Regime defections from February to August are listed in Christopher S. Chivvis,

Toppling Qaddafi: Libya and the Limits of International Intervention, New York: Cambridge University Press, 2014, Appendix C, pp. 214–22.

7. The Norwegian efforts are referred to in the report of the Norway Libya Commission, 'Evaluering av Norsk Deltakelse i Libya Operasjonene i 2011', 2018, 11.3, https://www.regjeringen.no/globalassets/departementene/fd/dokumenter/rapporter-og-regelverk/libya-rapporten.pdf; and in Norwegian media reports: see Nina Berglund, 'Støre Details Effort for Peace in Libya', News in English.no, 20 September 2018, https://www.newsinenglish.no/2018/09/20/norway-attempted-libyan-peace-talks; and Berglund, 'Norway Negotiated while Bombing Libya', News in English.no, 9 October 2018, https://www.newsinenglish.no/2014/10/09/norway-negotiated-while-bombing-libya. See also Joe Dyke and Imogen Piper, 'The Secret Talks That Nearly Saved Gaddafi', *Independent*, 19 March 2021.

8. UK Foreign and Commonwealth Office, 'FOI Release: Mohammed Ismail Meetings on Libya 2011', 10 June 2016, https://www.gov.uk/government/publications/foi-release-mohammed-ismail-meetings-on-libya

9. Peter Bartu, 'Libya's Political Transition: The Challenges of Mediation', International Peace Institute, December 2014, p. 3, https://www.ipinst.org/wp-content/uploads/publications/ipi_e_pub_mediation_libya.pdf

10. See Chapter 1.

11. Alex de Waal, 'African Roles in the Libyan Conflict', *International Affairs*, 89:2 (March 2013), p. 371.

12. Ban's telephone call is recounted in Jean Ping, *Eclipse sur l'Afrique: Fallait-il tuer Kadhafi?*, Paris: Michalon, 2014, p. 18.

13. African Union, Press Release, 'Meeting of the AU High-Level Ad Hoc Committee on Libya', Nouakchott, 19 March 2011, https://au.int/en/press-releases/20110319–0

14. Michael Clarke, 'The Road to War', in Royal United Services Institute (RUSI), 'Accidental Heroes: Britain, France and the Libya Operation', September 2011, p. 4, https://www.voltairenet.org/IMG/pdf/Accidental_Heroes.pdf

15. UK House of Commons, Foreign Affairs Select Committee, 'Libya: Examination of Intervention and Collapse and the UK's Future Policy Options', oral evidence, 19 January 2016, http://data.parliament.uk/writtenevidence/committeeevidence.svc/evidencedocument/foreign-affairs-committee/libya-examination-of-intervention-and-collapse-and-the-uks-future-policy-options/oral/23624.html

16. Quoted in Derek Chollet, *The Long Game: How Obama Defied Washington and Redefined America's Role in the World*, New York: Public Affairs, 2016, p. 107.

17. African Union, Press Release, 'Communiqué, Consultative Meeting on the Situation in Libya', Addis Ababa, 25 March 2011, https://au.int/en/pressreleases/20110325

18. Members of the Contact Group as of the London meeting are listed in Chivvis, *Toppling Qaddafi*, Appendix D, pp. 223–4.

19. Rob Weighill and Florence Gaub, *The Cauldron: NATO's Campaign in Libya*, London: Hurst, 2018, pp. 90, 93.

20. Harriet Sherwood, Ian Black and Patrick Wintour, 'Gaddafi's Deputy Foreign Minister Flies to Athens with Peace Proposal', *Guardian*, 3 April 2011.

21. Weighill and Gaub, *Cauldron*, p. 119.

22. Seumas Milne, 'Turkey Offers to Broker Libya Ceasefire as Rebels Advance on Sirte', *Guardian*, 27 March 2011.

23. Henri J. Barkey and Selin Nasi, 'Turkey and the Arab Spring: From Engagement to the Sidelines', in Sverre Lodgaard (ed.), *External Powers and the Arab Spring*, Oslo: Scandinavian Academic Press, 2016, p. 218.

24. Press Statement by Prime Minister Recep Tayyip Erdoğan on Libya, 7 April 2011, https://www.mfa.gov.tr/speech-delievered-by-h_e_-prime-minister-recep-tayyip-erdogan-on-libya-_ankara_-7-april-2011_.en.mfa

25. Weighill and Gaub, *Cauldron*, p. 130.

26. De Waal, 'African Roles in the Libyan Conflict', p. 372.

27. Described in Ping, *Eclipse sur l'Afrique*, pp. 111–12.

28. African Union, Press Release, 'The African Union High Level Ad hoc Committee on the Situation in Libya and the Transitional National Council (TNC) Have Had a Constructive Interaction in Benghazi', 11 April 2011, https://allafrica.com/stories/201104150557.html

29. Quoted in Mark Kersten, *Justice in Conflict: The Effects of the International Criminal Court's Interventions on Ending Wars and Building Peace*, Oxford: Oxford University Press, 2016, p. 142.

30. African Union, Press Release, 'The African Union High-Level Ad hoc Committee on Libya Convenes Its Fourth Meeting in Addis Ababa', 26 April 2011, https://au.int/pt/node/24302?page=4

31. 'Briefing by Al-Khatib, UN Security Council', 3 May 2011, S/PV.6527, p. 5, https://undocs.org/en/S/PV.6731

32. For an analysis of the different perspectives of African states, see Linnéa Gelot, 'Role and Impact on the African Union', in Dag Henriksen and Ann Karin Larssen (eds), *Political Rationale and International Consequences of the War in Libya*, Oxford: Oxford University Press, 2016, pp. 282–3.

33. African Union, 'Decision on the Peaceful Resolution of the Libyan Crisis', 25 May 2011, https://allafrica.com/stories/201105270681.html

34. Peter Fabricius, 'What Ended Zuma's Mediation in Libya?', Institute for Security Studies, 28 May 2015, https://issafrica.org/iss-today/what-ended-zumas-mediation-in-libya

35. Bartu, 'Libya's Political Transition', p. 5.

36. De Waal, 'African Roles in the Libyan Conflict', p. 374.

37. African Union, 'Proposals to the Libyan Parties for a Framework Agreement on a Political Solution to the Crisis in Libya', in UN Security Council, 'Letter Dated 22 July 2011 from the Secretary-General to the President of the Security Council', 26 July 2011, UN doc. S/2011/455, Annex 2, https://documents-

dds-ny.un.org/doc/UNDOC/GEN/N11/431/14/pdf/N1143114.
pdf?OpenElement

38. Ellen Barry, 'In Shift, Russia Agrees to Try to Talk Qaddafi into Leaving', *New York Times*, 27 May 2011.

39. Chivvis, *Toppling Qaddafi*, pp. 149–50.

40. 'Chess Tsar Says Gaddafi "Calm" as Uprising Rages', Reuters, 13 June 2011, https://www.reuters.com/article/ozatp-libya-gaddafi-chess-20110613-idAF-JOE75C0IP20110613

41. Andrew E. Kramer, 'Russia Meets with NATO in New Push for Libya Peace', *New York Times*, 4 July 2011.

42. Chivvis, *Toppling Qaddafi*, p. 151; Ruth Sherlock and Richard Spencer, 'Libya: France Risks Nato Split Over Call for Gaddafi Talks', *Daily Telegraph*, 11 July 2011; 'Paris dément négocier directement avec la Libye', *Le Monde* with AFP, 11 July 2011; 'France in Contact with Libyans over Gaddafi', Khamakar Press, 12 July 2011, https://khamakarpress.com/2011/07/12/france-in-contact-with-libyans-over-gaddafi; Henry Samuel, 'French Say Col Muammar Gaddafi "Prepared to Leave"', *Daily Telegraph*, 12 July 2011.

43. Bernard-Henri Lévy, *La guerre sans l'aimer: Journal d'un écrivain au cœur du printemps libyen*, Paris: Grasset, 2011, pp. 402–3; Jean-Christophe Notin, *La vérité sur notre guerre en Libye*, Paris: Fayard, 2012, p. 405.

44. David Cameron, *For the Record*, London: William Collins, 2019, p. 283.

45. Erdal Şafak, 'Türkiye'nin Libya formülü', Sabah.com, 15 July 2011, https://www.sabah.com.tr/yazarlar/safak/2011/07/15/turkiyenin-libya-formulu

46. Chair's Statement, Fourth Meeting of the Libya Contact Group, Istanbul, 15 July 2011, https://www.nato.int/nato_static/assets/pdf/pdf_2011_07/201109 26_110715-Libya-Contact-Group-Istanbul.pdf

47. Dyke and Piper, 'Secret Talks That Nearly Saved Gaddafi'.

48. Norway Libya Commission, 'Evaluering av Norsk Deltakelse i Libya Operasjonene i 2011', pp. 11–13.

49. Chollet, *Long Game*, p. 106.

50. 'Read-Out of Meeting, from Jake Sullivan to Hillary Clinton', 15 July 2011, Hillary Clinton Archive, WikiLeaks, https://wikileaks.org/clinton-emails/emailid/6234. For the account of another participant in the meeting, see Chollett, *Long Game*, p. 106.

51. Adel Al Taraifi, 'Mustafa Abdel-Jalil on Libya's Revolution', *Asharq Al-Awsat*, 21 October 2013.

52. Maria Golovnina, 'Gaddafi Can Stay in Libya if He Quits: Rebel Chief', Reuters, 3 July 2011, https://www.reuters.com/article/columns-us-libya-idIN-TRE7270JP20110703

53. Charles Levinson, 'Rebel Chief Says Gadhafi, Family Can Stay in Libya', *Wall Street Journal*, 25 July 2011; Dominique Soguel, 'Gaddafi's Deadline to Bow Out Whooshes Past', *Mail & Guardian*, 27 July 2011, https://mg.co.za/article/2011–07–27-gaddafis-deadline-to-bow-out-whooshes-past

54. For the assassination of Younis and consequent turmoil within the NTC, see Bartu, 'Corridor of Uncertainty', pp. 48–50.

55. Mark Muller Stuart, *Storm in the Desert: Britain's Intervention in Libya and the Arab Spring*, Edinburgh: Birlinn, 2017, pp. 162–3.

56. Quoted in Dyke and Piper, 'Secret Talks That Nearly Saved Gaddafi'.

57. Private communication.

58. UN Security Council, 'Maintenance of International Peace and Security: Conflict Prevention', 22 September 2011, S/PV.6621, pp. 6–7, https://undocs.org/en/S/PV.6621

59. See quotations in Weighill and Gaub, *Cauldron*, pp. 171, 182, 184–5.

60. William J. Burns, *The Back Channel: American Diplomacy in a Disordered World*, London: Hurst, 2019, p. 315.

61. Chollet, *Long Game*, p. 107.

62. 'Le colonel n'a jamais fait montre, à notre connaissance, de la moindre velléité de négocier. Nous n'avons jamais reçu de message nous indiquant qu'il avait compris ce que nous lui disions, qu'il réfléchissait à son départ ni qu'il prévoyait d'ouvrir des discussions.' Notin, *La vérité sur notre guerre en Libye*, p. 300.

63. For detailed assessments, see Kersten, *Justice in Conflict*, pp. 115–43; and Priscilla Hayner, *The Peacemaker's Paradox: Pursuing Justice in the Shadow of Conflict*, New York: Routledge, 2018, pp. 180–93.

64. Jo Becker and Scott Shane, 'Clinton, "Smart Power" and a Dictator's Fall', *New York Times*, 28 February 2016.

65. Kersten, *Justice in Conflict*, p. 133; Hayner, *Pursuing Justice*, pp. 187–8.

66. Quoted in Kersten, *Justice in Conflict*, p. 128.

67. Ibid., pp. 120–1.

68. Quoted in Hayner, *Pursuing Justice*, p. 186.

69. The influential cleric Ali al-Sallabi spoke on Libyan TV in September 2011 about reconciliation talks he had convened in Egypt with five people from the regime, with the knowledge of Abdul Jalil and Jibril: International Crisis Group, 'Holding Libya Together: Security Challenges after Qadhafi', 14 December 2011, p. 11, footnote 79, https://www.crisisgroup.org/middle-east-north-africa/north-africa/libya/holding-libya-together-security-challenges-after-qadhafi

70. On NTC attitudes, including interview testimony, see Kersten, *Justice in Conflict*, pp. 135–6.

71. Idriss Déby Itno, 'En Libye, l'histoire me donnera raison', *Jeune Afrique*, 26 December 2011, cited by Alex de Waal, '"My Fears, Alas, Were Not Unfounded": Africa's Responses to the Libya Conflict', in Aidan Hehir and Robert Murray (eds), *Libya: The Responsibility to Protect and the Future of Humanitarian Intervention*, London: Palgrave Macmillan, 2013, p. 58.

72. See examples cited in de Waal, 'African Roles in the Libyan Conflict', p. 369.

73. Gaddafi's past activities in Africa and within the AU are described in Ping, *Eclipse sur l'Afrique*, pp. 33–82; and de Waal, '"My Fears"', pp. 60–4.

74. Jean Ping, 'The African Union and the Libyan Crisis: Putting the Records Straight',

African Union Commission, 'Letter from the Chairperson', November 2011, https://reliefweb.int/sites/reliefweb.int/files/resources/Full_Report_2911.pdf. See also Gelot, 'Role and Impact on the African Union', pp. 279–80.
75. Ping, 'African Union and the Libyan Crisis'.

4. THE DAY AFTER: POST-CONFLICT PLANNING

1. See Chapter 1, footnote 103.
2. 'President Obama: Libya Aftermath "Worst Mistake" of Presidency', BBC, 11 April 2016, https://www.bbc.co.uk/news/world-us-canada-36013703
3. UK House of Commons, Foreign Affairs Select Committee, 'Libya: Examination of Intervention and Collapse and the UK's Future Policy Options', oral evidence, 13 October 2015, Q. 46–7, http://data.parliament.uk/writtenevidence/committeeevidence.svc/evidencedocument/foreign-affairs-committee/libya-examination-of-intervention-and-collapse-and-the-uks-future-policy-options/oral/22980.html
4. Barack Obama, *A Promised Land*, New York: Viking, 2020, p. 659.
5. UK Foreign and Commonwealth Office, 'London Conference on Libya: Chair's Statement', 29 March 2011, https://www.nato.int/nato_static_fl2014/assets/pdf/pdf_2011_03/20110927_110329_-London-Conference-Libya.pdf
6. I was brought to UNHQ to prepare for this role at the beginning of April, and my appointment was announced on 26 April.
7. The 1972 election was a vote for twenty representatives to a Council of the Federation of Arab Republics, an attempt by Gaddafi to unite Libya, Egypt and Syria.
8. I derived my early understanding in particular from Diederik Vandewalle, *A History of Modern Libya*, Cambridge: Cambridge University Press, 2006. Vandewalle uses the term 'statelessness' to describe 'the avoidance by Libya's rulers of creating a modern state'.
9. Professor Diederik Vandewalle of Dartmouth College.
10. From May 2011, the UN deployed two political officers in rotation to Benghazi, where there was also a presence of UN humanitarian agencies. I made visits to Benghazi in May, June and July.
11. See Prime Minister's Office, 'Libya Crisis: National Security Adviser's View of Central Coordination and Lessons Learned', 29 April 2013, pp. 12–14, https://www.gov.uk/government/publications/libya-crisis-national-security-advisers-view-of-central-coordination-and-lessons-learned
12. UK Department for International Development, 'Libya 20 May–30 June 2011: Report of the International Stabilisation Response Team', 7 September 2011, https://assets.publishing.service.gov.uk/government/uploads/system/uploads/attachment_data/file/67470/libya-isrt-June2011.pdf
13. Ian Black, 'Post-Gaddafi Libya "Must Learn from Mistakes Made in Iraq"', *Guardian*, 28 June 2011.

14. UN assessment from discussions in Benghazi.

15. Christopher S. Chivvis, *Toppling Qaddafi: Libya and the Limits of International Intervention*, New York: Cambridge University Press, 2014, p. 143.

16. Derek Chollet, *The Long Game: How Obama Defied Washington and Redefined America's Role in the World*, New York: Public Affairs, 2016, p. 109.

17. NTC document, 'A Roadmap for Libya', n.d. [early May].

18. Peter Bartu, 'The Corridor of Uncertainty: The National Transitional Council's Battle for Recognition and Relevance', in Peter Cole and Brian McQuinn (eds), *The Libyan Revolution and Its Aftermath*, London: Hurst, 2015, pp. 37–8.

19. There is an unpublished, detailed history of the Support Offices, the Tripoli Task Force and the Libya Stabilisation Planning Team by a non-Libyan who worked closely with Nayed in Edward Marques, 'Rebel Diplomacy as "Rebelcraft": Libya 2011', PhD thesis, Department of Politics and International Studies, SOAS, University of London, 2016. See also Nayed's own description in Aref Ali Nayed, *Radical Engagements: Essays on Religion, Extremism, Politics and Libya*, Abu Dhabi: Kalam Research and Media, 2017, pp. 139, 144–6.

20. NTC document, 'Transition Planning', n.d. [late May]. The work of the Tripoli Task Force and its dissolution is detailed in Marques, 'Rebel Diplomacy as "Rebelcraft"', pp. 138–57.

21. On the emergence of rival networks and tensions regarding the Tripoli Task Force, see Peter Cole with Umar Khan, 'The Fall of Tripoli: Part 1', in Cole and McQuinn, *Libyan Revolution and Its Aftermath*, pp. 64–71.

22. Ian Martin, 'Briefing by Special Adviser of the UN Secretary-General to Coordinate Post-Conflict Planning for Libya', Meeting of the Libya Contact Group, Istanbul, 15 July 2011.

23. 'Chair's Statement, Fourth Meeting of the Libya Contact Group', Istanbul, 15 July 2011, https://www.nato.int/nato_static_fl2014/assets/pdf/pdf_2011_07/20110926_110715-Libya-Contact-Group-Ista.pdf

24. There are accounts of both Dubai workshops in Marques, 'Rebel Diplomacy as "Rebelcraft"', pp. 163–9, 176–8.

25. Ian Martin, 'Briefing by Special Adviser of the UN Secretary-General to Coordinate Post-Conflict Planning for Libya', Meeting of the Security Council, 27 June 2011.

26. 'Letter Dated 7 September 2011 from the Secretary-General to the President of the Security Council', S/2011/542, https://digitallibrary.un.org/record/710335?ln=en

27. Ian Martin, 'Briefing by Special Adviser of the UN Secretary-General to Coordinate Post-Conflict Planning for Libya', Meeting of the Security Council, 9 September 2011.

28. 'Letter Dated 15 September 2011 from the Secretary-General to the President of the Security Council, Annexing Letter Dated 14 September 2011 from the Prime Minister of the National Transitional Council of Libya Addressed to the

Secretary-General', S/2011/578, https://digitallibrary.un.org/record/710 902?ln=en

29. UN Security Council, Resolution 2009(2011), 16 September 2011, https://undocs.org/en/S/RES/2009%20(2011)

30. Marques, 'Rebel Diplomacy as "Rebelcraft"', p. 191. See also Peter Cole with Umar Khan, 'The Fall of Tripoli: Part 2', in Cole and McQuinn, *Libyan Revolution and Its Aftermath*, pp. 95–6.

31. See Bartu, 'Corridor of Uncertainty', pp. 48–50.

32. On the role of Ali al-Sallabi, see Cole with Khan, 'Fall of Tripoli: Part 1', pp. 67–72.

33. Quoted in Mary Fitzgerald, 'Finding Their Place: Libya's Islamists during and after the Revolution', in Cole and McQuinn, *Libyan Revolution and Its Aftermath*, p. 194.

34. Quoted in Nicolas Pelham, 'Libya, the Colonel's Yoke Lifted', Middle East Research and Information Project, 7 September 2011, https://merip.org/2011/09/libya-the-colonels-yoke-lifted. See also Patrick J. McDonnell, 'Islamists Take Aim at Libya Rebels' Secular Leaders', *Los Angeles Times*, 13 September 2011.

35. Cole with Khan, 'Fall of Tripoli: Part 2', pp. 94–8.

36. Marques, 'Rebel Diplomacy as "Rebelcraft"', pp. 189–90.

37. 'Jibril Vows to Quit after Libya "Liberation"', Al Jazeera, 4 October 2011, https://www.aljazeera.com/news/2011/10/4/jibril-vows-to-quit-after-libya-liberation

38. This summary is based on the account in Cole with Khan, 'Fall of Tripoli: Part 2', pp. 81–104.

39. Frederic Wehrey, *The Burning Shores: Inside the Battle for the New Libya*, New York: Farrar, Straus and Giroux, 2018, p. 66.

40. Note from Jacob J. Sullivan, director of policy planning, Jeffrey D. Feltman, assistant secretary of state for Near Eastern affairs, and William B. Taylor, special coordinator for Middle East transitions, 28 September 2011, quoted in US House of Representatives, 'Final Report of the Select Committee on the Events Surrounding the 2012 Terrorist Attack in Benghazi', 7 December 2016, p. 301, https://www.congress.gov/114/crpt/hrpt848/CRPT-114hrpt848.pdf. See also Wehrey, *Burning Shores*, pp. 66–9.

41. Jeffrey Goldberg, 'The Obama Doctrine', *The Atlantic*, April 2016, p. 81.

42. Ambassador Richard Northern and Jason Pack, 'The Role of Outside Actors', in Jason Pack (ed.), *The 2011 Libyan Uprisings and the Struggle for the Post-Qadhafi Future*, London: Palgrave Macmillan, 2013, p. 139.

43. UK Department for International Development, 'Libya 20 May–30 June 2011: Report of the International Stabilisation Response Team', 7 September 2011, p. 27.

44. See Joseph Walker-Cousins, 'Security Sector Transformation in Arab Transitions: Working for Change', Background Paper on Libya, Carnegie

Middle East Center, 17–18 December 2012, p. 16, https://carnegieendowment.org/files/Walker_Cousins_-_Libya_-_English.pdf

45. Chollet, *Long Game*, p. 105.
46. General David Richards, *Taking Command*, London: Headline, 2014, p. 319.
47. UK House of Commons, Foreign Affairs Select Committee, 'Libya: Examination of Intervention and Collapse and the UK's Future Policy Options', oral evidence, 19 January 2016, Q. 342, http://data.parliament.uk/writtenevidence/committeeevidence.svc/evidencedocument/foreign-affairs-committee/libya-examination-of-intervention-and-collapse-and-the-uks-future-policy-options/oral/23624.html
48. Rob Weighill and Florence Gaub, *The Cauldron: NATO's Campaign in Libya*, London: Hurst, 2018, pp. 53, 167–8, 209–10.
49. Ibid., p. 242.
50. Chivvis, *Toppling Qaddafi*, p. 145.
51. Ibid., pp. 162–3.
52. Peter Ricketts, *Hard Choices: What Britain Does Next*, London: Atlantic Books, 2021, p. 4.
53. Florence Gaub, 'Libya in Limbo: How to Fill the Security Vacuum', NATO Research Report, 1 September 2011, https://www.files.ethz.ch/isn/137840/Report_Libya_1Sep11Gaub.pdf
54. Christopher S. Chivvis and Jeffrey Martini, 'Libya after Qaddafi: Lessons and Implications for the Future', RAND Corporation, 2014, pp. 71–3, https://www.rand.org/pubs/research_reports/RR577.html
55. Ibid., p. 5.
56. Richard Haass, 'Libya Now Needs Boots on the Ground', *Financial Times*, 22 August 2011.
57. Chivvis, *Toppling Qaddafi*, p. 184.
58. Weighill and Gaub, *Cauldron*, pp. 194–5.
59. See for example Chivvis and Martini, 'Libya after Qaddafi', pp. 75–6; Bruce Jones, *Still Ours to Lead: America, Rising Powers, and the Tension between Rivalry and Restraint*, Washington, DC: Brookings, 2014, p. 135.
60. For example, Wolfram Lacher, 'Was Libya's Collapse Predictable?', *Survival*, 59:2 (April–May 2017), p. 1: 'An international stabilization mission was not a realistic option either in 2011, or thereafter, since it would have been widely rejected by Libyans and thereby hastened the collapse of the political process. Indeed, Libya's National Transitional Council (NTC) consistently rejected proposals for such a mission in the intervention's final days.'

5. THE INTERIM GOVERNMENT AND THE FIRST ELECTION

1. UN Security Council Resolutions S/RES/2017(2011), https://undocs.org/en/S/RES/2017%20(2011), and S/RES/2022 (2011), https://undocs.org/en/S/RES/2022%20(2011)

2. For the US perspective and efforts, see Andrew J. Shapiro, 'Addressing the Challenge of MANPADS Proliferation', US State Department, 2 February 2012, https://2009–2017.state.gov/t/pm/rls/rm/183097.htm

3. C. J. Chivers, 'List of Unexploded Arms in Libya Is Seen as Limited', *New York Times*, 25 June 2012.

4. 'NATO–UN Lessons Learned on Cooperation and Coordination during the Crisis in Libya 2011'.

5. UN, 'Letter Dated 17 January 2012 from the Secretary-General Addressed to the President of the Security Council', forwarding 'Report of the Assessment Mission on the Impact of the Libyan Crisis on the Sahel Region 7 to 23 December 2011', S/2012/42, 18 January 2012, https://digitallibrary.un.org/record/720045?ln=en

6. See 'Briefing on the Impact of the Libya Crisis on the Sahel Region', Security Council Report, 26 January 2012, https://www.securitycouncilreport.org/whatsinblue/2012/01/briefing-of-the-impact-of-the-libya-crisis-in-the-sahel-region.php; and 'Debate on Transnational Organised Crime (West Africa and the Sahel)', 20 February 2012, https://www.securitycouncilreport.org/whatsinblue/2012/02/debate-on-transnational-organised-crime-west-africa-and-the-sahel.php

7. For example, NTC Chairman Abdul Jalil had said on 25 August: 'We promise to favour those countries which have helped us … We will treat them according to the support they gave us', quoted in Jean-Christophe Notin, *La vérité sur notre guerre en Libye*, Paris: Fayard, 2012, p. 482; French Foreign Minister Juppé spoke on 24 August of 'a fantastic opportunity for us, for our businesses', ibid., p. 514.

8. UN Security Council, S/PV.6622, 26 September 2011, pp. 6–7, https://undocs.org/en/S/PV.6622

9. Ahmed Jehani and Jalal Elhassia, 'A New Start for Libya', 28 March 2018, https://archive.org/details/2018.03.28ANewStartForLibya

10. Quoted in International Crisis Group, 'Holding Libya Together: Security Challenges after Qadhafi', 14 December 2011, p. 1, https://www.crisisgroup.org/middle-east-north-africa/north-africa/libya/holding-libya-together-security-challenges-after-qadhafi

11. Ibid., pp. 8–15, where these are well elaborated.

12. Ibid., pp. 30–1.

13. See the detailed account in Peter Bartu, 'The Corridor of Uncertainty: The National Transitional Council's Battle for Recognition and Relevance', in Peter Cole and Brian McQuinn (eds), *The Libyan Revolution and Its Aftermath*, London: Hurst, 2015, pp. 50–3.

14. See Sean Kane, 'Barqa Reborn? Eastern Regionalism and Libya's Political Transition', in Cole and McQuinn, *Libyan Revolution and Its Aftermath*, pp. 215–17.

15. See Mary Fitzgerald, 'Finding Their Place: Libya's Islamists during and after the Revolution', in Cole and McQuinn, *Libyan Revolution and Its Aftermath*, p. 186.

16. See European Union Electoral Assessment Team, 'Libya: Final Report; General Congress Election 7 July 2012', 21 October 2012, p. 10, https://eeas.europa.eu/archives/eueom/missions/2012/libya/pdf/eueat-libya-2012-final-report_en.pdf; Carter Center, 'General National Congress Elections in Libya: Final Report, July 7, 2012', Atlanta, 2012, pp. 21–3, https://www.cartercenter.org/resources/pdfs/news/peace_publications/election_reports/libya-070712-final-rpt.pdf

17. POMED (Project on Middle East Democracy), 'POMED Backgrounder: Previewing Libya's Elections', 5 July 2012, pp. 7–8, https://pomed.org/backgrounder-previewing-libyas-elections. Ten candidates' applications had been returned for not being filled out properly.

18. Often referred to as 'brigades' or 'militia'. On the inappropriate translation of *katiba* as 'brigade', see Wolfram Lacher and Peter Cole, 'Politics by Other Means: Conflicting Interests in Libya's Security Sector', Small Arms Survey, October 2014, p. 17, https://www.smallarmssurvey.org/resource/politics-other-means-conflicting-interests-libyas-security-sector-working-paper-20. A more appropriate translation of *kata'ib* is 'battalion'. I have used 'battalions' for those *kata'ib* that formed and fought during the revolution and 'armed groups' for the wider category that have existed since the end of the 2011 fighting. I have avoided generalised use of the derogatory term 'militia'.

19. An outstanding early account of the situation facing the interim government is the International Crisis Group report 'Holding Libya Together: Security Challenges after Qadhafi', 14 December 2011, which is largely the work of then ICG Senior Analyst Peter Cole.

20. Brian McQuinn, 'After the Fall: Libya's Evolving Armed Groups', Small Arms Survey, September 2012, https://www.smallarmssurvey.org/resource/after-fall-libyas-evolving-armed-groups

21. See also the analyses of the 2011 emergence of armed groups in Lacher and Cole, 'Politics by Other Means', pp. 16–19, and in Emadeddin Badi, 'Exploring Armed Groups in Libya: Perspectives on Security Sector Reform in a Hybrid Environment', DCAF—Geneva Centre for Security Sector Governance, 2020, pp. 11–15, https://www.dcaf.ch/sites/default/files/publications/documents/ExploringArmedGroupsinLibya.pdf. On the history of the LIFG and its participation in the revolution, see Fitzgerald, 'Finding Their Place', pp. 177–204.

22. International Crisis Group, 'Holding Libya Together', pp. 16–17.

23. Libyan Programme for Reintegration and Development (previously Warriors Affairs Commission), 'From Conflict to State Building: LPRD Progress Report 2011–2015', July 2015, https://www.libya-businessnews.com/wp-content/uploads/2015/07/LPRD-Progress-Report-2011–2015-English.pdf

24. McQuinn, 'After the Fall', p. 13.

25. Lacher and Cole, 'Politics by Other Means', p. 18.

26. Note by Salem Joha dated 13 December 2011, presented to UNSMIL on 21 December 2011.

27. See International Crisis Group, 'Divided We Stand: Libya's Enduring Conflicts', 14 September 2012, pp. 14–15, https://www.crisisgroup.org/middle-east-north-africa/north-africa/libya/divided-we-stand-libya-s-enduring-conflicts

28. Oliver Holmes, 'New Libyan PM Seeks Cash, Reassures Fighters', Reuters, 9 November 2011, https://www.reuters.com/article/uk-libya-pm-fighters-idUKTRE7A86F320111109

29. Umar Khan, 'Armed Protestors Try to Storm Prime Minister's Headquarters: 1 Killed', *Libya Herald*, 8 May 2012.

30. See Chapter 4.

31. See International Crisis Group, 'Divided We Stand', pp. 12–13; Lacher and Cole, 'Politics by Other Means', pp. 30–5.

32. For a description of the state of the army in 2011 by the then US defense attaché, see Brian E. Linvill, 'Retaking the Lead from Behind: A New Role for America in Libya', US Army War College, April 2013, pp. 6–7, https://apps.dtic.mil/sti/pdfs/ADA592903.pdf

33. Lacher and Cole, 'Politics by Other Means', pp. 23–4. See also Florence Gaub, 'The Libyan Armed Forces between Coup-Proofing and Repression', *Journal of Strategic Studies*, 36(2) (2012), pp. 13–17.

34. TV interview, 6 July 2012, cited in International Crisis Group, 'Divided We Stand', p. 14.

35. Note by Salem Joha dated 13 December 2011.

36. Described in Sean William Kane and Kenny Gluck, 'Mediation after Revolution in Libya', Oslo Forum, 2012.

37. International Crisis Group, 'Divided We Stand', pp. 17–20; Lacher and Cole, 'Politics by Other Means', pp. 39–43.

38. Lacher and Cole, 'Politics by Other Means', p. 47.

39. International Crisis Group, 'Divided We Stand', pp. 15–16; Lacher and Cole, 'Politics by Other Means', pp. 15–16.

40. Peter Cole, 'Borderline Chaos? Stabilizing Libya's Periphery', Carnegie Endowment for International Peace, 2012, p. 11, https://carnegieendowment.org/files/10–18–12_Cole-LibyasBorders.pdf

41. Lacher and Cole, 'Politics by Other Means', p. 32.

42. See Wolfram Lacher, *Libya's Fragmentation: Structure and Process in Violent Conflict*, London: I.B. Tauris, 2020, pp. 25–7.

43. For an analysis of border control under Gaddafi and the effect of the conflict, see Cole, 'Borderline Chaos', pp. 3–9.

44. See Chapter 2.

45. 'Qatar Fielded Hundreds of Soldiers in Libya', AFP, 26 October 2011, https://english.ahram.org.eg/News/25193.aspx

46. Lord Ahmad, DFID spokesperson in the House of Lords, 'Security Sector Capacity-Building in Libya', letter to Lord Chidgey, 12 November 2012,

http://data.parliament.uk/DepositedPapers/Files/DEP2012–1728/ LettertoLordChidgeyfromLordAhmad.pdf. The very limited US defence assistance is described in Linvill, 'Retaking the Lead from Behind', pp. 10–13.

47. UNSMIL, 'Non-Paper on Potential Initiatives for the Libyan Government to Improve the Security Situation', 9 October 2012.

48. On the emergence of the Barqa Council and the reasons for its limited appeal, see Kane, 'Barqa Reborn', pp. 217–25.

49. See especially European Union Electoral Assessment Team, 'Libya: Final Report'; Carter Center, 'General National Congress Elections in Libya'.

50. Frederic Wehrey, 'Libya's Revolution at Two Years: Perils and Achievements', Carnegie Endowment for International Peace, 11 February 2013, https://carnegieendowment.org/2013/02/11/libya-s-revolution-at-two-years-perils-and-achievements-pub-50881

51. See Chapter 2.

52. On the transitional justice debate, see Marieke Wierda, 'Confronting Qadhafi's Legacy: Transitional Justice in Libya', in Cole and McQuinn, *Libyan Revolution and Its Aftermath*, pp. 153–74.

53. See Chapter 2.

54. United Nations, Human Rights Council, 'Report of the International Commission of Inquiry on Libya', 2 March 2012, A/HRC/19/68, https://www.refworld.org/docid/4ffd19532.html

55. For example, Amnesty International, 'Libya: Rule of Law or Rule of Militias?', 5 July 2012, https://www.amnesty.org/en/documents/mde19/012/2012/en; Human Rights Watch, 'Libya: Candidates Should Address Torture, Illegal Detention', 18 June 2012, https://www.hrw.org/news/2012/06/18/libya-candidates-should-address-torture-illegal-detention

56. See in particular 'Briefings by Special Representative of the Secretary-General and High Commissioner for Human Rights, Meeting of the Security Council', S/PV.6707, 25 January 2012, https://undocs.org/en/S/PV.6707

57. POMED, 'POMED Backgrounder', p. 7.

58. Abdurrahim el-Keib, untitled, sent to the author 3 December 2012, translated from Arabic. His TV broadcast was on 13 November 2012.

59. Lisa Anderson, 'Libya: A Journey from Extraordinary to Ordinary', in Jason Pack (ed.), *The 2011 Libyan Uprisings and the Struggle for the Post-Qadhafi Future*, London: Palgrave Macmillan, 2013, pp. 231–2.

60. Diederik Vandewalle, 'After Qaddafi: The Surprising Success of the New Libya', *Foreign Affairs*, November/December 2012, p. 15.

61. Derek Chollet, *The Long Game: How Obama Defied Washington and Redefined America's Role in the World*, New York: Public Affairs, 2016, p. 112. See also Ben Fishman, 'How We Can Still Fix Libya', Politico, 28 February 2016, https://www.politico.com/magazine/story/2016/02/libya-intervention-hillary-clinton-barack-obama-213686

62. On the Political Isolation Law, see Wierda, 'Confronting Qadhafi's Legacy', pp. 159–62.

63. For an excellent summary of the slide into civil war between July 2012 and June 2014, see Lacher, *Libya's Fragmentation*, pp. 28–37.

64. See for example International IDEA, 'Support to Libya's Transition to Democracy: Key Considerations', 29 August 2011; Dawn Brancati and Jack L. Snyder, 'The Libyan Rebels and Electoral Democracy', *Foreign Affairs*, 2 September 2011.

65. 'Former UN Envoy: Libya Held Its Elections Too Soon', *Al-Hayat*, 12 October 2014. See also Tarek Mitri, *Arduous Paths: Two Years in and for Libya*, Beirut: Riad el-Rayyes, 2015, pp. 13–27 (in Arabic).

66. United Nations General Assembly, 'Strengthening the Role of the United Nations in Enhancing the Effectiveness of the Principle of Periodic and Genuine Elections and the Promotion of Democratization: Report of the Secretary-General', A/70/306, 7 August 2015, paragraph 33, https://digitallibrary. un.org/record/801968?ln=en

67. International Crisis Group, 'Holding Libya Together', p. 30.

68. Dirk Vandewalle and Nicholas Jahr, 'Libya's Unexpected Strength', *New York Times*, 8 May 2014.

69. Australia, Ireland and Malta.

70. On the negotiations within the Electoral Committee, see John M. Carey, Tarek Masoud and Andrew S. Reynolds, 'Institutions as Causes and Effects: North African Electoral Systems during the Arab Spring', Harvard Kennedy School Faculty Research Working Paper Series, November 2016, pp. 27–30, https:// www.hks.harvard.edu/publications/institutions-causes-and-effects-north-afri- can-electoral-systems-during-arab-spring

71. Christopher S. Chivvis, *Toppling Qaddafi: Libya and the Limits of Liberal Intervention*, New York: Cambridge University Press, 2014, p. 185.

72. International Crisis Group, 'Holding Libya Together', p. 30.

73. 'Briefing by Special Representative of the Secretary-General, Meeting of the Security Council', S/PV.6768, 10 May 2012, https://undocs.org/en/S/ PV.6768

74. Frederic Wehrey, 'Ending Libya's Civil War: Reconciling Politics, Rebuilding Security', Carnegie Endowment for International Peace, September 2014, p. 8, https://carnegieendowment.org/2014/09/24/ending-libya-s-civil-war-rec- onciling-politics-rebuilding-security-pub-56741

75. Frederic Wehrey, 'Electing a New Libya', Carnegie Endowment for International Peace, 2 July 2012, https://carnegieendowment.org/2012/07/ 02/electing-new-libya-pub-48715

76. International Crisis Group, 'Holding Libya Together', p. 34.

77. Rupert Wieloch, *Belfast to Benghazi: Untold Challenges of War*, Cirencester: Mereo Books, 2016, pp. 275, 288–9.

78. Frederic Wehrey, 'The Lost Decade: DDR and SSR Lessons in Libya since 2011', in Emadeddin Badi, Archibald Gallet and Roberta Maggi (eds), 'The

Road to Stability: Rethinking Security Sector Reform in Post-Conflict Libya', Geneva Centre for Security Sector Governance, 2021, p. 17, https://www. dcaf.ch/road-stability-rethinking-ssr-post-conflict-libya

79. Later efforts and their failures are summarised and analysed in Hamzeh al-Shadeedi, Erwin van Veen and Jalel Harchaoui, 'One Thousand and One Failings: Security Sector Stabilisation and Development in Libya', Clingendael Institute, April 2020, pp. 23–32, https://www.clingendael.org/pub/2020/one-thousand-and-one-failings. See also Frederic Wehrey, *The Burning Shores: Inside the Battle for the New Libya*, New York: Farrar, Straus and Giroux, 2018, pp. 153–9.

80. Al-Shadeedi, Van Veen and Harchaoui, 'One Thousand and One Failings', pp. 2–4. See also recommendations in Badi, 'Exploring Armed Groups in Libya', pp. 91–3; and Wehrey, 'Lost Decade', pp. 26–7.

81. Emily O'Brien, 'In Libya, UN Finds New Model for Postconflict Engagement', World Politics Review, 26 July 2012, https://www.worldpoliticsreview.com/articles/12202/in-libya-u-n-finds-new-model-for-postconflict-engagement. See also Richard Gowan and Tristan Dreisbach, 'Taking Risks: Sustaining Political Missions in Unstable Environments', in 'Review of Political Missions 2012', Center on International Cooperation, 2012.

82. See Chapter 4.

83. UK House of Commons, Foreign Affairs Select Committee, 'Libya: Examination of Intervention and Collapse and the UK's Future Policy Options', oral evidence, Q. 282, 19 January 2016, http://data.parliament.uk/writtenevidence/committeeevidence.svc/evidencedocument/foreign-affairs-committee/libya-examination-of-intervention-and-collapse-and-the-uks-future-policy-options/oral/25384.html

84. Ibid., Q. 100, 27 October 2015, Dominic Asquith, former UK ambassador to Libya, http://data.parliament.uk/writtenevidence/committeeevidence.svc/evidencedocument/foreign-affairs-committee/libya-examination-of-intervention-and-collapse-and-the-uks-future-policy-options/oral/23624.html

85. Jehani and Elhassia, 'New Start for Libya'.

6. REFLECTIONS AND REASSESSMENT

1. Wolfram Lacher, 'Was Libya's Collapse Predictable?', Survival, 59(2) (April–May 2017), p. 149.

2. Described in Chapter 4.

3. Briefing by Ian Martin, meeting of the Security Council, 27 June 2011.

4. United Nations, 'Report of the Panel on United Nations Peace Operations', A/55/305-S/2000/809, 21 August 2000, paragraph 53, https://peacekeeping.un.org/sites/default/files/a_55_305_e_brahimi_report.pdf

5. United Nations, 'Report of the High-Level Independent Panel on Peace Operations', A/70/95-S/2015/446, 17 June 2015, paragraph 122, https://www.un.org/en/ga/search/view_doc.asp?symbol=S/2015/446

6. Bruce D. Jones, Richard Gowan and Jake Sherman, 'Can the UN Clean Up Libya?', *Foreign Policy*, 11 April 2011.

7. See Chapter 4.

8. The term 'light footprint' is associated with Lakhdar Brahimi and his proposed approach to peacebuilding in Afghanistan. For his own reflections on Afghanistan and Iraq, see Lakhdar Brahimi, 'State Building in Crisis and Post-Conflict Countries', 7th Global Forum on Reinventing Government, Vienna, 26–29 June 2007, https://constitutionnet.org/sites/default/files/Brahimi%20UNPAN 026305.pdf

9. Ian Martin, 'All Peace Operations Are Political', in Center on International Cooperation, 'Review of Political Missions 2010', 2010, p. 9, https://cic.nyu. edu/sites/default/files/political_missions_2010_full.pdf

10. See Astri Suhrke, 'Virtues of a Narrow Mission: The UN Peace Operation in Nepal', *Global Governance*, 17(1) (January–March 2011), pp. 37–55.

11. Rory Stewart, 'Introduction', in Rory Stewart and Gerald Knaus (eds), *Can Intervention Work?*, 2nd edn, New York: Norton, 2012, pp. ix–xviii.

12. Adrian Pelt, *Libyan Independence and the United Nations: A Case of Planned Decolonization*, New Haven: Yale University Press, 1970; republished Tripoli: Libyan Institute for Advanced Studies, 2016.

13. Ibid., pp. 110–23. For example: 'First of all, the staff, from top to bottom, must know what it is working for. All members should be fully and intelligently informed, not only of the Mission's terms of reference, but also of the manner in which its job is to be carried out. Hence, rather frequent staff meetings permitting free interchange of opinions and the circulation of internal information bulletins and files including, to the largest possible extent, confidential papers, are essential.'

14. Ibid., pp. 415–17.

15. Ibid., pp. 112–13. The administering powers were those that would lead the 2011 intervention: the UK, which after the defeat of Italy and Germany in Libya at the end of 1942 had instituted separate military administrations in Cyrenaica and Tripolitania, and France in the Fezzan. Pelt describes how each manoeuvred to protect its perceived national interests during the transition to Libyan independence, as did Italy and Egypt. All four, together with Pakistan, the US and four Libyan representatives, were members of the Council for Libya, whom the commissioner was required to consult and be guided by.

16. Ibid., p. 883.

17. Mustafa Ben-Halim, *Libya's Hidden Pages of History: A Memoir*, rev. edn, Nicosia: Rimal Publications, 2014, pp. 85, 97–9. Ben-Halim, who was an advocate of these proposed changes, says that Pelt was initially 'fiercely opposed to the republican idea' and warned against a hasty change to a unitary constitution, 'perhaps desperately defending a system he had instituted of which he was very proud'. On Pelt's views expressed in the 1955 consultation, see also Majid Khadduri, *Modern Libya: A Study in Political Development*, Baltimore: Johns

Hopkins University Press, 1963, pp. 265–6. Pelt says nothing about these consultations in his 'Afterthoughts', where he refers to the 1963 change to a unitary constitution.

18. Available on YouTube, https://www.youtube.com/watch?v=VJwErGFnjpA. Its abbreviated account of UN General Assembly decisions should not be relied upon.

19. Briefing by Ian Martin, meeting of the Libya Contact Group, Istanbul, 15 July 2011.

20. The two categories of UN peace operations are (1) peacekeeping operations, including uniformed military and police contingents with a mandate to use force in certain circumstances, managed by the Department of Peacekeeping Operations (since 2019, Department of Peace Operations); and (2) special political missions, with no mandate for the use of force, managed by the Department of Political Affairs (since 2019, Department of Political and Peacebuilding Affairs). For a further description, including the different funding arrangements, see United Nations, 'Report of the High-Level Independent Panel on Peace Operations'.

21. See Chapter 4.

22. Described in Chapter 4.

23. See Chapter 5.

24. Marc Lynch, The New Arab Wars: Uprisings and Anarchy in the Middle East, New York: Public Affairs, 2016, p. 90.

25. For example, Virginie Collombier, 'Libya Urgently Needs New Mechanisms for Dialogue', FriEnt, 29 June 2016, https://old.frient.de/en/news/details?tx_ggnews_newsdetailsplugin%5Baction%5D=details&tx_ggnews_newsdetailspl ugin%5Bcontroller%5D=News&tx_ggnews_newsdetailsplugin%5Buid%5D= 1061&cHash=5632632ad5b336fee52164f1e5971f33

26. Quoted in Rob Weighill and Florence Gaub, The Cauldron: NATO's Campaign in Libya, London: Hurst, 2018, p. 48.

27. Report of the Norway Libya Commission, 'Evaluering av Norsk Deltakelse i Libya Operasjonene i 2011', 2018, p. 160, https://www.regjeringen.no/globalassets/departementene/fd/dokumenter/rapporter-og-regelverk/libya-rapporten.pdf

28. Mary Fitzgerald, 'Finding Their Place: Libya's Islamists during and after the Revolution', in Peter Cole and Brian McQuinn (eds), The Libyan Revolution and Its Aftermath, London: Hurst, 2015, p. 178. See also Noman Benotman, Jason Pack and James Brandon, 'Islamists', in Jason Pack (ed.), The 2011 Libyan Uprisings and the Struggle for the Post-Qadhafi Future, London: Palgrave Macmillan, 2013, especially pp. 206–23. For an early US assessment, concluding that 'Islamists appear weak and exert low influence over the Libyan uprising', see Varun Vira and Anthony H. Cordesman, 'The Libyan Uprising: An Uncertain Trajectory', Center for Strategic and International Studies, Washington, DC,

20 June 2011, pp. 68–9, https://www.csis.org/analysis/libyan-uprising-uncertain-trajectory

29. Benotman, Pack and Brandon, 'Islamists', p. 223.

30. These and other attacks are described in Frederic Wehrey, *The Burning Shores: Inside the Battle for the New Libya*, New York: Farrar, Straus and Giroux, 2018, pp. 110–12.

31. Quoted in International Crisis Group, 'Holding Libya Together: Security Challenges after Qadhafi', 14 December 2011, p. 21, https://www.crisisgroup.org/middle-east-north-africa/north-africa/libya/holding-libya-together-security-challenges-after-qadhafi

32. Quoted in David Kenner, 'Oil, Guns and Money: Libya's Revolution Isn't Over', *Foreign Policy*, 21 December 2011.

33. Ambassador Richard Northern and Jason Pack, 'The Role of Outside Actors', in Pack, *2011 Libyan Uprisings*, pp. 124–5.

34. Quoted in Nicolas Pelham, 'Losing Libya's Revolution', *New York Review of Books*, 10 October 2013. The role of Salwa Bughaighis in the uprising and after, and her murder, are described in Wehrey, *Burning Shores*, especially pp. 23–8, 73–4, 166–7, 175–9.

35. See Chapter 4.

36. United Nations, 'Report of the High-Level Independent Panel on Peace Operations', paragraphs 175–7, 184.

37. For a critical view, including of the UN's efforts, see Michael G. Smith, 'Opportunities Missed: The Failure of Security Sector Reform in Libya', June 2015. Smith was the director of UNSMIL's Security Sector Advisory and Coordination Division from July 2011 to June 2013.

38. For a discussion of the difficulties and possibilities of accountability of a NATO operation to the UN Security Council, see Karin Wester, *Intervention in Libya: The Responsibility to Protect in North Africa*, Cambridge: Cambridge University Press, 2020, pp. 237–51, 298–302.

39. Jonathan Eyal, 'Responsibility to Protect: A Chance Missed', in Adrian Johnson and Saqeb Mueen (eds), 'Short War, Long Shadow: The Political and Military Legacies of the 2011 Libya Campaign', London: Royal United Services Institute, 2012, pp. 61–2, https://rusi.org/explore-our-research/publications/whitehall-reports/short-war-long-shadow-the-political-and-military-legacies-of-the-2011-libya-campaign

40. Leading examples are Aidan Hehir and Robert Murray (eds), *Libya: The Responsibility to Protect and the Future of Humanitarian Intervention*, London: Palgrave Macmillan, 2013; Wester, *Intervention in Libya*. For the reflections of the leading proponent of R2P, see 'Gareth Evans on "Responsibility to Protect" after Libya', *The World Today*, London: Chatham House, October 2012, https://www.chathamhouse.org/publications/the-world-today/2012–10/gareth-evans-responsibility-protect-after-libya. For a persuasive analysis of the problems exhibited by the Libya intervention, see Roland Paris, 'The "Responsibility

to Protect" and the Structural Problems of Preventive Humanitarian Intervention', *International Peacekeeping*, 21(5) (2014), pp. 569–603.

41. International Commission on Intervention and State Sovereignty, 'The Responsibility to Protect: Report of the International Commission on Intervention and State Sovereignty', Ottawa: International Development Research Centre, 2001, p. 39, https://www.idrc.ca/en/book/responsibility-protect-report-international-commission-intervention-and-state-sovereignty

42. Wester, *Intervention in Libya*, p. 311.

43. Wolfram Lacher, *Libya's Fragmentation: Structure and Process in Violent Conflict*, London: I.B. Tauris, 2020, p. 56.

44. Jacob Mundy, *Libya*, Cambridge: Polity Press, 2018, p. 213.

45. Hisham Matar, *The Return*, London: Viking, 2016, p. 137.

46. Ibid., pp. 140–1.

47. Ibid., p. 235.

INDEX

INDEX